S0-BDM-866

An Intercultural Approach
to English Language Teaching

LANGUAGES FOR INTERCULTURAL COMMUNICATION AND EDUCATION

Editors: Michael Byram, *University of Durham, UK* and *Alison Phipps, University of Glasgow, UK*

The overall aim of this series is to publish books which will ultimately inform learning and teaching, but whose primary focus is on the analysis of intercultural relationships, whether in textual form or in people's experience. There will also be books which deal directly with pedagogy, with the relationships between language learning and cultural learning, between processes inside the classroom and beyond. They will all have in common a concern with the relationship between language and culture, and the development of intercultural communicative competence.

Other Books in the Series
Audible Difference: ESL and Social Identity in Schools
  Jennifer Miller
Context and Culture in Language Teaching and Learning
  Michael Byram and Peter Grundy (eds)
Critical Citizens for an Intercultural World: Foreign Language Education as Cultural Politics
  Manuela Guilherme
Developing Intercultural Competence in Practice
  Michael Byram, Adam Nichols and David Stevens (eds)
How Different Are We? Spoken Discourse in Intercultural Communication
  Helen Fitzgerald
Intercultural Experience and Education
  Geof Alred, Michael Byram and Mike Fleming (eds)

Other Books of Interest
Foreign Language and Culture Learning from a Dialogic Perspective
  Carol Morgan and Albane Cain
The Good Language Learner
  N. Naiman, M. Fröhlich, H.H. Stern and A. Todesco
Language, Culture and Communication in Contemporary Europe
  Charlotte Hoffman (ed.)
Language Learners as Ethnographers
  Celia Roberts, Michael Byram, Ana Barro, Shirley Jordan and Brian Street
Language Teachers, Politics and Cultures
  Michael Byram and Karen Risager
Motivating Language Learners
  Gary N. Chambers
New Perspectives on Teaching and Learning Modern Languages
  Simon Green (ed.)
Teaching and Assessing Intercultural Communicative Competence
  Michael Byram

Please contact us for the latest book information:
Multilingual Matters, Frankfurt Lodge, Clevedon Hall,
Victoria Road, Clevedon, BS21 7HH, England
http://www.multilingual-matters.com

LANGUAGES FOR INTERCULTURAL COMMUNICATION AND EDUCATION 7
Series Editors: Michael Byram and Alison Phipps

An Intercultural Approach to English Language Teaching

John Corbett

MULTILINGUAL MATTERS LTD
Clevedon • Buffalo • Toronto • Sydney

Library of Congress Cataloging in Publication Data
Corbett, John
An Intercultural Approach to English Language Teaching/John Corbett.
Languages for Intercultural Communication and Education: 7)
Includes bibliographical references and index.
1. English language–Study and teaching–Foreign speakers.2.Intercultural
communication. 3. Multicultural education. 4. Language and culture.
I. Title. II. Series.
PE1128.A2C6933 2003
428'.0071–dc21   2003008656

British Library Cataloguing in Publication Data
A catalogue entry for this book is available from the British Library.

ISBN 1-85359-684-1 (hbk)
ISBN 1-85359-683-3 (pbk)

Multilingual Matters Ltd
UK: Frankfurt Lodge, Clevedon Hall, Victoria Road, Clevedon BS21 7HH.
USA: UTP, 2250 Military Road, Tonawanda, NY 14150, USA.
Canada: UTP, 5201 Dufferin Street, North York, Ontario M3H 5T8, Canada.
Australia: Footprint Books, PO Box 418, Church Point, NSW 2103, Australia.

Copyright © 2003 John Corbett.

All rights reserved. No part of this work may be reproduced in any form or by any
means without permission in writing from the publisher.

Typeset by Archetype-IT Ltd (http://www.archetype-it.com).
Printed and bound in Great Britain by the Cromwell Press Ltd.

For Maria Augusta Rodrigues Alves

O problema de uma língua internacional é uma questão de arrependimento. Quando recorremos a essa forma de língua, não estamos, na verdade, à procura de nada de novo, mas daquilo que perdemos.

The problem of an international language is a problem of remorse. When we seek such a language, we are seeking, indeed, not what will be new, but what we lost.

Fendando Pessoa,
'Língua Internacional'
in *A Língua Portuguesa*
(São Paulo, Companhia das Letras, 1997)

Contents

Acknowledgements

The process of turning this volume into a finished product has been a long one. I am grateful to all the inspirational colleagues and students from my time living and teaching in Italy, Britain, Russia and Brazil, and to those I met elsewhere at seminars usually organised by Nick Wadham-Smith of the British Council. A smaller number of scholars, colleagues and friends substantially influenced the final outcome: you will recognise yourselves in the pages that follow, and I am indebted to you all. I am also grateful to the Department of English Language at the University of Glasgow for sparing me for an academic session, so that I could write the first full draft of the manuscript. Christian Kay, Alan Pulverness and Mike Byram generously read versions of the work in progress and made constructive comments. Alison Phipps spurred me to get the job done. Throughout, Augusta Alves has been a constant source of ideas, support and love – to her this work is dedicated. The errors that remain are, obviously, my own responsibility.

The Scottish Cultural Resources Access Network (www.scran.ac.uk) kindly gave permission under its licence to reproduce the following copyright images: a statue of the Buddha and a print of a Highland soldier accompanied by a slave (National Museums of Scotland). *The Four Horsemen of the Apocalypse* and Duane Hanson's *Tourists* are reproduced with the kind permission of the National Gallery of Scotland and the Design and Artists Copyright Society.

Foreword

Dr Martin Montgomery

An Intercultural Approach to English Language Teaching draws upon a range of intellectual traditions to explore the cultural contexts of language and of language learning. Although some learners acquire another language for quite specific and limited purposes, increasingly we adapt our language and learn new ones under the pressures of migration and out of the need to reach a settlement with new contexts of communication. These new contexts are not simply contexts for language use but structured instances of a culture at work in all its richness and density. How language works, how we make sense in language, how we mean things to each other – all take place within specific contexts. And in these contexts, cultures are in play as habitual patterns of interaction, routine forms of social practice, recurrent uses of symbol, sedimented frameworks of value and belief. As a dense backdrop, culture is implicated in every instance of language in use.

But if culture is a constant backdrop to the everyday use of language, how is it best to equip the learner with cultural knowledge? For while any language as a code is finite, cultures are boundless and it is difficult to anticipate what features of context will be significant for communication. The approach adopted by this book is to equip the learner with ways of analysing and interpreting culture. Fundamentally it provides the learner with methodologies for exploring cultural difference enabling them to explore their own culture as well as the target culture. For if we are to bridge the gap between our cultural origins and our destinations we need ways of observing, interpreting, and understanding the cultures we encounter and the differences between them and our own.

Raymond Williams – a representative of one tradition discussed in the pages that follow – once commented that 'culture is ordinary', emphasising its immediate and all-pervasive presence. Culture is at play in forms of politeness, in culinary practice, in popular song, in fashion and in the many ways we symbolise our distance from or our solidarity with others. But if culture is ordinary, it is also – like language itself – in flux. Increasingly global patterns of communication threaten to erode cultural differences in the long term; at the same time, however, those very cultural differences become more palpable, come to symbolise the resistance of the local to the global and take on new vitality as a result. Williams also described culture as 'the whole way of life of a people'. In settled societies this whole way of life could be invisible: it was all that people knew. But, as change accelerates, as societies fragment and cultures divide, culture itself and degrees of cultural difference become more visible.

A central thesis of this important book is that we need to re-consider a long-established goal of language teaching. An understandable aspiration of language teachers was to inculcate a native-speaker like linguistic competence in the target language. This book offers a different picture of learning language as an open-ended and continuing process in which we move from one set of linguistic and cultural contexts into others, each of which demands new efforts of translation and interpretation. The language learner moving between cultures is an intercultural learner and hence, as this book argues and exemplifies in rich detail, needs an intercultural approach to language teaching. The approach offered in these pages promises to enrich the learning of a language; in addition, however, it promises to alert learners to the operation of cultural difference by providing techniques for comparing one culture with another, ultimately enabling the learner better to negotiate the distance between their own and another culture. In this way the learner becomes not just a competent speaker and hearer of another linguistic code but a mediator between cultures – a cultural diplomat.

Chapter 1

An Intercultural Approach to Second Language Education

This chapter introduces intercultural language teaching by addressing the following issues:

- *The limitations of a 'communicative' model of linguistic interaction.*
- *Intercultural communicative competence, and its relevance to both state sector and commercial ELT.*
- *The main theoretical influences on intercultural communicative competence.*
- *A review of the role of 'culture' in ELT.*

What is an 'Intercultural' Approach to Second Language Education?

Since the mid to late 1980s, a number of teachers and educationalists have been arguing that an 'intercultural approach' to second language teaching prompts us to re-examine the most basic assumptions about what language does, and what a language course should seek to achieve. Current 'communicative' methods of second language teaching generally view language as a means of bridging an 'information gap'. Communicative language learning also assumes that by bridging a series of information gaps, learners will 'naturally' develop their linguistic knowledge and skills, ultimately to the point where they will acquire native-speaker competence. This view of language and linguistic development has tended to underrate culture. Stern (1992: 206) notes that, despite a sustained and consistent body of work, particularly in America, drawing attention to the importance of culture in language teaching, 'the cultural component has remained difficult to accommodate in practice'. In fact, cultural content was often stripped from learning materials. Pulverness (1996: 7) says of English language teaching (ELT) in the 1970s:

English was seen as a means of communication which should not be

1

bound to culturally-specific conditions of use, but should be easily transferable to any cultural setting. Authenticity was a key quality, but only insofar as it provided reliable models of language in use. Content was important as a source of motivation, but it was seen as equally important to avoid material which might be regarded as 'culture bound'. Throughout the 1970s and much of the 1980s, syllabus design and materials writing were driven by needs analysis, and culture was subordinated to performance objectives.

However, more recently, there have been fresh attempts to integrate 'culture' into the communicative curriculum. While acknowledging the obvious importance of language as a means of communicating information, advocates of an intercultural approach also emphasise its social functions; for example, the ways in which language is used by speakers and writers to negotiate their place in social groups and hierarchies. It has long been evident that the ways in which these negotiations take place vary from community to community. A language course concerned with 'culture', then, broadens its scope from a focus on improving the 'four skills' of reading, writing, listening and speaking, in order to help learners acquire cultural skills, such as strategies for the systematic observation of behavioural patterns. Moreover, as learners come to a deeper understanding of how the target language is used to achieve the explicit and implicit cultural goals of the foreign language community, they should be prompted to reflect on the ways in which their own language and community functions. The intercultural learner ultimately serves as a mediator between different social groups that use different languages and language varieties.

The ultimate goal of an intercultural approach to language education is not so much 'native speaker competence' but rather an 'intercultural communicative competence' (e.g. Byram, 1997b; Guilherme, 2002). Intercultural communicative competence includes the ability to understand the language and behaviour of the target community, and explain it to members of the 'home' community – and vice versa. In other words, an intercultural approach trains learners to be 'diplomats', able to view different cultures from a perspective of informed understanding. This aim effectively displaces the long-standing, if seldom achieved, objective of teaching learners to attain 'native speaker proficiency'. Obviously, one key goal of an intercultural approach remains language development and improvement; however, this goal is wedded to the equally important aim of intercultural understanding and mediation.

English language teaching has long been a multidisciplinary field in practice, but it has drawn mainly upon research into linguistics and psychology for its theoretical insights. An intercultural approach continues to draw upon these disciplines, but gives equal weight to other areas of research and practice in the humanities and social sciences. Some of these disciplines, such as anthropology and literary studies, are well established; others, such as media and cultural studies, are relatively young and still developing. Since the theoretical frameworks that have stimulated intercultural approaches are diverse, and potentially bewildering, much of the remainder of this chapter seeks to summarise them and clarify their contribution.

Much recent work on the intercultural approach to second language education has been done in state schools and colleges, particularly in Europe, and in courses and seminars sponsored by state institutions such as the British Council. An intercultural approach has been slower to impact upon ELT in the commercial sector. The commercial sector clearly is not motivated by exactly the same ideological considerations that govern state education. Modern languages education in state schools usually has to conform to goals that explicitly embed foreign language teaching in a broader humanistic curriculum. For example, a Working Group preparing modern language teachers in England and Wales for a revised national curriculum defined the curricular aims of modern languages teaching in a manner wholly in accord with the goals of an intercultural approach. The Working Group proposed that learners should have the opportunity to:

- appreciate the similarities and differences between their own and cultures of the communities/countries where the target language is spoken;
- identify with the experience and perspective of people in the countries and communities where the target language is spoken;
- use this knowledge to develop a more objective view of their own customs and ways of thinking. (DES, 1990: 3, cited in Byram _et al._, 1994: 15)

Such goals are more likely to be part of a liberal state-sponsored educational curriculum than a commercially driven one. However, there are benefits for the commercial sector in adopting and possibly adapting aspects of an intercultural approach. The skills of social observation and explanation that are taught in the intercultural classroom give a coherent rationale for the teaching of the traditional 'four skills'. Communicative language teaching has always demanded that classroom activities have a _purpose_. An intercultural approach gives teachers and learners a clearly defined and consistent set of purposes. Furthermore, while a fully developed intercultural approach, as such, has not yet been systematically or widely adopted by commercial language schools, many English language teachers will nevertheless recognise in the contents of this book aspects of what they already do. Many teachers have a long-standing interest in cultural activities, and their interests and individual experience of some of the 'tributary disciplines' of the intercultural approach (such as literary or media studies) no doubt will have led them to adopt some of the practices described in this book. Indeed, most English language teachers will recognise the possibilities afforded by the intercultural approach as an extension of their current methods, and a re-examination of the rationale governing them. The intercultural approach does not seek to replace or undermine the advances made by task-based learning or learner-centred curricula (see, for example, Nunan, 1988; Willis, 1996 and the various contributions to Carter & Nunan, 2001). Rather, it seeks to build on these advances, and to channel them towards useful and realistic goals. Few learners achieve 'native speaker' linguistic competence. Many, however, can achieve the valuable skills of observation, explanation and mediation that contribute to 'intercultural' communicative competence (cf. Byram 1997b).

This book recognises the wide diversity of English language teaching throughout the world, and consequently does not seek to detail a single, all-purpose approach to meet all situations and requirements. Over the past few decades, there rightly has been a suspicion of 'one size fits all' approaches to second language education. Charges of 'linguistic imperialism' have been brought against those who impose competence in English as a prerequisite to access to broader education (cf. Pennycook, 1994; Phillipson, 1992). Critics argue that the adoption of 'English through English' policies in certain contexts encourages economic and educational dependence on textbooks and teachers from anglophone countries. The adoption of an intercultural approach cannot hope to equalise the patterns of economic domination and subordination that characterise international relations. Nevertheless, its reflective stance can encourage learners to be critically aware of the roles that different languages play in their lives. The *inter*cultural element of this kind of second language education also requires teachers and learners to pay attention to and respect the home culture and the home language. Learning materials have to incorporate aspects of the home culture, and non-native teachers become particularly valued for their own ability to move between the home and target cultures.

This book, then, does not provide a series of 'ready to use recipes' for those wishing to adopt an intercultural approach. It offers instead a systematic outline of the main principles of an intercultural approach, an 'intellectual history' of the influences upon it, and some practical examples of how to implement an intercultural approach in ways that complement current 'communicative' practices. To begin, we shall consider the main research disciplines that have provided insights into intercultural language education.

Tributary Disciplines

'Culture' is the object of study of a range of different research disciplines. For example, _anthropology_ investigates in general how membership of a particular social group is related to particular sets of behaviour; _ethnography_ seeks, partly through structured exposure to other cultures, to explore and describe how the speech systems and behaviours of groups are related to their social structures and beliefs; and _cultural studies_ seeks to understand and interpret the way that members of a group represent themselves through their cultural products (whether those products are poems, songs, dances, graffiti, or sports events). Each of these disciplines has its own intellectual history and methodology, and each alone easily constitutes an entire university programme. From the perspective of the intercultural approach, they can be thought of as 'tributary' disciplines, each shaping the practices and concerns of the intercultural classroom and intercultural courses. To make sense of their contributions to ELT it is worth summarising some of the arguments about culture found in the main 'tributary disciplines', that is, the various branches of linguistic, anthropological and cultural studies. These summaries should be understood as thumbnail sketches, intended to give general points of reference in a complex set of discussions.

Linguistics

English language teaching is generally considered a branch of _applied_ linguistics: in ELT, linguistic knowledge is not sought for its own sake but in order to facilitate the more effective teaching of English to speakers of other languages. Linguistics 'proper' has a different set of disciplinary objectives from ELT. It would, in fact, be a mistake to assume that linguists such as grammarians, discourse analysts, phoneticians and phonologists, all have a similar set of objectives. Given the diversity of their interests, we would expect linguists to disagree to some extent about the primary goals of linguistic investigations and the methods of gathering and validating evidence. For example, some linguists consider native speaker intuitions about language to be the primary source of valid data, while others prefer to collate and analyse large computerised data archives of what other people have written and uttered. Most academic disciplines are characterised by arguments about priorities and methodology – in linguistics one of the sources of dispute is about the status of culture and its relationship to language.

Linguistics in North America

In North America, formal linguists have tended to abstract language from its social and cultural context. The structural linguists who followed Bloomfield (1933) were interested in devising systematic procedures that would first break the sentence down, constituent by constituent, until its smallest grammatical components were discovered, and then would explore the relations holding between the different constituents. The transformational-generative linguists who followed Chomsky (1957) are more concerned with devising rules for the generation of sentences, arguing that such a set of rules models human grammatical knowledge. Both Bloomfield's and Chomsky's theories of grammar have influenced ELT theory and practice. Structuralist theories of language combined with behaviourist psychology to produce the audiolingual method in ELT. The audiolingual curriculum was organised according to increasingly complex grammatical constructions, and learners were drilled in these constructions in the hope that they would form the habit of producing grammatically correct utterances. This method held sway from about the 1950s to the 1970s. Following Chomsky's criticism of both the behaviourist theories of learning and structuralist theories of language, audiolingualism gave way to the communicative approach, the preferred set of approaches from the early 1980s to the present day. Linguistic theory became much more cognitively oriented, and attention was directed towards how learners' 'interlanguage' could be understood and its development supported.

Formal linguistics in the traditions of Bloomfield and Chomsky made a deep, if at times indirect, impact upon ELT, first in audiolingualism, and later in cognitive models of second language acquisition. However, the communicative approach was never as monolithic as audiolingualism, and it has also been susceptible to different linguistic approaches. In particular, speech act theory, developed by Searle (1969) from the British linguist, Austin's (1962) study, also influenced early communicative curricula that attempted to redefine language as a taxonomy of notions and functions (cf. Wilkins, 1976). For the moment, however, it is sufficient to note that communicative language teaching has been influenced by Chomsky's view of language as a cognitive faculty that allows humans to develop an internalised model of the target language through exposure to it and interaction with its speakers. Instead of doing language drills, learners are encouraged to develop language skills (reading, writing, listening and speaking) through *tasks* that involve interaction with 'authentic' written and spoken texts. Although it might be supposed that interaction with authentic texts might encourage cultural exploration, the communicative approach focused instead on the transfer of information as the core of the language-learning task. Interaction between speakers and with texts concentrated on this aspect of communicative behaviour, and, as the structure drill had been the typical classroom activity of the audiolingual method, so the information-gap activity became the heart of the archetypal task in the communicative classroom (cf. Breen & Littlejohn, 2000; Nunan, 1989).

Cultural exploration was not considered essential to the theories of language and language acquisition that influenced either audiolingualism or cognitive approaches to second language learning. For example, Stephen Pinker (1994: 18–19) writes in his popular account of linguistics:

> Language is no more a cultural invention than is upright posture. It is not a manifestation of a general capacity to use symbols: a three-year old . . . is a grammatical genius, but is quite incompetent at the visual arts, religious iconography, traffic signs, and the other staples of the semiotics approach.

From Pinker's point of view, language is not a cultural construct but the result of a long process of biological evolution – it is an instinct that is no more or less remarkable than the instincts which allow bats to navigate at night or migratory birds to fly home (Pinker, 1994: 19). Pinker, like Chomsky before him, is interested in language organisation and development as a universal phenomenon. They are less interested in asking why a particular person produces a particular utterance on a given occasion. Nevertheless, the question is significant, since we also use language partly to construct and maintain group identity, and to establish and negotiate social norms of belief, attitude and value. Particular linguistic choices therefore come imbued with cultural significance, and this relationship is a valid area of investigation. As we shall shortly see, it has been a valid area of investigation even in America, when interest in language has overlapped with an interest in anthropology.

Linguistic anthropology

In America, cultural investigation has been less associated with linguistics than with anthropology, beginning with the late 19th and early 20th century anthropologists Franz Boas (1911), Edward Sapir (1958) and Benjamin Lee Whorf (1956). These scholars were initially motivated by a concern that the languages of the Native Americans were rapidly disappearing, and they embarked on a programme to analyse and record these languages before they were lost forever. The work of Boas in particular led to the concern with grammatical 'discovery procedures' that helped to shape Bloomfield's work on English. However, there is a long-standing tension between the interests of linguistic anthropology and linguistics in North America. Pinker's dismissal of the importance of culture should be understood in the context of a debate about the Sapir–Whorf Hypothesis, the name given to an argument about the degree to which language determines thought. That is, how much do the different forms of expression that are available in different languages to articulate concepts like time, duration and completion determine the possibility of thinking in a particular way? This hypothesis originated in the observations of Whorf, whose work with certain Amerindian languages, most notably Hopi, suggested that the Hopi's grammatical categories resulted in a radically different means of conceptualisation from that of those who speak European languages. From this observation, he made the following generalisation:

> We dissect nature along lines laid down by our native languages. The categories and types that we isolate from the world of phenomena we do not find there because they stare every observer in the face; on the contrary, the world is a kaleidoscopic flux of impressions which has been organized in our minds – and this means largely by the linguistic systems in our minds. (Whorf, 1956: 213)

Although the more extreme of Whorf's views have been discredited, modified and weakened versions are still influential, and he is still quoted as an authority in the introductory essays to a recent series of 'cultural lesson plans' for ELT teachers (Fantini, 1997). However, as we have seen, some American theorists are dismissive of such views. For example, Pinker argues that language is fundamentally the expression of a universal 'mentalese' (1994: 82):

> People do not think in English or Chinese or Apache; they think in a language of thought. This language of thought probably looks a bit like all these languages; presumably it has symbols for concepts, and arrangements of symbols that correspond to who did what to whom.

In other words, it is ridiculous to argue that thought is determined by the language (or languages) that any individual speaks. The language of thought goes beyond the boundaries of any spoken language, and it is that which determines our cognitive limits.

This position seems sensible, and accounts for the observation that translation between even quite different languages is possible, even if at times explanatory circumlocution and paraphrase are necessary. A modified version of the Sapir–Whorf Hypothesis would therefore be that languages provide maps of *cultural priorities*, not *cognitive possibilities*. Speech communities transform mentalese into languages which serve their cultural needs, and these languages can be verbal, or visual. Analyses of languages are ways of investigating the structures of other cultures, other ways of looking at a shared world. This position, in fact, marks a return to that of Boas, who, in 1911, discussed with speakers of Kwakiutl on Vancouver Island modifications they would need to make to their language in order to express generalisations – every statement in Kwakiutl had to be tied down grammatically to a specific person, animal or thing, through the mandatory use of the possessive pronoun. Boas concluded that by omitting the possessive pronoun, Kwakiutl could express generalisations quite adequately, and its speakers could understand what was meant – they just found such abstract thought unnecessary, and therefore unidiomatic. Boas concluded:

> It does not seem likely, therefore, that there is any direct relation between the culture of a tribe and the language they speak, except in so far as the form of the language will be moulded by the state of the culture, but not in so far as a certain state of culture is conditioned by morphological traits of the language. (Boas [1911], reprinted in Valdes, 1986: 7)

Linguistic anthropology has traditionally been a discipline in which North American linguists with an interest in culture can discuss many topics that are also relevant to an intercultural approach. Learners of a second language clearly have a need to be able to discover how, for example, language is used to establish and maintain status in a social group in the target culture. Linguistic anthropology also bridges the disciplines of formal linguistics and anthropology. Until recently, as we have seen, ELT has been largely influenced by developments in linguistics and psychology. The intercultural approach has applied anthropological techniques, particularly those taken from ethnography.

Ethnography

Ethnography technically refers to an anthropologist's description of a community through systematic observation, usually accomplished by someone who has lived amongst the community as a 'participant observer' over many months, or even years. Ethnographers often give detailed descriptions of language behaviour within the community. In later years, ethnography has widened to encompass a variety of research techniques in media research and cultural studies, as well as in anthropology. Moreover, teachers, materials designers and learners of foreign languages have been urged to develop ethnographic skills (Holliday, 1994; Roberts *et al.*, 2001), and the development of such skills is a fundamental part of the intercultural approach. Ethnographic research is sometimes described, half sardonically, as 'loafing and lurking' but the strategies used to observe, interpret and explain social behaviour are sophisticated, practical and at the very heart of the intercultural language curriculum. Ethnography is a recurring theme in the remainder of this book, particularly Chapter 5.

Sociolinguistics

Although North American linguistics has been dominated by grammatical modelling in the tradition of Bloomfield, and then Chomsky, other, more socially based, approaches to language exploration and description exist. Of these, sociolinguistics would seem to promise most to anyone interested in culture. Loveday (1981) gives a lucid account of ways in which sociolinguistics promised to contribute a cultural perspective to communicative language teaching. For example, sociolinguists are interested in the structures of discourses like conversation, joke-telling and teacher–pupil interaction. Sociolinguistics is associated most strongly, perhaps, with ways in which linguistic markers and procedures identify speakers and writers as members of a particular group, whether that group is bound together by age, gender, class, region, nationality, ethnicity or some other common affiliation. It is also interested in the way bilingual speakers use language. For example, sociolinguists ask when and why bilingual speakers switch codes, and they consider whether the fact that they command two or more languages alters their perception of their personal identity.

Not surprisingly, it was from sociolinguistics that the most powerful critique of Chomsky's linguistics arose. Hymes (1972: 277) attacked the narrowness of Chomsky's idealised view of competence, which might be characterised as knowledge of how to construct grammatically acceptable sentences. Hymes coined the term 'communicative competence' to include:

> knowledge of sentences, not only as grammatical, but also as *appropriate*. [A child with normal abilities] acquires competence as to when to speak, when not, and as to what to talk about, with whom, when, where and in what manner.

The term 'communicative competence' became common currency among ELT professionals in the 1970s; however, this did not prevent cultural aspects of communicative competence from being relatively neglected. Even so, sociolinguistics has had a powerful impact on the practice of English language teaching. Stern (1992: 211) argues unequivocally that 'a foreign language must be studied sociolinguistically', that is, foreign language teaching must make the connection between linguistic features and 'social events, social structure, and social stratification'. Stern also appeals for ELT to focus not just on the target language, but on 'the people who use the language, the way they live, what they do, think and dream' (ibid.). While the sociolinguistic influence on ELT has embraced some topics that are relevant to different cultures – for example, the study, description and teaching of politeness formulae – there are other topics, such as the social construction of the self and others, which have been comparatively neglected. An intercultural approach redresses this balance.

British and Australian linguistics

In North America, as we have seen, distinct research traditions have developed in which culture is seen as either central or marginal to language study. Culture may be considered irrelevant to language development, if such development is thought to be a biological universal. Alternatively, language can be related to sociocultural hierarchies, or language can be considered part of more general cultural patterns. In Britain and Australia, and in occasional outposts elsewhere, further linguistic traditions have appealed directly to the concept of culture to provide explanations of linguistic behaviour. One prominent school that adopts this approach is 'systemic-functionalism', which derives mainly from the work of the British linguist Michael Halliday. Halliday's work was, in turn, influenced by the British linguist J.R. Firth, and Eastern Europeans such as the anthropologist Malinowski (cf. Butler, 1985). This approach subsequently helped to shape educational practices in Australia, where it is currently associated with Eggins, Martin, Matthiessen and others. Compared to the North American tradition in linguistics, this European and Australian school has a greater interest in 'performance' than 'competence' – the preferred source of data is not native-speaker intuition but examples of discourse, situated in their concrete social and cultural contexts. The main principles of systemic-functional linguistics may be summarised as follows.

First of all, language is considered to be a system of choices. That is, a speaker may choose from a limited set of expressions the one deemed most appropriate to a particular situation, that is, he or she may choose to thank another person by using one of various expressions such as *Ta; Gee, thanks; thank you; thank you very much; thank you so much; thanking you for your kind consideration* and so on. Secondly, the choice made will depend on situational factors, usually referred to as the 'context of situation'. In any situation, the number of options available to a speaker is limited. The range of options available constitutes the 'system' at that point in the language. The systemic-functional linguist is interested in describing the options available, and in giving a functional explanation for why a particular choice is made in a particular utterance or written text. The characterisation of the 'context of situation' will determine whether the researcher adopts a mode of investigation known as 'register analysis' or 'genre analysis'.

Register analysis

Register analysis is adopted by linguists wishing to account for the influence of the immediate situation upon the shape of a stretch of language. Three main situational variables are taken into consideration, usually referred to as the field, tenor and mode of discourse. These factors refer respectively to the topic of the discourse (field), the relationship between participants in the discourse (tenor), and the channel or type of discourse, for example, whether it is a written editorial or a spoken conversation (mode). Together, the consideration of field, tenor and mode constitute *register analysis*, which was developed from the 1960s through the 1990s (Ghadessy, 1988, 1993; Halliday *et al.*, 1964; Halliday & Hasan, 1989). For example, all the expressions listed above fall into the field of 'expressing thanks'. However, 'ta' would imply informality (tenor) and conversational speech (mode), while 'thanking you for your kind consideration' would imply formality (tenor) and written text, probably a letter (mode).

The impact of register analysis on language teaching materials produced during the later 1960s and 1970s cannot be underestimated. This was the period in which 'English for Special/Specific Purposes' (ESP) courses and textbooks began to blossom, and register analysis gave materials designers a way of abstracting 'the language of science' or 'the language of business' from the seemingly inchoate mass of 'general English'. Learners could now be taught about the features relevant to, say, an oral business presentation, or a written technical report. Ironically, the impact of register analysis and the rise of ESP courses and materials gave credence to the idea that language could be described and taught without reference to a wider culture. If the vocabulary and grammar of the typical scientific report, for example, could be described and taught, then a set of teaching techniques that were purely instrumental could be devised and implemented across cultures. As we shall see in Chapter 4, this assumption is questionable. While register analysis has been influential in the communicative approach, particularly in its earlier manifestations, it is genre analysis that holds more promise for an intercultural approach.

Genre analysis

During the 1980s it became clear to those working directly and indirectly with systemic-functional linguistics that there was a context beyond the immediate context of situation. Register analysis helped identify predictable aspects of varieties of specialised English, but consideration of the variables of field, tenor and mode does not itself tell us *why* a text had been produced in the first place. The social purposes that a text serves can also contribute to the explanation of why it has the form it does. When considering the social purposes of a text, we are putting it into its context of culture, and this process came to be known as *genre analysis*. Chapter 4 deals in greater detail with the procedures of genre analysis than is possible here; however, it is worthwhile noting from the outset that there are different ways of analysing genre. Within the systemic-functional tradition (Eggins & Slade, 1997; Hasan, 1984; Martin 1985; Ventola, 1983), texts are broken down into goal-directed stages, the purpose of each of which is realised by particular linguistic exponents. A related but distinct tradition, arising directly from the teaching of English for specific purposes, combines ethnography with textual analysis (Bex, 1996; Bhatia, 1993; Candlin & Hyland, 1999; Hyland, 2000; Swales, 1990). Genre analysts in this tradition seek specialist information from members of the discourse community that the texts serve about how members of that community see the texts functioning. Despite differences in methodology, both schools of genre analysis are concerned with *why* texts exist and they both seek to determine the cultural function of texts. By focusing on the reasons why particular texts exist, they attempt to justify linguistic choices through reference to cultural contexts.

Critical discourse analysis

One branch of linguistics that has regularly employed systemic-functional analyses of texts is critical discourse analysis (CDA). CDA is relevant to a discussion of the intercultural approach in part because it is sometimes argued that language education should promote critical awareness (cf. Melde, 1987: Pennycook, 2001). In other words, an intercultural approach should not simply provide information about the target culture, but it should provide a set of skills that allows the learner to evaluate critically products of the target culture, and, where relevant, the home culture. CDA promises to provide learners with such skills, since its proponents claim that it is a socially responsive mode of text analysis. Associated primarily with the work of Norman Fairclough (Fairclough, 1989, 1992, 1995), CDA attempts to come to a deep understanding of how language is used by combining textual and sociological analysis and political critique. As Fairclough states (1995: 97):

> The approach I have adopted is based upon a three-dimensional conception of discourse, and correspondingly a three-dimensional method of discourse analysis. Discourse, and any specific instance of discursive practice, is seen as simultaneously (i) a language text, spoken or written, (ii) discourse practice (text production and text interpretation), (iii) sociocultural practice.

Fairclough's 'three-dimensional' model of analysis informs many of the examples of discourse discussed later in this book. In Chapter 3, for example, the mealtime discussion can be viewed as (1) a generic text conforming to certain formal conventions, (2) a dynamic flow of conversational turns, each of which can only be understood in the unique context of the other turns, and (3) a means by which the participants actively enact their individual status in the sociocultural institution of the family. In Chapters 7 and 8, visual and cultural texts are also considered as forms, as discourse practices and as sociocultural events, although sometimes the focus is more on one 'dimension' than the other. The model of discourse processing, discussed in Chapter 8 in relation to media texts, also draws as much on institutional context (and technological means) as on the formal constituents of the texts themselves.

The links Fairclough draws between language use, textual interpretation and sociocultural explanation have an obvious value in cultural analysis. In his analyses, Fairclough draws upon various key concepts, including *genre, orders of discourse* and *hegemony*. He defines 'genre', in systemic-functional terms, as texts designed to fulfil socially ratified purposes, such as interviews or editorials. The concept of an 'order of discourse' is adapted from social theorists such as Foucault (1981) and refers to the language associated with a particular social domain, such as academia, religion, marketing, and so on. It is broadly similar to the concept of 'field' in register analysis, and encompasses different genres. As such, the 'order of discourse' is extremely pertinent to the teaching of English for Specific Purposes. Where a CDA perspective differs from a traditional 'register' or 'genre' approach to discourse, is in its recognition of the differences in power enjoyed by different members of discourse communities. In Chapter 4, 'academic' and 'scientific' English are considered across a spectrum of perspectives: from the 'authority' who can enlighten students or general readers from a secure institutional base, to the writer of research articles who has to impress gatekeepers and fellow members of the 'peer' community. The equations of power and the modes of persuasion depend absolutely on the context in which writing occurs.

The concept of 'hegemony' is often discussed in CDA. It is taken from the Italian theorist Antonio Gramsci (Gramsci, 1971). Gramsci followed Marx in arguing that the governments of capitalist societies function to sustain the domination of the working class by a small, elite class. Governments, of whatever political colour, preserve the interests of the elite class before the interests of the workers. Gramsci's contribution to the debate was to argue that in developed capitalist societies, this domination of the mass by the elite is not by coercion but by consent. In other words, in a hegemonic society, the elite dominates the masses not by force or coercion, but by ongoing persuasion. Clearly, even reasonably stable societies exhibit stresses and strains, as the various factions within them contest the distribution of status, power and resources. In Gramsci's model, language – through which persuasion is articulated and consent negotiated – becomes a key social issue. Language is the weapon of hegemonic cultures in which an unequal distribution of power is maintained by negotiation and consent.

The teaching of English language itself comes into any discussion of hegemonic practices that threaten non-anglophone cultures and non-

English modes of expression, as recent voices in ELT have reminded us (Pennycook, 1994, 1998; Phillipson, 1992; Skuttnab-Kangas, 2000). Proponents of English as a 'global lingua franca' face reasonable accusations that the near monopoly English enjoys in the world's information-driven economy disenfranchises at least as many as it empowers. The arguments are complex and it is not the function of this volume to explore them in detail. However, one of the hopes of the present volume is that by embedding language teaching in an explicitly intercultural curriculum, rather than vice versa, the home language and the home culture of the learners (and of the many non-native teachers) will be valued in the classroom alongside the often glamorised target language, English.

Literary, Media and Cultural Studies

There is now a long tradition of using literature and the media (film, television and newspapers) as staple resources in the communicative classroom. Cultural studies (CS) is a newer arrival. As a field of academic inquiry, cultural studies is often linked in the popular imagination with literary studies – for example, the two disciplines are yoked together in the IATEFL Special Interest Group 'Literature and Cultural Studies'. Moreover, many cultural studies courses at university level are located within literature departments. However, it is to some extent misleading to associate the two disciplines too closely: cultural studies has indeed been criticised for the neglect of literature in its work (cf. Kenneth Parker, cited in Montgomery, 1998: 4). What, then, is cultural studies, what is its relationship to literary and media studies, and how does it relate to an intercultural approach?

Cultural studies is sometimes referred to as 'British' cultural studies, not primarily because British culture is being studied (though it often is), but because a particular set of problems and a methodology for studying them were developed in Britain. In the initial stages these developments were closely linked with certain British and Commonwealth theorists (e.g. Richard Hoggart, Raymond Williams, Stuart Hall) and certain institutions (e.g. the Centre for Contemporary Cultural Studies at the University of Birmingham). A number of introductions to British cultural studies are currently available (e.g. Turner, 1990) and so the following summary will be brief.

Cultural studies in Britain developed out of a reaction against the dominant university tradition of teaching English literature which had developed since the 19th century. This dominant tradition had its seeds in Matthew Arnold's *Culture and Anarchy* (1869; reprinted 1960) and in the 20th century it was principally associated with influential literary critics such as T.S. Eliot, F.R. Leavis, Q.D. Leavis and L.C. Knights. These critics generally viewed literature as a storehouse of civilised values, and the appreciation of a defined canon of 'great' literature was effectively synonymous with being able to discriminate between the civilised values of the minority and the barbarism of the masses. Changes in this view of literature teaching were themselves the result of social changes. In the post-war years there was an incursion of 'grammar school boys' into the socially superior bastions of English academia and, as some of these students graduated and took up teaching posts themselves, they began to re-evaluate their own educational experiences. In 1957, Richard Hoggart's *The Uses of Literacy* was published. This book is partially a defence of the working-class culture of Hoggart's youth, and although it regards some aspects of modern popular culture with distaste, it opened the way for a re-evaluation of 'culture' and the narrowness of the 'great tradition' as defined by the reading lists of university courses. Later, Raymond Williams in a series of books and articles, particularly *The Long Revolution*, developed his thesis that culture is 'ordinary' and refers to 'a whole way of life' (1961: 63). Williams contributed to early development of media studies (*Communications*, 1962; *Television: Technology and Cultural Form*, 1974), another instance of the widening of academic interest beyond the traditional literary canon. In 1964, under the directorship of Richard Hoggart, the Birmingham Centre for Contemporary Culture (CCC) was established. Particularly under the later directorship of Stuart Hall, the CCC further broadened the scope of cultural studies to encompass other aspects of popular culture, such as youth fashion (Hebdige, 1979), the dances of girls and young women (McRobbie, 1993), and family television (Morley, 1986). Increasingly, those working at the CCC, and those they influenced and inspired, developed a theoretical methodology for describing the cultural phenomena in which they were interested – a methodology based on Gramsci's theory of hegemony (see above); Barthes theories of semiology (cf. Chapter 7); and principles of ethnography and participant observation (cf. Chapters 5 and 6).

There has not, of course, been uncritical acceptance of cultural studies – and specifically cultural studies as it has developed in Britain – within academia (Montgomery, 1998). There has been a typical hegemonic struggle within the domain of literary studies about the dominant paradigm: for example, should students be doing close textual study of Shakespeare's texts or analysing the way Shakespearian quotations are appropriated by such Hollywood films as *The Last Action Hero, Star Trek VI: The Undiscovered Country* and *Schindler's List* (Drakakis, 1997)? The tensions between cultural studies and literary studies are accessibly summarised by Culler (1997). One broad area of concern is the 'canon' of texts which form the basis of study – in crude terms, are the literary 'greats' being replaced by the equivalent of soap operas?

Culler (1997) argues that cultural studies in America has few of the links with political movements that have energised the discipline in Britain, and it could be seen in the USA as primarily a resourceful, interdisciplinary, but still primarily academic study of cultural practices and cultural representation. Cultural studies in Britain is supposed to be radical, as is critical discourse analysis, but the opposition between an activist cultural studies and a passive literary studies may be sentimental exaggeration (Culler, 1997: 53–4). However, as we shall see, the debate in America stirred up by Hirsch (1987) and the responses to him (Murray, 1992) demonstrate that the USA may not be as immune as Culler suggests to political questions of the kind that prompted the development of British cultural studies in the 1950s to 1980s. It may be that the cultural theorising, the struggles for academic territory, and even the very content of cultural studies seems irrelevant to the practising teacher of English as a second language.

Byram (1997a) gives a detailed critique of cultural studies and its relationship to foreign language teaching, and ELT in particular. Seen from the perspective of a language education pedagogy that has been concerned with learning processes and methodological effectiveness, cultural studies is found wanting:

> It [cultural studies] does not work with explicit learning theories, or with issues of adapting methods to particular age groups. It does not address issues of affective and moral development in the face of challenges to learners' social identity when they are confronted with otherness in the classroom or, just as significantly, in the hidden approach of the informal learning experiences of residence in the country. CS discourse does not, furthermore, include discussion of teaching methods and learning styles appropriate to different kinds of classroom interaction, in different environments inside or outside the country in question. (Byram, 1997a: 59)

Byram's work focuses on teenagers learning European languages in state schools, and particularly on the exploitation of school trips to the target country for raising intercultural awareness. Therefore his priorities lie in developing frames of reference and 'decentring skills' that will facilitate intercultural communication, rather than in the intellectual abstractions of cultural studies and its focus on ideological critique and interpretative disciplines. He observes that cultural studies and foreign language teaching could happily go their own ways, but also acknowledges the potential value to foreign language teaching of a critical cultural analysis, albeit one with greater emphasis on the processes of learning, and greater sensitivity to the demands of non-native speakers in a variety of learning situations.

Despite Byram's reservations, there is substantial evidence that cultural studies has influenced ELT indirectly. The revival of literature in communicative language learning, after a period of relative neglect, has emphasised the non-canonical: no longer is literature included in the syllabus to inculcate the values embodied in a 'great tradition' (e.g. Brumfit & Carter, 1986; Lazar, 1993; McRae, 1991). Instead, literature is exploited largely for its value in promoting language acquisition and, to a lesser extent, cultural awareness.

Similarly, the broadening of the canon, and in particular the rise of media and cultural studies, is reflected in activities in recent ELT coursebooks, like *True to Life,* and in specialised textbooks such as Edginton and Montgomery's *The Media* (1996). As a result of projects sponsored by the British Council, school books and curricula have been developed in different countries which attempt to combine the 'four skills' of language teaching with the 'fifth skill' of cultural interpretation (e.g. the Romanian textbook *Crossing Cultures,* Chichirdan *et al.*, 1998; cf. the intercultural curriculum developed for Bulgarian schools, Davcheva & Docheva, 1998). In these materials, task-based methodologies familiar to ELT are put to the service of issues which are familiar to cultural studies: for instance, how are social categories like gender, youth, and nationality constructed across different cultures; and how do advertising, popular television and the press represent social groups in the media? In such materials, cultural studies absorbs some of the lessons of a task-based ELT methodology while ELT absorbs some of the curricular aims of cultural studies. No longer are the students simply 'learning language' – they are learning ways of viewing others and reviewing themselves. By no means all of Byram's anxieties have so far been addressed, and there is much still to achieve and debate, but the process of merging ELT and cultural studies has already resulted in a range of innovative materials (see further, Chapter 8).

Defining 'culture' across disciplines

The above discussion has shown that the disciplinary influences on the intercultural approach are extraordinarily diverse, ranging from North American anthropology to Australian genre theory and the tensions found in British literary scholarship. Nevertheless, a consensus is emerging about the curricular aims of an intercultural approach, and even about how to implement it. The object is sometimes vaguely expressed as the 'whole way of life' of the target community, but it is clear that this formulation is a product of the desire to be inclusive rather than elitist. Cultural exploration demands, as Stern (1992) argues, a focus on people rather than on language as such. To understand how a community uses language it is deemed necessary to understand the community: the dynamic system of its beliefs, values and dreams, and how it negotiates and articulates them. While earlier language learning textbooks might invite an uncritical celebration of the target culture, current intercultural curricula suggest a more cautious description and critical evaluation. The home culture as well as the target culture may well come under scrutiny in such programmes. Stern (1992: 207) also identifies some fundamental problems in implementing a cultural syllabus:

> In our view the following four issues have to be dealt with: (a) the vastness of the culture concept; (b) the problem of goal determination and the lack of accessible information; (c) questions of syllabus design and the difficulty of according an appropriate place to culture in a predominantly language-oriented approach; (d) questions of teaching procedures and the difficulty of handling substantive subject-matter in a mainly skill-oriented programme.

According to Stern, the first two of these issues hindered the proliferation of cultural syllabuses, certainly up until the early 1990s. If culture is indeed 'the whole way of life', or 'the dynamic belief-system of a community', then it is certainly difficult to know how these vast concepts can be approached, particularly in language classrooms where communication is already constrained. However, from the various, interacting traditions of linguistics and anthropology, as well as literary, media and cultural studies, we can adapt techniques of observation and description, as well as the analysis and evaluation of texts and social practices, in order to equip learners with ways of making sense of target cultures. A redefinition of the goals of the communicative curriculum, and a skills-based orientation towards intercultural exploration, go some way towards addressing Stern's remaining anxieties. We do not have to prepackage the vast and changing target culture for learners if developing appropriate tools for intercultural exploration becomes one of the central goals of language education.

It should also be clear from the above that the concept of 'culture' is not necessarily related – or even best related – to nationalities. British culture is not just made up of English, Northern Irish, Scottish and Welsh cultures, but of communities characterised by a range of factors, including age, gender, class, ethnicity and even such things as leisure pursuits. We can talk about 'Welsh culture' but we can also talk about 'youth culture', and the cultures of football fans, soap opera viewers and different academic disciplines. Most recent writing on 'culture' and ELT has assumed a more-or-less anthropological view of culture as an entire way of life. The concept was in fact clearly defined in one of the early discussions of the communicative approach:

> [Culture] involves the implicit norms and conventions of a society, its methods of 'going about doing things', its historically transmitted but also adaptive and creative ethos, its symbols and its organisation of experience. (Loveday, 1981: 34)

Loveday's definition of culture incorporates a number of key concerns that will be evident in later chapters of this book. A society (or any cohesive group of individuals) constructs for itself a set of beliefs and presuppositions that it will come to regard as 'common sense'. These beliefs relate to the behaviour of the group, and also to the kinds of things it produces to celebrate or assert its identity and values. The language of the group – its 'symbols' – in turn serve to organise its experience, and to construct and maintain group identity and cohesion. However, we must always be aware that the norms, beliefs, practices and language of any group are not static but dynamic – the group is forever negotiating and renegotiating its norms and values among its membership. Therefore, the core beliefs – and the language that articulates them – will necessarily change over time. The 'culture' of a group can be considered the *relationship* between its core beliefs and values, and the patterns of behaviour, art and communication that the group produces, bearing in mind that these beliefs and values are constantly being negotiated within the group.

Foreign language learners are in the position of someone who is outside the target language group, looking in. Learners may not wish to adopt the practices or beliefs of the target culture, but they should be in a position to understand these practices and beliefs if they wish fully to comprehend the language that members of the target culture produce. It is this recognition that language is more than the transfer of information – it is the assertion, negotiation, construction and maintenance of individual and group identities – that has led to the development of an intercultural approach to language education.

Culture-free communicative competence?

Having surveyed the 'tributary disciplines' that feed into an intercultural approach to second language education, we now focus in particular on reasons why the exploration of culture has been marginal to communicative language teaching. In many ways, the marginalising of culture in communicative curricula has been surprising. After all, the key idea of communicative competence was adapted from the work of a sociolinguist, Dell Hymes. In the late 1970s, the idea of 'rules of use, without which rules of grammar would be useless' (Hymes, 1972: 278) gave a powerful intellectual respectability to classroom practices which looked beyond grammatical accuracy as the primary goal of language teaching and learning. A concern for communicative competence prompted teachers and materials designers to contextualise the target language by placing it in 'real-world' situations, in the hope of making it 'authentic'. Even by the early 1980s, however, there were suggestions that ELT practitioners had distorted the notion of communicative competence. Loveday (1981: 61) argues:

> Unfortunately, many theorists and teachers have come to equate the concept of communicative competence with spontaneous self-expression, probably because they have taken the term absolutely literally as the ability to communicate. This interpretation is not only trite but also shows a grave lack of understanding of what is involved.

In order to transmit and decode meaning, we must do more than arrange our sounds and words in a special order. One has to be aware of the diverse ways of constructing a message, of the guidelines which, rarely obvious and definable, constitute unquestioned principles of presenting the sound and word patterns together with other symbols. This code for our verbal conduct is our communicative competence and it fulfils a multitude of social functions and is largely determined by the sociocultural system.

If it is perhaps overstating the case to argue that the notion of communicative competence had become 'trite', it is certainly true that its transactional character – that is, the focus on knowledge of how to *do* things with language – had overshadowed its cultural aspects. In the same year as Loveday's book was published, Morrow and Johnson's *Communication in the Classroom* (1981) set out to guide teachers in the classroom applications of the communicative approach. Addressing the issue of 'structural competence' existing alongside 'communicative incompetence', Johnson sees the solution lying in the adoption of a notional-functional syllabus and the implementation of needs analysis, while Morrow advocates the use of information gap activities as the core type of classroom activity. These components of communicative language teaching were enormously influential, and they assumed that language was largely concerned with 'doing things'. In time, whole branches of communicative language teaching – the 'procedural' or 'task-based' approach to learning – grew out of this intimate association of language use and transactional purpose.

In Europe, the notional-functional syllabus enjoyed strong institutional backing – indeed it grew out of an initiative by the Council of Europe to develop a pan-European system of teaching suitable for the languages of all of the Council's member countries. Wilkins (1972, 1976) proposed a syllabus organised not according to increasingly complex grammatical structures, but according to (1) the range of concepts or 'notions' that a language can express (such as frequency, duration, and quantity), and (2) the communicative functions that speakers perform through language (such as offering, inviting, accepting and declining). Language, then, did two things: it expressed meanings and it was used in the performance of tasks. Communicative language teaching materials of this period bear witness to the impact of Wilkins' work. ESP textbooks in particular asked students to express quantities, measure volumes, describe cyclical and linear processes – in short, to articulate abstract notions verbally. More general EFL textbooks concentrated more on 'doing things', as can be seen in the titles of books such as Leo Jones' *Functions of English* (1977).

The 'information gap' or 'information transfer' task became the archetypal communicative activity. Typically, one learner would be given access to information that was denied to another learner. Then, in pairs or groups, the learners would exchange the information. Information gap activities were intended to ensure 'genuine' or 'authentic' communication. The information gap remains fundamental to communicative teaching. Any exercise or procedure which claims to engage the students in communication should include some transfer of information or opinion, and one of the main jobs of the teacher is consistently seen as setting up situations where information gaps exist and motivating the students to bridge them in appropriate ways. By the time of Nunan's *Designing Tasks for the Communicative Classroom* (1989), the information gap task had been analysed into constituent parts, including goal of task, activity type, input, learner roles, teacher role and setting, and graded in terms of difficulty. However, it was still the transactional nature of the task that was emphasised: language was a medium for getting things done, as can be seen from the example that Nunan gives of a simple communicative task from a popular textbook (Maley & Moulding, 1981: 3; Nunan 1989: 11):

Goal:	Exchanging personal information
Input:	Questionnaire on sleeping habits
Activity:	(i) Reading questionnaire
	(ii) Asking and answering questions about sleeping habits
Teacher role:	Monitor and facilitator
Learner role:	Conversational partner
Setting:	Classroom/pair work

This communicative task sets up an information gap activity whereby learners exchange personal information; however, there is no consideration given in the textbook or in Nunan's analysis of the task to *why* learners might want to exchange this kind of information. Personal information is exchanged for its own sake.

That language is primarily a means of exchanging information is not an unreasonable view, and it is one which was acceptable to the commercial growth of English language teaching world-wide during the 1970s, sometimes in cultures which were suspicious of the Western cultural values espoused by Britain and America. A focus on transactional functions also made sense to course book publishers, who could promote the purely instrumental value of their textbooks across a range of cultures. Even so, the transactional view of language is a narrow one, as Loveday (1981: 123) observes:

> Now English is increasingly recognized as approaching the status of a world lingua franca and because of this fact there are many involved in its teaching who seek and support its de-ethnicization and de-culturalization. Whatever the outcome of this particular debate will be, L2 teaching should not blindly follow the extreme utilitarianism of the Zeitgeist and reduce communicative competence to the mere acquisition of skills. Perhaps this is all that is needed for English as an international medium, but I doubt it, because the cultural background of the L2 speakers of English will still be present in their communicative activity if this consists of more than booking into a hotel or answering business letters or writing scientific reports, and even these will involve specific cultural presuppositions.

Loveday argues that by focusing only on the transactional level, a communicative language teaching course neglects important cultural information that can help anticipate and make sense of differences in how even simple transactions operate in different countries. For example, in Moscow in 1988, I found it difficult to purchase half a dozen eggs in a shop, not only because of my poor Russian, but simply because the shopkeeper was accustomed to selling eggs in multiples of ten. Loveday argues that the communicative classroom should find a place for cultural information of this kind.

Obviously, many good teachers will have been introducing cultural information during their communicative language teaching lessons, despite little encouragement from the materials themselves, just as good teachers during the years of the audiolingual method would have come up with 'communicative' activities before they were systematically incorporated into the curriculum. Stern calls this kind of *ad hoc* introduction of cultural information 'cultural asides' (1992: 224). A good Russian teacher might simply have pointed out to a learner, like me, that Russians do not use imperial measures. However, both teachers and students require systematic support from language teaching materials, not only in devising communicative tasks, but also in dealing with cultural differences. Furthermore, Stern voices concern with the sheer scale of the curriculum designer's task: given the vastness of culture, how is cultural knowledge to be addressed in the classroom?

One reason why, perhaps, writers who championed the cause of culture were nevertheless comparatively neglected until the later years of the 1980s was that, having identified the problem, they were seldom in a position to provide the solution. Books such as Loveday's (1981) are given over to providing examples of cross-cultural difference: for instance, how classifiers work in Amerindian and Asiatic languages, or the interpretation of long periods of silence in Amerindian, West Indian and Quaker communities. Loveday identifies what he calls 'framing and symbolising patterns' (1981: 65–100) which seem to equate loosely to (1) knowledge of what are later called spoken and written genres, and (2) the verbal and non-verbal means by which people construct messages (e.g., speech, writing, intonation, voice quality, kinesics, mime, visual symbols). However, having identified these as areas of theoretical exploration, he does not provide ways of integrating them in the communicative language teaching classroom. Clearly, it is impossible to tell the learner everything he or she needs to know about the target culture, for example, how people buy eggs, socially acceptable and unacceptable greetings and leave-takings in face-to-face situations, on the phone, by email, and so on. Instead, we need to attune the learner to the possibility of difference, and seek to explore how 'decentring from one's own taken-for-granted world can be structured systematically in the classroom' (Byram & Fleming, 1998: 7). This endeavour means going beyond the information gap and making people's use of language a topic of classroom exploration.

Despite the mainstream emphasis on the transactional nature of language, and the complexities of deciding just what culture is, since the late 1980s there has been a renewed interest in the integration of 'culture' in the language classroom in Europe, Asia and the United States. This interest is evident in a proliferation of articles and books on the subject, ranging from *Culture Bound: Bridging the Cultural Gap in Language Teaching* (ed. Valdes, 1986), to *Target Culture –Target Language?* (Seago &McBride, 2000). Such studies draw upon various disciplines and theoretical frameworks, and they consequently define 'culture' in different ways and have different views of its application to language teaching. The diffuse nature of the concept of culture, and the varied, and sometimes suspect, aims of those who have tried to incorporate culture into their classes might also have contributed to its marginal status in ELT. The main approaches to teaching culture in a communicative curriculum can be summarised as follows.

Using 'culture' to motivate communication

Some publications focus squarely on classroom practice. Tomalin and Stempleski (1993: 6–7) talk about culture with a 'little c' as incorporating *products* such as literature, art and artefacts, *ideas* such as beliefs, values and institutions, and *behaviours* such as customs, habits, dress, foods and leisure. They present a series of lesson plans that explore the relationship between the language taught in the classroom, and the products, ideas and behaviour that impact upon its meaning. The cultural products, ideas and behaviours are presented primarily as a means of motivating language use. In his introduction to a similar anthology of 'cultural' lesson plans, Fantini (1997: 5) reverses the definition of anthropologist Edward Hall to assert that 'communication *is* culture' [original emphasis]. Fantini and his collaborators dwell on the way that individual languages divide up the world of the learner into different categories, labelled by different words and related by different grammars. As the Whorfian view asserts, learning a new language involves recategorising your world and reformulating the relationship between its constituent parts. Both of these selections of 'cultural lesson plans' assume that language and culture are inseparable, and that learners will be interested in and motivated by cultural topics.

Language learning as acculturation

The North American approach to language teaching has emphasised 'acculturation' as a curriculum goal, largely because English language learners have usually been immigrants. 'Acculturation' is the process by which learners are encouraged to function within the new culture, while maintaining their own identity (Byram *et al.*, 1994: 7). Valdes' selection of articles focus on those values and beliefs that are shaped by one's environment, and in her introduction she argues that 'Once people . . . recognize that they are, truly, products of their own cultures, they are better prepared and more willing to look at the behavior of persons from other cultures and accept them non-judgmentally' (Valdes, 1986: vii). Like Valdes, Stern assumes that the ultimate goal of language education is to create a 'bicultural' learner, that is, one who acquires 'a generalized sociocultural competence . . . certain sociocultural skills, or . . . specifically socioculturally appropriate behaviour' (1992: 218). His far-sighted discussion of the 'cultural syllabus' (1992: 205–42) also draws on insights from anthropology and cross-cultural education. Stern and Valdes represent a strong North American tradition of teaching culture in order that immigrant learners adapt more smoothly to their new social environment.

While the North American context focuses on the experience of immigrant learners, the European Community has been learning to cope with the gradual formation of a single political body that is both multilingual and multicultural. The Council of Europe has long been active in exploring issues related to diversity in the EC (Council of Europe, 1989) and some textbooks are beginning to emerge that directly address the challenges of learning languages in a multicultural context (e.g. de Jong, 1996).

Language learning as 'enculturation': the 'critical literacy' debate

The integration of culture into the language classroom has a profound impact on the overall goals of the language curriculum, prompting us to reconsider why we are teaching learners to communicate in an L2 at all. For most of the history of ELT, there has been the largely unquestioned assumption that we are training learners to become as close to native speakers as possible, in the gloomy knowledge that few will reach that particular goal. A controversial alternative to acculturation is 'enculturation', the assimilation of learners into the host culture. Enculturation involves indoctrinating learners in a 'common culture' consisting of facts and myths which have the power of binding the nation into one. Proponents of this goal in the USA take their cue from Hirsch's (1987) *Cultural Literacy: What Every American Needs to Know*; and Hirsch *et al.*'s (1988) *The Dictionary of Cultural Literacy*. Their belief that the social function of culture is to preserve fundamental civilised values has parallels in earlier British debates, and echoes, for example, the views of Matthew Arnold in *Culture and Anarchy* (1869; reprinted 1960) and F.R. Leavis in *Mass Civilisation and Minority Culture* (1930). Arnold and Leavis saw 'Culture' as being the preserve of an elite minority, and they argued that the values expressed by literature, music and art acted as a defence against the 'anarchy' that would follow upon the adoption of the corrupt, vulgar values of the uneducated masses. Hirsch's work also implies that elite culture is a repository of basic values, but unlike Arnold and Leavis, his aims are explicitly inclusive: immigrants and members of ethnic minorities are advised to demonstrate their readiness to become American citizens by speaking English and becoming knowledgeable about the eurocentric culture that is shared by the elite groups in American society. Hirsch portrays the relationship between ethnic minorities and mainstream American society as being that of candidates for membership of a club:

> Getting one's membership is not tied to class or race. Membership is automatic if one learns the background information and the linguistic conventions that are needed to read, write, and speak effectively. (Hirsch *et al.*, 1988: 22)

As Walters (1992: 4) observes, this offer is disingenuous at best, misleading at worst. Full access to the opportunities offered by any society is fundamentally affected by just such factors of class, race, ethnicity, gender and colour.

Moreover, the argument that elite, eurocentric culture is uniquely qualified to serve as the universal repository of civilised values has been subject to a strong intellectual challenge since the 1950s, particularly in Britain (cf. Hall & Whannel, 1964; Hoggart, 1957; Thompson, 1963; Williams, 1958, 1965).

A narrow view of cultural literacy as associated with a specific set of elite values, sometimes labelled 'culture with a capital C' (Tomalin & Stempleski, 1993), at least provoked reconsideration of the overall goals of introducing culture into the ELT classroom. Is the ideal goal for a learner to be indistinguishable from a native speaker – in particular, an educated native speaker who is well versed in the cultural values and products of the elite group in society? This in fact seems to be the unspoken assumption behind many ELT curricula. Many learners might well align themselves with this goal, and be motivated strongly by lessons which indeed introduce them to 'culture with a capital C' – and teachers should consequently be open to this possibility and exploit it where appropriate. But what if learners resist this social positioning as a betrayal of their own cultural identity, or see it as an irrelevance to their personal goals in learning an L2? Murray (1992) sets out explicitly to challenge the narrow view of cultural literacy, and presents an alternative definition which celebrates cultural diversity as a 'resource' in the American ELT classroom, rather than denigrating it as a social stigma and mark of exclusion.

It would be ill-advised to polarise the debate about 'whose culture' should be represented in the ELT classroom by arguing that 'elite culture' should be actively excluded because it is irrelevant to the concerns of learners. 'Elite culture' – literature, music, art, philosophy – can be a marvellously rich resource and some learners are strongly motivated by its use in the L2 classroom. However, the very fact that it is associated with 'educated' or 'elite' groups in the target society may demotivate other students, who view interest in such cultural products as irrelevant to their own cultural concerns. In such cases, the 'home culture' of the learners can be exploited as a valuable classroom resource. This involves teachers finding out about students' production and consumption of cultural products – whether 'home culture' in this sense means ethnic culture, class culture or professional culture. This can be done in class initially through questionnaires (for a detailed example, see Murray *et al.*, 1992) which can target specific topic areas.

Questionnaires about language use in everyday life can serve as a starting-point for learners and teachers to become more keenly aware of their own linguistic practices. Vasquez' (1992) observations of literacy events in a Mexicano community in the USA noted a rich range of uses for English and Spanish in the home: from listening to the advice of community workers, getting the latest news and gossip from the local baker, listening to the tales of the older generation, to engaging in prolonged cross-generational, bilingual discussions about the behaviour of characters in popular soap operas. Lucas (1992) notes that different cultural profiles may influence how a learner responds to types of instruction in the L2 – someone who keeps a diary in the L1, for example, may be better primed for personal writing than someone who does not. Lucas also warns that each learner is an individual, and should not be stereotyped with generalisations such as 'Japanese learners do not respond well to personal writing'. Lack of experience of a given genre does not mean a learner would lack interest in it. A cultural profile can serve as a preliminary stage before a negotiated statement of language needs (e.g. 'I don't use English to speak to my grandparents, but I do need to improve the way I speak with my fellow-students in seminars'), but it also serves to raise awareness that language and culture are many-faceted and vary from individual to individual. It may also prompt a preliminary analysis of how class discussions, for example, are different from casual conversations (Chapter 3).

To summarise: in multilingual and multicultural classrooms, particularly in the USA, the proposed imposition of a narrowly defined 'cultural literacy' has been countered by a call to celebrate diversity (Murray, 1992). The principle applies mainly to this ESL setting (that is, where learners are long-term immigrants into an anglophone culture), but it can be extended to those settings where learners who share a single L1 are studying English as a foreign language. Celebrating diversity is principally about acknowledging that learners are already proficient users of language and inheritors of a rich culture. Extending their proficiency should not entail denial of that fact, but rather their current proficiency as language users and cultural beings can serve as a launching-point for their further education.

Language Learning as Social and Political Education: The Rise of British Studies

In the preface to a British collection of articles, Harrison states his and his contributors' concerns as 'the procedural culture of the classroom', 'the effect of political decisions on the content of language teaching programmes', and 'how adequately [teaching materials] reflect, or how they distort, the culture they purport to represent' (Harrison, 1990: 1). This represents a critical concept of 'culture', that is, one that is sensitive to the individual learner's relationship to the intricate webs of power and domination that characterise society from the arena of international relations to the microcosm of the classroom. Various textbooks and teachers' resource books continue this theme; for example, Bassnett, (1997) explores critical approaches to the construction of British identity. The topics range from the study of Shakespearean quotation in popular culture (Drakakis, 1997), to a description of the multiplicities of identity masked by the single term denoting a nation, in this case 'Scotland' (Crawford, 1997). The relevance of such topics to the foreign language learner is also explored (Byram, 1997a; Durant, 1997). In her introduction, Bassnett (1997: xiv) paraphrases Williams by asserting that culture is 'always . . . fragmented, partly unknown and partly unrealized' and calls for an inquiry into cultural practices that respects no disciplinary boundaries. Such an inquiry would draw upon literary studies, sociology, history, anthropology and linguistics, and it could as easily stand alone as form part of a foreign language curriculum.

Both Harrison's and Bassnett's anthologies represent a critical strain in the teaching of culture to learners: the curricular goal is less 'acculturation' and more to do with sociopolitical education, specifically an increased awareness of how various social and political pressures shape their own and others' national identity. This 'cultural turn' in British ELT has not been without institutional backing. In 1992, the British Council began publishing a newsletter called *British Studies Now*, which aimed in part to encourage:

> the multidisciplinary study of contemporary Britain calling on history, literature and the social sciences to explore the distinctive features of British culture and society. (Wadham-Smith, 1992; reprinted 1995: 12)

To this end, the British Council also published course materials (Edginton & Montgomery, 1996; Montgomery and Reid-Thomas, 1994; Raw, 1994) and, as well as *British Studies Now*, it supported journals such as the *Journal for the Study of British Cultures* (Germany), *Perspectives* (Czech Republic) and *LABSA Journal* (Latin American British Studies Association), all dedicated in whole or in part to developing the connections between ELT and the critical study of British and other cultures into social groups, which negotiate and share common beliefs, attitudes and practices.

The British Council is financed by the British government to promote cultural, educational and technical links between Britain and other countries; it forms policies and then seeks to influence teachers' behaviour by supporting educational initiatives and publications. It has its own agenda, which has come under intensive critical scrutiny (Phillipson, 1992), and which may or may not coincide with the agendas of individual teachers and students or of the overseas institutions with which it co-operates. Having Britain and the British as the focus of attention (even critical attention) of academic subjects in schools, colleges and universities across the world can be seen as indirectly promoting British trade and commercial interests. The British 'brand name' is at least kept alive among educated overseas elites. However, during the 1990s it undoubtedly did much to stimulate and sustain interest in culture, in a broad sense, through materials production, and the support of short and longer-term courses in Britain and overseas (see, for example, Raw's description of the first months of a British cultural studies course in Turkey in Byram *et al.*, 1994: 125–34).

Moving culture from the margins to the centre

The foregoing discussion attempts to tease out approaches to the teaching of culture that at times are closely interwoven. The everyday practice of language teachers has long borrowed eclectically from different educational approaches, and so the goals of systematic acculturation, or enculturation, or indeed sociopolitical education are unlikely to have been sustained consistently within curricula whose primary drive remains towards language proficiency. The intercultural approach assimilates some of the features of earlier approaches to culture in the communicative curriculum. For example, an intercultural approach assumes that:

- cultural topics (e.g. exploring how personal and group identities and values are constructed) are interesting and motivating;
- acculturation (the ability to function in another culture while maintaining one's own identity) is important;
- 'cultural awareness-raising is an aspect of values education' (Maley's introduction to Tomalin and Stempleski, 1993: 3);
- intercultural language education should cast a critically reflective eye on its own workings.

However, the intercultural approach differs from earlier approaches to teaching culture by moving intercultural knowledge and skills centre-stage, and making them an integral part of the curriculum. This means adopting strategies from ethnography as well as linguistics, and defining, teaching and testing intercultural knowledge and skills, as well as language skills. Most radically, it means redefining the aims of language education to acknowledge 'intercultural communicative competence' rather than 'native-speaker proficiency' as the ultimate goal. Not all language teaching professionals or institutions will want to embrace intercultural curricula in their entirety. Nevertheless, the following chapters, which give a detailed discussion of the intercultural approach, should be of interest to all those who enjoy reflecting on the means and methods of second language education.

Chapter 2

Implementing an Intercultural Approach

This chapter focuses more directly on intercultural communicative competence by addressing the following issues:

- *Defining intercultural communicative competence (the 'savoirs').*
- *The desirability of intercultural learning.*
- *Learners as ethnographers.*
- *The needs of different learners.*
- *Replacing 'native speaker competence' with 'intercultural communicative competence'.*
- *Task design in the intercultural classroom.*

Beyond the Information Gap: Defining Intercultural Learning

As we saw in the previous chapter, in a 'general' communicative language curriculum, cultural competence has traditionally been considered as knowledge about the 'life and institutions' of the target culture. By contrast, immigrant learners have been urged to learn and mimic the cultural behaviours of the host community, in order to pass as 'normal' members of the target culture. Cultural knowledge in the latter case has been directed at prompting learners to modify their behaviour patterns towards those favoured by the target community. Increasingly, however, in modern languages teaching, 'intercultural communicative competence' (ICC) is being seen as a complex combination of valuable knowledge and skills. Byram (1997b) has produced what is to date the most fully worked-out specification of intercultural competence, which involves five so-called *savoirs*, that is, five formulations of the kinds of knowledge and skills needed to mediate between cultures. Together these *savoirs* indicate the student's ability to reach Kramsch's 'third place', that is, a vantage point from which the learner can understand and mediate between the home culture and the target culture (Kramsch, 1993). These are specified as follows (adapted from Byram, 1997b: 34):

(1) Knowledge of self and other; of how interaction occurs; of the relationship of the individual to society.
(2) Knowing how to interpret and relate information.
(3) Knowing how to engage with the political consequences of education; being critically aware of cultural behaviours.
(4) Knowing how to discover cultural information.
(5) Knowing how to be: how to relativise oneself and value the attitudes and beliefs of the other.

This set of *savoirs* incorporates and transforms the goals of communicative curricula, even those in which culture found some kind of place. In an intercultural curriculum, the learner is still expected to accumulate facts about the target culture, and know something of how people from the target culture might be expected to behave. To these stipulations are added an ethnographic perspective (in so far as students are expected to demonstrate 'discovery' skills), a critical stance (knowledge of the behaviours of the target culture should prompt comparison and reflection rather than automatic imitation), and a liberal morality (learners should demonstrate the skills of decentring and valuing, or at least tolerating, other cultures).

However, developing intercultural competence does not mean doing away with the information gap or related activities, but developing them so that (1) culture becomes a regular focus of the information exchanged, and (2) learners have the opportunity to reflect upon *how* the information is exchanged, and the cultural factors impinging upon the exchange. There has always been a range of information gap activities: some involving the exchange of knowledge between partners, some involving the building up of knowledge from diverse sources (e.g. 'jigsaw' reading and listening), some involving the transfer of information (from visual images to verbal descriptions, and vice versa), and some involving the expression of differing personal opinions (e.g. ranking exercises, where learners must discuss their preferred holiday destination, their favourite artwork, and so on). These activities lend themselves not only to the promotion of fluency, but also, potentially, to increased awareness of culture.

A common criticism of some 'general' ELT courses in the past is that the content is frequently banal: the emphasis on skills trivialises the content. In the later 1980s there was a movement towards teaching foreign languages through a variety of topics, and, at its most radical, through instruction in some other discipline – in a some schools a subject such as Geography was taught through a modern language, such as French. At its logical extreme, this tendency led to 'immersion' courses, the best-known being the Canadian schools in which anglophone children received much or all of their education in French, and vice versa. Taking 'culture' as a topic has the advantage of direct relevance to the learning of another language, and the motivational factor of simultaneously encouraging enquiry into and review of one's own cultural habits. Intercultural enquiry can be used as the topic base of a curriculum. At the same time, cultural enquiry and reflection can shape and reshape *how* the information is exchanged in other arenas: factual writing, spoken conversation, role plays, simulations and the other staples of the language curriculum. In short, the intercultural language course involves the designing and implementing of tasks which encourage the learner actively and systematically to seek cultural information, which then impacts upon his or her language behaviour.

In order to design and implement such a course the ELT professional needs certain types of information and knowledge of certain strategies – for example, the way that language genres serve cultural needs, how language can negotiate cultural identity, and how written, spoken and visual texts can be 'read' as messages about cultural affiliation. This chapter shows how established means of task design for communicative teaching can be adapted to serve intercultural ends. Succeeding chapters seek to impart key knowledge about topics relevant to intercultural teaching across a range of subjects, as well as practical suggestions about how this knowledge can be transformed into classroom practice.

Is an Intercultural Approach Necessary?

It might be argued that it is unnecessary to teach culture explicitly in an ELT programme because it is already implicitly there in the lessons. Indeed, Valdes (1990: 20) argues that any method of language teaching and learning is inevitably cultural:

> From the first day of the beginning class, culture is at the forefront. Whatever approach, method or technique is used, greetings are usually first on the agenda. How can any teacher fail to see the cultural nature of the way people greet each other in any place in any language? The differences made in formal greetings, casual greetings, in greetings of young to old and vice versa, of employee to employer, in who shakes hands, bows, or touches the forehead, who may be called by first names, etc. are certainly not universal and serve as an excellent introduction to the culture of the people who speak the language, as well as to the language itself.

Valdes sees the inevitability of cultural content in language teaching as an argument for making it explicitly part of the ELT lesson. It has already been argued that good teachers have always made cultural 'asides' when required, and it may also be claimed that, since culture is implicitly built into ELT courses, learners will automatically acquire cultural knowledge. These arguments assume that there will always be an informed teacher ready to elucidate obscure cultural points for the learner, or that the learner's experience of the culture will not extend beyond the bounds of any one course. However, by encouraging learners to be active analysts and interpreters of culture (including their own), we help them along the road to independent intercultural analysis and interpretation in a range of situations where they might otherwise be at a loss, and where authoritative guidance is unavailable.

Learners, of course, have varying levels of interaction at different times with the culture and language they are learning. For some, English and anglophone culture might never be more than an occasional school subject in their home country. Others, however, might find themselves interacting with the target language and culture on a variety of levels: they might be conducting business in the L2, studying in an L2-speaking university, or living for a substantial period of time in an L2-speaking community. For the last group, whose interaction with the culture is more immediate, there is a correspondingly greater urgency in mastering the genres that have developed in the target culture to serve the needs of the community the learners find themselves in.

Absolute and universally applicable recommendations about how explicit a cultural component should be in a language course, therefore, cannot be given. Knowledge about how a community's beliefs and values are linguistically constructed and negotiated might well be a higher priority for learners who are likely to have direct contact with the L2-speaking community. For others, for whom the L2 is only ever likely to be a school subject, explicit cultural training might be treated as a lower priority. Even so, in the latter situation, an intercultural approach still offers a way of enriching the language-learning experience and contributing to the wider educational goals of better understanding one's own community as well as those of others.

Learners as Ethnographers

As we observed in Chapter 1, intercultural learning involves an element of ethnography, that is, the systematic observation and description of how a community behaves. Again, it might be objected that learners are interested in becoming proficient in the target language, not in becoming pseudo-anthropologists. The introduction of ethnography, defined broadly as 'the scientific study of different races and cultures', into secondary school and university foreign language learning is most closely associated in Britain with the work of Michael Byram and his associates (e.g. Byram, 1993; Byram, 1997b; Byram & Fleming, 1998; Byram & Morgan, 1994; Roberts *et al.*, 2001). Proponents of the ethnographic approach to language learning acknowledge that it involves accepting a new set of purposes for language learning and teaching. Effectively, it fundamentally reconfigures the long-accepted goals of communicative language teaching by seeking:

- an integration of linguistic and cultural learning to facilitate communication and interaction;
- a comparison of others and self to stimulate reflection on and (critical) questioning of the mainstream culture into which learners are socialised;
- a shift in perspective involving psychological processes of socialisation;
- the potential of language teaching to prepare learners to meet and communicate in other cultures and societies than the specific one usually associated with the language they are learning. (Byram & Fleming, 1998: 7)

This framework for encouraging learning through ethnography itself is culturally situated: it assumes learners will be part of the mainstream culture and therefore require critical decentring from its normative assumptions. However, given that 'decentring' should be sensitive to where the learners' 'centre' actually is, these precepts can serve as a general guide to curriculum and task design.

The question of whether learners necessarily require a range of ethnographic skills as a key part of their language learning experience is not ultimately one which will be decided by this book or by any one learner or teacher. The design and implementation of materials and methods require consensus by a number of parties, which, in different contexts, might include the materials designer, the teacher, the learner, the learner's family, the institution of learning, whether that is a private language school or a state school. However, as Byram and his colleagues are showing, it is possible to design and teach courses in which language learning is part of a richer, cultural exploration of the target community, and its 'whole way of life'. Chapter 5 further discusses what is meant by the ethnographic approach, and attempts to show how it might be implemented as much in the commercial ELT sector as in the language classrooms of state secondary schools, colleges and universities.

Addressing the Needs of Different Learners

Pulverness (1996) argues that in the 1980s, ELT materials and syllabuses were driven largely by needs analysis, rather than cultural considerations. The intercultural approach also recognises the fact that different learners have different needs, and that these needs should be taken into consideration when devising curricula and courses. Learners may have more or less immediate contact with the target culture; and they may have, as individuals, more or less interest in the range of products produced by that culture (some might be motivated by a focus on literature, art, music, television, or films, while others might not). Some learners might wish to integrate seamlessly into an L2 subculture (for example, an academic or professional community) whereas others might wish to retain a distinct cultural identity while also requiring to communicate with a range of L2 speakers. These various needs and wants will impact upon the type of input that the materials and course designer will wish to use, and also impact upon the goals of the course, whether the learner is being trained to be mainly a cultural observer or to be an active member of a specific subcultural group, such as academics.

The following chapters of this book cater for a range of these needs. First of all, the learner is seen as a cultural observer and analyst – as a kind of 'ethnographer'. The explicit observation and analysis of the relationship between language and cultural settings may be seen as a highly specialised skill, but it is a skill which is extremely useful for L2 learners, for the reasons given above. Primarily, it is a skill that will equip them for areas of possible misunderstanding in the target culture, and, one hopes, by promoting better understanding, this skill will promote tolerance and enjoyment of the target culture. Secondly, most learners will wish to participate at some level in the target culture – whether as casual conversationalists or as members of specific subcultural communities. Other factors (such as race, colour, class and ethnicity) notwithstanding, linguistic membership of these subcultures entails competence in the genres which serve them. The succeeding chapters on this book therefore give advice and suggestions on (1) training learners to be cultural observers, and (2) demonstrating to learners how different genres (spoken and written) are products of subcultural communities with specific cultural needs.

There is a danger in packaging the cultural content of courses too neatly, because culture is a dynamic concept, forever being negotiated and renegotiated by its members. No sooner has an ELT materials designer codified the norms of behaviour of a particular community than these norms have shifted. For this reason, training in cultural observation should be part of most courses.

A thorny political question is how much learners should be expected to conform to the norms and values of a target culture, if these are alien or irrelevant to an individual's concerns. Casanave (1992) gives a case study of 'Virginia', a Hispanic woman who joined a doctoral programme in sociology at an American university, only to find that the theoretical concerns and demands of that subculture (i.e. the culture of quantitative sociologists) did not meet her needs as a woman who wished to tackle practical social issues. She dropped out after a year. Casanave (1992: 165–6) notes that the conflict between her 'home' culture and the target 'academic' culture was realised partly in her rejection of technical language in favour of 'everyday' terms:

> Language in some ways lay at the heart of her self-identity by helping define who she was and with which reference group she would align herself. By 'using Dr. Bernstein's language' she was aligning herself with scientists, not with the populations with whom she wished to communicate at home and in future work: women, ethnic minorities, educators in racially and culturally mixed neighbourhoods. She rejected this alignment, but had no convenient linguistic substitute because so many of the new concepts seemed to be created out of the specialized language itself.

Casanave notes that the university's academics were trying to do their best for their students – rigorous application of theoretical modes of validation is highly valued in academic circles and its mastery leads to status and influence in that community. However, Virginia's particular needs were not met by the course she was offered. Casanave (1992: 179) concludes by suggesting that in cases where prospective new members come from diverse backgrounds, it is the subculture that has to rethink its norms and values:

> A program that admits half or more of its doctoral students from outside the mainstream White middle-class culture needs to consider seriously the question of how relevant its socialization practices are to a culturally diverse group. If certain skills and values are deemed funda-mental, how can they be transmitted more meaningfully to people who may have no inherent interest in the intellectual inventions of White males?

In short, there are profound consequences when an L2 speaker participates in an L1 culture – not just for the learner but potentially for the members of the target culture, who risk having their cherished values challenged by the new or aspiring members. The language teacher supporting learners like Virginia is faced with the options of training them either to assimilate invisibly into the L2 culture, or to articulate their resistance to its values. Equipping learners to resist the values of an education system is clearly a high-risk option. More generally, the question of how many cherished values should be up for negotiation is an awkward one. Barrow (1990: 9) argues that English teachers should not be embarrassed about presenting their cultural values to non-native speakers:

> I am not suggesting that teachers of English as a Second Language should see themselves as missionaries for the cultural heritage that is enshrined in the English Language or that they should disparage the cultural backgrounds of their students. But I am suggesting that they should have no qualms about the fact that they are directly introducing certain patterns of thought and values to students, and, indirectly, introducing various other beliefs, values and ways of thinking. It is true that at a sophisticated level of language use students will encounter much that is foreign to their thinking, but we can reasonably argue that much of what they are introduced to is desirable, in some instances we may even say superior to alternatives. Besides which, provided we avoid indoctrination, we are not forcing anybody to accept anything: we are merely presenting them with the possibility of thinking in certain ways.

The final point made here is disingenuous: educators seldom, if ever, 'merely present the possibility of thinking in certain ways'. Learners invest time, energy and money in educational programmes, usually in the expectation that their career prospects and social standing will be improved. To gain a qualification they need to demonstrate mastery of (and implicit alignment with) L2 cultural norms as presented, implicitly or explicitly, by the faculty staff. Students can always choose to leave programmes, as 'Virginia' did, but otherwise they are in a relatively powerless position with respect to academic cultures which are powerful and usually conservative. An issue facing intercultural language education is the negotiation of forums, acceptable to colleagues as well as learners, whereby students can explore the political nature and consequences of their education in an informed and unthreatening way.

At least university students are at a level of maturity when they are capable of reflecting on educational issues critically and articulating their own concerns. Byram *et al.* (1994: 16–24) consider the relatively unexplored issue of developmental psychology in intercultural education: at what age can learners be expected to benefit from an intercultural curriculum? Their review of available research suggests that, although individuals differ in their capacity for 'decentring' and 'empathy', by the time they reach young secondary school age (12 years and upwards), we should be able to expect learners to engage in tasks that involve intercultural exploration. From the early teenage years on, then, a focus on culture may have two desirable outcomes: (1) the ability to interpret the cultural norms governing the community to which the learner desires access, and (2) the ability to negotiate alternative ways of obtaining desired goals within the target culture. Johns' (1992) study of a successful learner from Lao suggests that her ability to interpret the sometimes alien demands of the faculty and her enjoyment in meeting those demands were a key factor in her success:

> Her rational approach to cultural acquisition enabled her to stand back and examine the rules – rules that enabled her to make analogies about tasks, to understand the nature of higher order thinking skills (e.g. analyzing), to exploit models and to structure new discourse. She found pleasure in coming to terms with this foreign culture and its distant faculty. (Johns, 1992: 195)

Clearly, not every learner gains pleasure from identifying and conforming to the demands of educators – some, like 'Virginia', will actively or passively resist conforming, and challenge the norms of their instructors. However, an intercultural approach – the recognition that communities cluster around a set of common goals, values and beliefs which are articulated in and through different types of language and behaviour – should help learners identify more clearly those communities with which they wish to align themselves, to observe the way they work, and to negotiate more effectively their own place in these communities.

More Than a Native Speaker?

In the end, if all instruction has been successful, what should our 'intercultural' L2 learner look like? As already noted, the spoken or unspoken goal of L2 instruction and learning has been 'native-speaker proficiency', a nebulous and rarely attained goal. As Kramsch (1998) observes, the concept of native-speaker competence has been subject to re-evaluation over the past two decades (e.g. Davies, 1991; Kachru, 1986; Widdowson, 1994), and Byram's promotion of 'intercultural' communicative competence' further prompts a re-examination of 'native-speaker' competence as the ultimate goal of language learning. Intercultural L2 learners are both less and more skilled than a monolingual native speaker. They are less skilled in so far as they do not have complete mastery of the L2 language system. Errors have always been judged harshly by L2 teachers, but probably less harshly by those outside the educational system (cf. Loveday, 1981: 147–8). Loveday (1981: 125–75) observes that the criterion for 'correct' spoken English for the L2 learner is standard English, which is itself based on a codification of a written variety of the language used by the educated and powerful. Few native English-speakers entirely conform to 'standard English' in their own output, but even today, when recordings have introduced a great variety of accents into the L2 classroom, there is still relatively little systematic attention paid to non-standard dialects (cf. Corbett, 2000). It is ironic that L2 learners are often required institutionally to conform to standards that are more rigorous than those applied to native speakers. Of course, dialect-speakers' 'errors' do not arise because of incomplete mastery of the L1 system – the stigmatised 'errors' of dialect-speakers are only regarded as such in relation to the standard variety. Dialect features are usually completely systematic and intelligible within their own context, and they are used at least in part to signify alignment with a particular social or regional group of speakers, in the same way that use of the standard variety shows affiliation to elite, educated or powerful groups.

In the intercultural curriculum, near-native mastery of the elite L2 variety is not the unspoken goal. Instead, the 'intercultural' or 'trans-cultural' speaker is the ideal (cf. Kramsch, 1998; Risager, 1998). Kramsch (1998) sees the 'intercultural' speaker as one who moves easily between discourse communities – communities encountered at home, school, work and play – observing and applying the language that is appropriate to each community. Language learners' knowledge of different languages and cultures makes them more skilled than monolingual native speakers. Intercultural communicative competence, for Kramsch, is not knowledge, but 'shared rules of interpretation' that are applied judiciously to familiar and new contexts to make sense of the world (Kramsch, 1998: 27). Risager's notion of learning to be a 'transcultural' speaker is also conditioned by the fact that it is increasingly apparent that learners do not belong to a single monocultural and monolinguistic bloc:

> The transcultural approach takes as its point of departure the interwo-ven character of cultures as a common condition for the whole world: cultures penetrate each other in changing combinations by virtue of extensive migration and tourism, world wide communication systems for mass and private communication, economic interdependence and the globalisation of the production of goods. (Risager, 1998: 248)

If even national identity is a consequence of a group's construction of a powerful 'imagined community' (cf. Anderson, 1991) then the cultural affiliations that the individual learner forges or renounces by travel, corre-spondence, participation in email discussion groups, education, immigration, and so on, are likely to be equally powerful and important in determining his or her language use and preferences. The 'intercultural' or, in Risager's terms, 'transcultural' learner is one who is linguistically adept (although not 'native-speaker' proficient), who has skills which enable him or her to identify cultural norms and values that are often implicit in the language and behaviour of the groups he or she meets, and who can articulate and negotiate a position with respect to those norms and values. In achieving this, the learner may become more skilled – in Kramsch's (1998) terms, more 'privileged' – than a mere monolingual speaker of the target language.

Having discussed at length the objectives of the intercultural curriculum, we turn now to the question of how it is to be implemented in the classroom. As noted earlier, implementing an intercultural curriculum does not mean that the teacher has to abandon communicative tasks. These can be adapted to provide materials for raising intercultural awareness by reflecting on culturally specific patterns of behaviour. The tasks may range from a 15-minute activity to a long-term project and report. However, the framework devised by Nunan (1989) for designing communicative tasks can be adapted as the basis for many intercultural tasks.

Designing Tasks for the Intercultural Classroom

Nunan's framework sees the *task* as consisting of six components which have to be specified for any communicative activity:
These components can be modified if the aim of the task is to raise cultural awareness as well as to develop communicative skills. Let us consider the components in turn.

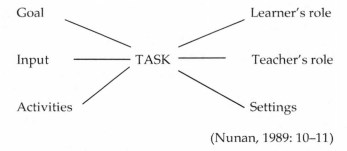

Goal   Learner's role

Input   TASK   Teacher's role

Activities   Settings

(Nunan, 1989: 10–11)

Goals

Goals refer to the pedagogical purpose of the task. The goals of cultural tasks will normally involve a combination of intercultural exploration and linguistic development. For example, the following goals might be met by specific intercultural tasks:

- to investigate how everyday conversation maintains the solidarity of social groups; to investigate how the individual's status in a group is negotiated through casual conversation; to observe the different roles

played by men and women in conversation in the target culture (see Chapter 3);
- to consider how the expectations of the academic community in the target culture affect the language used in research articles; to compare how the different expectations of the academic community and the general public affect the language of research articles and their popularisations (see Chapter 4);
- to research, describe and explain patterns of behaviour in a certain community, such as youth subcultures, professional business people or scientists, or Scottish country dancers (see Chapters 5 and 6);
- to explore the cultural messages conveyed by visual images, literary and media texts (see Chapters 7 and 8).

As noted above, the goals selected for any given course will depend upon various factors: how much access do the learners have to the target culture (exchange visits, broadcast media, email contacts), and what is the level and nature of the learners' participation in the target culture (are they learning mainly for tourism, education, business, or immigration)?

Input

'Input' refers to the stimulus provided by the teacher for the learning to occur. The input may be a written or spoken text for discussion, or a visual image for interpretation and evaluation, or a media text for analysis. As in communicative language teaching in general, 'authentic' materials are valuable classroom resources – 'authentic' materials being those written or spoken texts that have not been produced primarily for teaching purposes. In communicative methodology, there has been much debate about the 'authentic use' of authentic materials – a newspaper, for example, is perceived to have lost some of its 'authenticity' if it is used for, say, jigsaw reading and information exchange, rather than for the kind of reading that people normally do with newspapers. The terms of this debate shift somewhat in the intercultural classroom. Authentic materials are not necessarily there to be used in the same way as members of the target culture use them – they are there as evidence of how a culture operates. Thus an L2 newspaper or magazine can be compared with an L1 counterpart, to see how each culture constructs news values, or travel agency advertisements might be used to see how different cultures represent foreign countries, or leisure priorities. The tasks used in the intercultural classroom may be 'inauthentic' in that they sometimes involve *more* interpretation than the native speaker would engage in; however, this is another consequence of the L2 learner becoming an intercultural observer, rather than a simulacrum of a mythical L1 speaker.

Not all input in the intercultural classroom needs to be authentic. The input may be constructed by the teacher: a set of outlines for conducting and reporting on an interview or an ethnographic observation; a proposition for debate etc. The material used as input will correspond to the goals of the cultural task – political campaign posters from different countries might be used to investigate the way different cultures use images for propaganda purposes (see Chapter 7).

It is obvious that a broadening of input in the intercultural classroom to include L1 material has implications for the teacher – bilingual teachers will be at an advantage over their monolingual colleagues. However, the monolingual teacher can work with visual materials from the L1 culture, and co-operate with bilingual colleagues – and learners! – in finding appropriate materials for comparison activities.

Activities

A full range of communicative activities can also be used to serve the goals of an intercultural task. Students may collect and share information through class presentation or group work (which will necessarily involve information gap activities), and they may evaluate and discuss their different observations and findings. Having observed cultural behaviours in action, they may be asked to reconstruct that behaviour in role plays or simulations, or by writing parallel texts.

Learner's role

The learner's role will vary from activity to activity, and from stage to stage within each activity. As courses progress there will probably be a gradation in the learner's role according to how much responsibility he or she must take for the collection, organisation, evaluation, reporting, and / or reconstructing of materials exemplifying cultural behaviour. In the early stages of a course the learners will need support or 'scaffolding' for the activities – the teacher will probably need to provide guidelines, models if needed, and lead the learners through the tasks. Later, as the learners become more confident, they may wish to negotiate an agenda, initiate a series of tasks, or contribute more actively to the construction and implementation of intercultural tasks.

Teacher's role

The teacher's role is the mirror-image of the learner's. Again, in the early stages of a course, it will be primarily the teacher's responsibility to provide materials for the tasks, to suggest and show how they may be used to increase intercultural competence, to provide models of evaluation, and to suggest language that might be used to explore or reconstruct cultural behaviour. In later stages of a course the role of the teacher may change to one of negotiator, or mediator between the interests of the learners and the demands of the institution. Again, as learners become more confident and independent, the teacher's role is much more of a guide and that of adviser, rather than initiator and authority. The changing roles of teacher and learner themselves offer opportunities for cultural exploration. In different cultures, even within the same school, college or university, the teacher–student relationship varies. In some cases the teacher is expected (by both parties) to be a distant, authority–figure; in others, a friendlier guide and mentor. In a university context, Casanave (1992) and Johns (1992) both demonstrate how important it is for students to be able to negotiate aspects of their courses with their lecturers and tutors – in some cases impersonal and irrelevant tasks can be made much more meaningful and rewarding if they can be personalised within a framework in which the relevant skills are still being taught. As long as faculty staff can be convinced that the skills *are* being covered, a negotiated project can motivate students to a higher level of performance. The negotiated syllabus is advocated more generally by intercultural teachers such as de Jong (1996: 71–90). Learners can clearly benefit from being encouraged to identify the goals of a task, see where their own interests fit into the educational purpose, and to articulate reasons why their own procedures would satisfy the educational demands of the institution (or simply those of the teacher). Having said this, students must also realise that in many educational contexts – particularly at university level – they are negotiating from a relatively powerless position. Even so, if they can argue rationally that their own interests meet educational criteria, they may benefit from being permitted to integrate their own interests into the educational programme, and may even be rewarded for showing initiative.

Settings

Intercultural tasks, like communicative tasks, allow for a range of settings: from individual work, pair work and group work to whole-class activities. Settings should ideally vary throughout a course, so that learners can benefit from peer-group interaction as well as reflect upon their learning in some solitude. However, no one setting is inherently better than another – each has advantages and disadvantages – and it should be remembered that even group-work, that most privileged of settings in communicative language teaching, carries cultural connotations and may be viewed less favourably by some students. Johns (1992) reports in her case study of a successful student from Lao that the learner avoided peer reviews of her work because she felt she understood what the teachers wanted better than her fellow students, and she found it useful to practise and memorise exam essay responses on her own, to improve her speed in examinations. In contrast, my own experience of working with university students from Hong Kong over several years is that they benefited from organising themselves into study groups where the stronger students saw it as their responsibility to help the weaker ones. Johns concludes (1992: 197): 'It is my contention that rather than impose native speaker 'rules', we should encourage diverse students to do what works for them, whether it is theoretically correct at this point or not.' Allowing for a range of settings throughout a series of tasks will have the advantages of satisfying most learners at some point, and also training them in what most teachers see as useful strategies of co-operation as well as individual development.

The components listed above can act as a framework for the teacher who is designing intercultural tasks. Furthermore, it has the advantage of adapting a set of components that will be familiar from communicative task design. For example, a teacher might wish to demonstrate to learners how gossip is used to negotiate group values in anglophone culture (see further, Chapter 3). As input, she may supply role cards that prompt the learners to talk about an absent third party, what he or she has done, and to evaluate whether or not that action was socially acceptable. The teacher's role would be to set up the activity, the learners' role would be to carry it out, and the setting would be small groups of perhaps three or four. Having acted out the role-play, however, there should be a pause for reflection, and the opportunity to refine learners' observations and their reconstruction of cultural behaviour. In this case, the function of gossip in different cultures might be reflected upon – is it ethical to gossip about an absent third party? Do men gossip more or less than women? What kind of people are gossiped about (friends, family, celebrities)? What happens if the people gossiping cannot come to a consensus about the moral evaluation of the absent party's actions?

Gossip tends to end with consensus – the participants move towards some kind of agreement or compromise about how they are going to judge the absent party's actions. In this way, group solidarity is strengthened, and its value system is re-affirmed. Learners might not have thought of gossip in these terms before, and having run through a gossip task once, they may wish to explore its limits by re-running it again, several times, varying the extent of disagreement and consensus. This refinement of the task has the effect both of strengthening their language skills and making them aware of the range of possible variations within this culturally conditioned genre.

The main point is that learners should be as aware as the teacher is of the pedagogical goals of the intercultural tasks, and they should have the opportunity both to reflect upon the cultural behaviour targeted, and to refine their own simulations of this behaviour, once it has been reflected upon. In other words, tasks should offer opportunities for reflection, and activities should be recycled if learners are to benefit fully from them.

Chapter 1 and this chapter have established the general framework of an intercultural approach to teaching English as a foreign language, and suggested that an adaptation of task-based communicative activities can well serve the goals of an intercultural curriculum. The following chapters consider in greater detail some of the key issues already raised.

Chapter 3

Culture and Conversational English

This chapter turns to the more specific focus of conversational English, and argues that casual conversation is quintessentially cultural. It addresses the following issues:

- *The difference between transactional and interactional talk.*
- *The neglect of interactional talk in the language classroom.*
- *The exploration of the cultural functions of talk through a case study.*
- *Genres of conversational English.*
- *Power relations and participant goals in conversation.*
- *Constructing intercultural activities to teach conversation.*

What is 'Casual Conversation'?

If you think of all the reasons for which you use spoken language during the day, from the time you wake up to the time you go to sleep, you will quickly come up with a long list of reasons for speaking. Sometimes speech is *transactional*: it is 'message' oriented, and involves the communication of information to achieve some goal, such as buying and selling, instructing, describing, and so on. At other times speech is *interactional*: it is social in nature, and includes greetings, compliments, telling jokes, and making 'casual conversation' or 'chat'. Even when the interactional function of speech is acknowledged, teacher training in the communicative tradition has tended to dismiss its importance. For example, Ur (1996: 131) makes the following claim:

> The way interactional talk is carried out in different languages is very culture-linked, and it is difficult to explain the conventions that govern it in a foreign language; it is dubious therefore whether it is worth investing very much effort in teaching and practising them. My own opinion is that given general language proficiency, and a knowledge of the more obvious courtesy conventions, most learners will be able to cope adequately with interactional speech on the basis of their own cultural knowledge and common sense.

47

An intercultural approach to language learning addresses the 'difficulty' underlying the conventions of interactional speech more directly than Ur recommends (although, to be fair, some of the role play activities she suggests do deal with casual conversation). If the conventions are indeed difficult, then it seems likely that learners will appreciate guidance in this respect that extends beyond a general proficiency, some ritual expressions, and their 'common sense'. This chapter seeks to untangle some of the complexities of interactional speech in ways that will facilitate in particular the teaching of 'casual conversation'.

The Difficulties of Casual Conversation

There are various difficulties associated with interactional speech, and, in particular, casual conversation. These difficulties do pose challenges but, as we shall see, they can be overcome. Some of the key difficulties are as follows.

Conversational patterns vary across cultures

As Ur suggests, one difficulty is the variability of patterns of social interaction across cultures. Some differences can be quite marked; for example, silence can be interpreted differently in different cultures, as can the paralinguistic features of body language and personal space. Once the learner has been made aware of these potential differences, however, they can become the focus of ethnographic investigation: how long can participants in a conversation endure silence before one feels compelled to speak? How close do participants in conversations stand? What gestures do they make and do they touch each other?

Many cultural differences are, however, subtler; for example, many discourse analysts have argued that males and females in English-speaking societies take different roles in mixed-sex conversations: males tend to initiate while females tend to support (Tannen, 1984). Learners can also be encouraged to investigate these kinds of interactional patterns, not only in the target culture, but also in their home culture. Do they have mealtime conversations within their families? If so, who initiates topics for discussion? Who or what provides the content of the discussion? How do members contribute? In the following sections of this chapter, we will consider a transcript of a mealtime conversation as an illustration of this kind of description.

Interpreting conversational implicatures

A considerable difficulty for non-native speakers tackling casual conversation in English is that much of what is said is indirect. People do not mean what they literally say. Participants in conversations, then, have to infer what is meant from what is actually said. The name usually given to an expression that demands some kind of inference to make sense is *conversational implicature*. Both transactional and interactional talk make frequent use of implicatures. For example, it might be taught that an indirect (and therefore polite) way of asking someone to close a window is to say, 'It's cold in here, isn't it?' The listener is presented with an utterance that is literally a statement plus a request for confirmation; however, he or she is likely to infer that it is in fact a request for action. Bouton's (1999) research suggests that non-native speakers find certain kinds of conversational implicature difficult to comprehend, given only general language proficiency and 'common sense'. Most difficult were examples of irony, understated criticism, and indirect affirmation or denial of the kind 'Is the Pope Catholic?' and 'Do cows fly?' Examples of these kinds of exchange (based on Bouton, 1999) include:

Irony

On hearing that his friend, Bill, has been seen out dancing with his wife while he was away on business, Peter remarks, 'Bill knows how to be a really good friend, doesn't he?'

Understated criticism

Jill: Do you like my new dress?
Angela: It's certainly different!

Indirect affirmation/denial

George: Are you going to the office party?
Alex: Do dogs have fleas? (i.e. 'Yes, of course.')
          Do chickens have lips? (i.e. 'Of course not.')

Bouton reports that learners respond well to explicit instruction in these kinds of implicature, although other kinds were less susceptible to instruction. The teaching consisted of giving handouts of examples of irony, understated criticism, and indirect affirmation and denial, and discussing possible meanings. Learners then searched authentic texts (such as the 'Calvin and Hobbes' cartoon strips) for further examples, and also came up with their own variants, such as 'Does a frog have hair?' or 'Do fish walk?' (Bouton, 1999: 70). Bouton suggests that such 'cultural' aspects of conversation respond well to explicit instruction. However, the acquisition of inferencing skills is only one part of conversational competence. We now turn to a more general consideration of conversation as a whole.

Towards a 'prosodics' of interaction

Hall (1999) takes a wider view than Bouton of the nature and function of conversation. She writes of everyday conversation (1999: 138):

> Much of this talk consists of interactive practices, that is, goal-oriented, recurring moments of face-to-face interaction, through which we manage our family relationships, engage in a variety of community-and-work-related tasks, and nurture our social networks.

Up to a point, then, Hall dissolves the boundary between interactive and transactional talk – both are goal-oriented. Interactional talk, however, is implicitly directed towards managing our membership of a range of communities. This is the ongoing cultural function of 'casual conversation', and it is managed differently by different communities within a single society, whether these communities are defined by age group, social class, gender, ethnicity, profession, or indeed leisure interest. Hall advocates advanced learners becoming ethnographers, and proposes a framework for analysing what she calls 'the prosodics of interaction', that is, the elements that combine to structure interactional talk. Judd (1999: 162) proposes a similar model, and the synthesis below contains elements of both:

> *Setting*: Physical location, time, and duration of speech events.
> *Participants*: Their age, ethnicity, gender, and geographic origin. What is the relative status of the participants (inferior to superior; peers)?
> *Expected goals/outcomes*: These may be transactional ('to make a purchase') or interactional ('to strengthen social bonds by telling a story that affirms group values').
> *Topics*: The situation will influence what gets talked about. At social events, we might expect gossip about the transgressions of absent community members, while in classroom situations, we would expect talk to be determined by the objects of study.
> *The constitutive speech acts and their development*: How are the utterances to be interpreted? Here we focus on the form and function of the utterances; for example, in what kinds of situation do we find questions answered by indirect affirmations such as 'Is the Pope Catholic?', and in what kinds of situation might questions be responded to by understated criticism, such as 'Well, it certainly is different'? How structured is the speech event – is it ritualised, as for example a religious service might be, or is it relatively unstructured, as in a casual conversation?
> *The participation structures*: How is the taking of conversational 'turns' managed among the participants? Are speakers self-selecting or nominated? How many can speak at one time? Who interrupts and who 'yields the floor'? What strategies do speakers use to take the floor,

maintain the floor, and keep the conversation going? Again, participation structures will vary from context to context: in a classroom, the teacher will usually keep the floor and nominate other speakers, while in a casual conversation the floor will be negotiated more freely.

Formulaic openings and closings: Some speech events have ritualised or expected openings and closings. Transactions often begin with 'Can I help you?' while story-telling within a conversation might start with a cue such as 'Well . . . '.

Relevance to learners: Will the learners ever encounter this kind of speech event? Does it have an equivalent in their home culture? If so, does the speech event in the home culture have similar or different characteristics to that of the target culture?

Hall and Judd's frameworks for the analysis of speech events usefully guide learners towards an ethnographic analysis of the speech event – one that will raise to their consciousness salient aspects of the way language is used both transactionally and interactionally. Judd, however, is rightly cautious about enthusiastically recommending that learners become amateur ethnographers: this kind of analysis takes training, skill and time, and a certain level of maturity – only teenagers and above will be able to cope with the sophistication of this analysis. Moreover, it is not always easy for teachers and learners in EFL contexts to find examples of 'authentic' native-speaker discourse to analyse. Judd recommends that learners in EFL situations turn to media discourse for speech events to analyse but, as we shall see in Chapter 8, this strategy has its drawbacks.

If an intercultural approach is to be implemented, then, some guidance needs to be given both in ethnographic analysis and in developing classroom tasks that focus on the cultural functions of casual conversation. The following sections are intended to provide such guidance.

Mealtime Talk: Exploring the Cultural Functions of Conversation

Everyday conversation has always caused problems in communicative language teaching. When everyday conversations are transcribed and written down, they typically seem unstructured and banal. Despite the well-established efforts of conversation analysts to uncover the structures of conversation (for example, turn-taking rules, and conventions of topic maintenance and shifting), it has nevertheless been difficult to convert these insights into practical classroom activities. The problem, as I have suggested above, is that communicative task design focuses on the transactional nature of language – the goal of communication has been seen as the bridging of an information or opinion gap. However, the apparent banality of much conversation suggests that the transfer of information or even opinion is not the primary goal of much everyday conversation. Of course, in all conversations, information is transferred from one participant to another. However, the implicit purpose of transferring information in interactional talk is, as Hall suggests above, to manage membership of communities. Therefore the main goal of interactional talk is not to gain knowledge as such, but to find out your fellow participants' *attitudes* towards the topic being discussed, and thus indirectly establish their various beliefs. Staffroom discussions of learners' behaviour, and discussions of issues of 'discipline' are obvious examples of this kind of talk in a familiar educational context. Where the beliefs and attitudes of participants in interactional talk diverge, there will usually be some negotiation to modify the core beliefs and attitudes of some members of the group. In this way, group membership is established and maintained.

One source of examples of target language conversations, is, of course, academic studies of discourse. Eggins and Slade (1997) examine various conversations from a linguistic perspective that embraces the cultural. In this extract from their data, there are three conversational participants, Dave, Brad and Fran.

1	**Dave:**	You know . . . You know a lot of funny people, don't you Brad?
2	**Brad:**	Yeah, everyone at Uni is.
3	**Dave:**	They're ALL mad –
4	**Brad:**	They're all FREAKS
5	**Dave:**	Except you.
6	**Brad:**	Yeah.
7	**Fran:**	And they're all coming home now.
8	**Brad:**	Whaddya mean? Coming, oh
9	**Fran:**	Like, they're coming up the hill are they?
10	**Brad:**	No, this . . . For General Studies we've got this . . . tutor and he's German and he's insane.
11	**Fran:**	I didn't know you had to do General Studies.
12	**Brad:**	Yeah, I, I got exemption from . . . *[noise of passing bus]* Bastards!
13	**Fran:**	Last year.
14	**Brad:**	From half of it.
15	**Dave:**	When are you going to do . . . all your odds and sods subjects?
16	**Brad:**	Whaddya mean, 'odds and sods' subjects?
17	**Dave:**	Well, you know you can't just do languages can you?
18	**Brad:**	Whaddya talking about?
19	**Dave:**	If you're doing an Arts degree, you got a lot of other garbage to do.

20	**Brad:**	No. If I wanted to, I could do French, German and Russian.
21	**Fran:**	This year?
22	**Brad:**	In First Year.
23	**Fran:**	Oh this year.
24	**Brad:**	I could do . . . In FIRST year you can do whatever you WANT –
25	**Fran:**	Mmm.
26	**Brad:**	– in an Arts degree . . . as long as you do . . . a few General Studies subjects.
27	**Dave:**	That's what I mean. And when you gonna do your General Studies?
28	**Brad:**	I'm doin it NOW!
29	**Fran:**	Mmm
30	**Brad:**	That's what I'm talking about.

(Eggins & Slade, 1997: 68; presentation of data adapted)

The relationship between these participants might not be immediately obvious, and without contextual knowledge, some of the meanings may well seem opaque. We can begin an exploration of the extract by using the analytical framework based on Hall and Judd, discussed above:

Setting: Mealtime in an Australian household.
Participants: Dave and Fran are the parents of Brad, a student. They are white; from Dave's comments it is evident that neither he nor Fran is university educated.
Goals/outcomes: This is an interactional conversation; information about Brad's studies is exchanged and discussed, but the subtext is to 'position' Brad in relation to (1) his family, and (2) the university community.
Topics: This is a family conversation, and Brad and his studies form the topic of the conversation.
Speech acts and development: The conversation proceeds by question and answer. Dave asks Brad about the kind of people he knows at university; after he gives his opinion, Fran directs the conversation (indirectly) towards what he is studying (for more detail, see the discussion below).
Participation structures: Dave initiates the topic and asks direct questions; Brad answers and elaborates; Fran monitors, checks and seeks confirmation.
Formulaic openings and closings: There is little that is obviously formulaic in this extract. Openings and closings might well be exhibited elsewhere in the discourse.
Relevance to learners: Family mealtime conversations are subject to con-

siderable cultural variation. While learners might or might not expect to have to participate in family mealtime conversations in the target language, they can compare this example with their own experiences. Do they sit around a table as a family at mealtimes? If so, which meal(s)? What patterns of communication are evident in their own family mealtimes? If they do not have family conversations at mealtimes, what happens – do they watch television together, or eat at separate times?

The difficulties of using a transcription of a mealtime conversation such as this in a traditional 'communicative' textbook should be clear. There are ambiguities, non-sequiturs, occasional incoherence, and, above all, the amount of actual information transferred is low. A conversation like this must be understood not as an attempt to communicate information, but to negotiate cultural positions, here among family members. The focus of attention is the son, Brad. He is a student, and his contributions reflect a tension in his construction of his cultural identity: he is positioned (ambivalently) as a student, but also as a family member. To some extent, Dave and Fran's contributions support or challenge one or both of Brad's cultural affiliations. Let us look in more detail at how these negotiations are worked out in the opening exchanges. The numbers refer to the conversational 'turns' as shown in the extract above:

1–6   This is an exchange between Dave and Brad. At this point in the conversation, Brad has been criticising his university colleagues, and Dave seems by his question (1) to determine how Brad relates to them. Dave shares Brad's antipathy to university people, but Dave pushes him on this point, resulting in Brad's dissociation from his university fellows ('They're all FREAKS' with himself as the only exception).

7–10   Fran intervenes at this point, apparently making a joke, that all the 'freaks' are coming home. This joke seems to be a humorous attempt to prompt Brad to re-evaluate his position, to self-identify with the students again. She seems more concerned than Dave with Brad's antipathy towards the other students and staff. Brad does not understand her intervention at first, then ignores her when she rephrases, and he changes the subject to a supporting example of a mad General Studies tutor.

11–30   The conversation moves onto what is again at first sight a trivial series of questions and answers about the curriculum Brad has to follow. However, under the surface, the various positions are being restated: Fran's question diverts Brad from further elaborating on the insanity of university staff, Dave's questions further reveal his low opinion of university studies ('garbage', 'odds and sods') and Brad oscillates between being disparaging about university and being defensive about it ('Whaddya mean "odds and sods" subjects?')

To summarise, the work of the conversation is partly for Dave to distance Brad from the university community, and Fran to 'reposition' him in it, while Brad himself is ambivalent, both a critic of and an authority on university culture.

As Eggins and Slade point out, other aspects of the conversation are culturally significant. Brad accepts his dominant role as the main participant in the conversation, and all participants accept the fact that Brad's university experiences and career are a suitable topic of conversation. Most of the interaction is between Brad and his father, Dave. Dave makes authoritative statements and asks loaded questions, and while Brad aligns himself with Dave at certain points, he dissociates himself from him at others. This kind of affirmation of similarity and negotiation of difference is typical of many conversations. To confirm his status as family member to Dave, Brad distances himself from the university. Yet he is a university student, and his knowledge about the curriculum gives him authority with which to contest Dave. Fran's contributions are least regarded in the conversation: when she attempts to reconcile Brad with the university, she is ignored. She does, however, manage to divert Brad away from disparaging the university by asking questions and 'back-channelling', that is, echoing what Brad says, and making responsive 'mmming' and 'aahing' noises that prompt him to continue developing a topic. In the latter part of the extract, Fran's contributions serve to encourage Brad to take on the role of authority on university life. The conversation, then, can be read as a shifting negotiation, in which Brad's status as family member and as member of another community – the student community – is contested and redefined. The way this contest is performed is very probably culturally specific: in other cultures, sons might not challenge parents in this way – or swear, however mildly, in front of them – and fathers might not demean education in front of a child.

Conversational Genres

The above analysis of a family mealtime exchange suggests that the surface banality of conversations belies their significant cultural function. The banality is related only to the information content of the conversations, which is unfortunately the aspect of linguistic exchanges that communicative teaching methodology has always focused on. The strategies used by the participants to negotiate cultural identity are implicit and tend to have been neglected. However, other than as raw data for ethnographic analysis by advanced learners, it is not immediately obvious from the kind of extract given above how such a conversational transcript *could* be used in the classroom. We now turn from the function of everyday conversation to the transformation of these insights into classroom activities that focus on production rather than awareness-raising.

Clearly it would be ill-advised to use a recording such as that of Dave, Fran and Brad's conversation as a listening activity, or even as the basis of a dialogue to be reconstructed, even though it might conceivably form the basis for classroom discussions about family relationships, and how they are negotiated through interactional talk. The very transcription of the conversation has the effect of transforming a dynamic series of negotiations into a static object, for description and evaluation. However, an analysis of the way that these family members negotiate their own cultural identities does not directly give learners practice in negotiating their own identities. In order to turn cultural insights into teachable activities, the structure of the conversation has to be generalised, and the kind of language used in any stage of the structure has to be identified and described. Eggins and Slade (1997) go into exhaustive detail on the grammar, semantics and discourse structure of this kind of conversation. Here, I wish to simplify some of their findings by focusing on particular conversational genres that can be used as the basis of classroom activities.

Chat

The text above is an example of mealtime *chat* in a family group. Although Fran participates less explicitly than the other two, the conversational turns are fairly evenly distributed. The purpose of the conversation here, mainly, is to renegotiate and affirm well-worn family participant roles: the son is the focus of his parents' concern. He is oscillating between his membership of the university community and his role as a member of this particular family – reaffirming solidarity with his father, who is sceptical of university studies, and responding (or not) to his mother's consequent anxiety. Chat can often be characterised as a sequence of turns whose main purpose is to work out these issues of group identity – confirming solidarity and testing difference.

Stories in conversation

There are times when conversation seems to depart from the relatively even distribution of turns seen in the example of mealtime chat. Frequently, one participant will take the floor and indulge in a long, sustained turn that tells a *story*. There are different kinds of story that can be told in conversation, and they often have a cultural purpose. In their study of casual English conversation in Australia, Eggins and Slade (1997) identify four types of story that would seem to have a wider application, at least in English-speaking cultures. All include optional and compulsory stages that I shall not elaborate upon here (for further details, see Eggins & Slade, 1997: 227–72). In brief:

- *narrative* includes some kind of crisis, which is resolved and perhaps evaluated;
- *anecdote* also climaxes in a crisis – say, an embarrassing situation – but no resolution is offered. The crisis is simply offered as something to entertain and amuse – it is usually reacted to with laughter;
- *exemplum* is offered as a story with a moral – it tells us something about how the world should or should not be;
- *recount* is a simple, chronological relation of events that are deemed worthy of the listener's appraisal. Recounts are told so that the speaker and listener can share a similar reaction to the events related.

Looking at these story-telling genres culturally, we can see that they have a clear purpose in the way they establish relationships between conversational participants. There are also cultural variations in the way stories are realised. Eggins and Slade argue that, in Australian English-speaking culture at least, it is mainly men who tell *narratives* – narratives allow men to tell how a crisis occurred that they were able to resolve. This puts them in a heroic role, which gives them status in their community. Women are more likely to tell *anecdotes* that put them in embarrassing situations in which there is no resolution. In female-only conversations, anecdotes are generally the preferred option; unlike men, women seem to bond by offering examples of their personal vulnerability. *Exemplums* are used by both sexes to seek group approval for a particular ethical or moral stance, and *recounts* seek confirmation of what the group deems normal and what it deems strange, funny or disturbing. The genres listed above can be combined in more complex conversational exchanges such as 'second stories'.

Second-storying

'Second-storying', or 'story capping', is very common in conversation amongst friends and acquaintances. Let us say someone in a group of friends has just returned from having a minor operation in hospital. He or she tells the story of their operation, and shows a small scar. This recount is the 'first story'. Someone else then tells their own story of an operation, usually more horrible than the first, and perhaps even shows a bigger scar. This is the 'second story'. Then a third person tells a story of an even worse operation, which possibly happened to a friend, but the friend has a scar *this* big. And so it goes on, until the most horrible story has been told, and the biggest scar has been displayed, and the topic shifts to something new (cf. Morgan & Rinvolucri, 1986: 89–90, 'Scars').

The function of second-storying is largely cultural. Again, the point is not primarily that information is being exchanged. The point is rather that the participants are re-affirming their group identity by sharing experiences through a sequence of narratives, anecdotes, exemplums or recounts. The conversation is a way of identifying that they have shared common experiences and also share common attitudes and beliefs (e.g. 'hospitals are scary', 'nurses are overworked', 'doctors are too young'). There is also a competitive element in second-storying. The latest story should always be more exciting or more vivid than the preceding stories – by capping earlier stories, the 'second storyteller' therefore acquires a high status in the group. Some people always have to have the last word, the best story, the most attention. Other people might resist playing, and sit quietly on the edge of the group, ready to fade out. But most participants are happy to initiate or continue the sequence of second-stories, sometimes having the best story and sometimes being just part of the cycle.

Gossip

Gossip, too, has its own structure and conventions. Eggins and Slade (1997) give a narrow definition of gossip, arguing that its cultural function is to reinforce group norms by describing and discussing behaviour that falls outside the accepted norms of the community. Someone who initiates gossip usually begins by telling a story about an absent member of the community, often a friend or an acquaintance – although often a known celebrity or public figure serves the purpose. The story will often relate or refer to some aspect of the absentee's behaviour that the speaker finds unacceptable. This evaluation, and the account of the behaviour, may be confirmed or challenged by the other participants in the conversation. Usually some kind of compromise is found – perhaps the group agrees that a particular aspect of the behaviour is unacceptable, but the third party was under stress at the time, or egged on by a fourth party, or was brought up badly. The purpose of gossip, then, is to negotiate within a group what is and is not acceptable behaviour – the point of the conversation is to explore and confirm group solidarity through the discussion of shared ethical or moral sensibilities. By choosing an absent subject for gossip, conversational participants can safely draw, redraw and confirm the limits of acceptable behaviour in their group or community.

Clearly, conversational genres can be understood as sharing an important cultural function; namely, the positioning of an individual in relation to a group by (1) confirming of the individual's worth, (2) affirming shared characteristics or experience (e.g. of vulnerability), (3) negotiating a shared ethical standpoint, and / or (4) sharing a sense of the strange or funny.

Power Relations and Participant Roles

Now that we have a sense of why and how people use conversations, and have considered some key conversational genres, we are at the point where we can begin to apply this knowledge to materials design. However, one final point should be made. So far, the misleading impression might have been given that all conversations have the same status, that the contexts are interchangeable and the participants can be equal players. This is obviously not the case. A family mealtime conversation is not the same as, say, a conversation between near-strangers in a doctor's waiting room. There are things one can and cannot say in these situations. What can be said is also determined by cultural norms – it would be interesting to see reactions to the conversation between Dave, Brad and Fran if you switched the names of Fran and Dave around. Would Fran then look like an unacceptably bossy mother? Do we expect women in anglophone society to be the supporters and checkers of information, and leave the demanding of and replying to information mainly to the men?

What would happen if a man went into a male-only group and started telling stories about embarrassing things that happened to him at, say, the golf club? Would his conversational participants react in the same sympathetic way we expect women to react to anecdotes telling of their vulnerability? What about a woman who regales her female friends with stories of how she battled heroically against adverse circumstances? Would her friends regard her with sympathy or as someone who is rather pushy?

Power relations naturally determine what is and is not acceptable in conversation. For example, good friends might tease each other without giving offence – it might be a playful way of testing the boundaries of their relationship. But teasing takes on a very different colouring if the teaser is the boss and the teased is the employee. It goes without saying that gender also affects this relationship: in different societies, with different traditions of gender relationships, attitudes differ when a male boss teases a female employee, and vice versa. Offence is more or less likely depending on the degree of differential in power and status.

Participant roles – the relationship between interactants in a conversation – will therefore determine to some extent what is and is not said in conversation, and this too should be incorporated into materials design.

From 'Real' Conversations to Classroom Activities

As we observed above, research insights into the structure and purpose of conversations, and the distribution of participant roles, do not necessarily directly suggest relevant or useful classroom activities. The insights offered by researchers can nevertheless be used in a variety of ways in the intercultural ELT classroom. The remainder of this chapter offers some practical suggestions as to how interactional speech can be taught, and how an intercultural approach to teaching conversation can be implemented.

Designing conversational tasks

Conversation, as we have seen, involves a complex set of possible options. We can obviously break these down into discrete areas for practice of specific subskills, like opening a conversation or supporting a conversational partner. Furthermore, we can devise more global tasks that practise the realisation of different genres of conversation. The activities which follow suggest ways of practising (1) some of the subskills necessary to open and sustain a conversation, and (2) some of the global genres of conversation commonly used to construct and maintain cultural identity.

The tasks below realise the general components of communicative and cultural task design outlined in Chapter 2. In addition, I suggest that any conversational task should make explicit (at least to the teacher) the following points:

1. Participant roles

Are the speakers friends, colleagues, etc.; are they of equal or different status?

2. Conversational focus

Are the learners practising a specific subskill, e.g. opening moves or responding moves in chat, storytelling or gossip; or is the task more global?

3. Cultural purpose

Is the point of the conversation to negotiate the status of the individual in the group, to determine shared ethical norms, or to invoke group solidarity by sharing a funny experience, etc?

4. Procedure

How is the task to be achieved, e.g. what are the steps in the role-play or game? Does the task have a tangible outcome, e.g. does a group decision have to be made by the end?

5. Language exponents

Do the learners have the appropriate language to ask questions, make statements, give opinions, evaluate experience and people, etc.? Do they command the linguistic resources to ask indirect questions, and make understated criticisms, if appropriate?

6. Opportunity for reflection

Ideally, some learners' conversations could be recorded and used to generate discussion about alternative ways in which the conversation could have developed. For example, learners can be asked if the conversation would have been different if the participant roles had been altered.

The tasks suggested below begin with two key subskills, which are widely applicable to a range of conversational genres, then proceed to activities focusing on specific conversational genres discussed above, second-storying and gossip.

Initiating topics

For a conversation to begin, one participant must initiate a topic by making an 'opening move'. There are various ways of initiating conversations, some of which are more likely to be transactional in nature, others which are more likely to be interactional, although, at times, as we have seen, the boundaries between these two can be blurred. See Table 3.1 and Table 3.2.

A good way of practising opening moves is by playing the game 'Hidden Sentences', which can be found in *Keep Talking* (Klippel, 1984). In this activity, the class is divided into two teams, and each nominates a speaker. Each speaker is then given a 'hidden sentence' which he or she

Table 3.1 The language of opening moves

Opening moves	Examples
seek attention	Hey Joe! Hi there!
offer goods/services	Would you like some . . . ?
demand goods/services	Could I trouble you for . . . ?
offer fact	That reminds me of . . .
offer opinion	Your dress looks lovely.
demand fact	Who's that letter from? Is that letter from Bertie?
demand opinion	What do you think of . . . ? Isn't that terrible?

Table 3.2 The language of conversational support

Type of supporting move	Example of supporting move (in italics)
ask for repetition of a misheard element	'He disappeared into the sticks.' *'He disappeared into the what?'*
confirm that you have heard the right information	'He disappeared into the sticks.' *'Did he?'/'He didn't!'*
ask for additional information needed to understand the preceding move	'He disappeared into the sticks.' *'What exactly are 'the sticks'?'*
volunteer further, related, information for confirmation	'He disappeared into the sticks.' *'Was that because he wanted to run away?'*
show that you have understood and acquiesce with the information	'He disappeared into the sticks.' *'Yeah, I see.'*

must work into the conversation, within a given time, in such a natural way that the opposing team cannot identify it. Sentences might be something like 'I sometimes think of becoming a vegetarian' or 'A friend sent me a postcard from there'. The class then identifies a topic that the nominated speakers will begin to discuss (e.g. 'The Economic Crisis'). The object of the game is for the speakers to manage the conversation so that their own sentence can be embedded into it in as seamless a way as possible. In order to do this, they must open a series of moves which will lead them onto their own topic area. This is a good activity to record, and then discuss in class how moves might have been opened and how performances could be improved. With regular practice, learners' skill in opening conversations can be significantly improved.

It has been frequently observed that second-language learners are often not particularly good at giving conversational support. In particular, they do not 'back-channel' the kind of support that encourages a speaker to continue the conversation. The kind of language that is involved in supporting your conversational partner is seen in Table 3.2.

The activity described below raises awareness of the importance of giving conversational support through back-channelling. The role-play invites learners to compare self-assessed and peer-assessed ratings of the level of support given during a conversation. The learner can additionally decide how interested or bored he or she wishes to appear to be.

Supporting talk

(1) *Participant roles*: two friends or acquaintances.
(2) *Conversational focus*: to practise supporting moves when someone else is storytelling.

(3) *Cultural purpose*: to show sympathy and solidarity with the speaker by giving conversational support at appropriate points in the conversation.

(4) *Procedure*: One speaker tells a story, and the other chooses a level of sympathy with which to respond (e.g. on a scale from 1 to 5), and gives support appropriate to that level. After the conversation the speaker (and/or other class members) grade the listener's responses on the same scale, to see if they match.

(5) *Language exponents*: main focus is on useful types of supporting move (see Table 3.2.).

(6) *Opportunity for reflection*: a comparison of the 'sympathy scale' can generate discussion about the appropriate level of back-channelling and whether the speaker's and listener's cultural expectations match.

For example, the first speaker might be given a role card prompting him or her to tell a story about an unfortunate event – let us say the speaker went on a walk in the country, and got lost in bad weather. The second speaker chooses a level of sympathy with which to respond, from bored to over-enthusiastic, and gives an appropriate level of support (from virtual silence to interrupting with a variety of supporting moves). The first speaker, and the class, are then invited to rate the level of sympathy the second speaker has been giving.

The level of support expected in conversational interaction will vary from culture to culture. The point of this activity is not necessarily to impose a particular level of support on all learners of English, but to demonstrate that (1) giving support is an important aspect of conversation, and (2) perceptions of appropriate levels of support vary from participant to participant, and supporters should therefore try to be aware of the effect they are having. The type of conversational support given in English can be compared with that of the first language, for example, by introspection, observation and discussion of L1 behaviour, or by cross-curricular work in the L1 classroom.

Second-storying activities

The two previous tasks concentrate on conversational subskills; namely initiating a topic and supporting your conversational partner. The final two tasks focus on the generic level, and so approach full conversations. The cultural function of 'second-storying' was discussed briefly above: telling similar stories on the same topic offers the opportunity for people to demonstrate that they share both common experiences and evaluations of those experiences. A group affinity is therefore established. By 'capping' the previous story in a second-story sequence, however, the story-teller can gain prestige within the group. Second-storying, therefore, bonds groups together and negotiates status within the group.

Second-storying is relatively easy to teach. Most language courses encourage students to tell personal narratives on a topic such as 'my holiday disaster', or 'how I got this scar' (cf. Morgan & Rinvolucri, 1986: 89–90). From telling stories to second-storying is a small but significant step.

(1) *Participant roles*: three or four friends or acquaintances.
(2) *Conversational focus*: to share common experiences, and to try to 'cap' the previous person's story.
(3) *Cultural purpose*: to bond members of a group and negotiate status within the group.
(4) *Procedure*: one speaker tells a story on a given topic (e.g. 'My fear of spiders' or 'The day I outsmarted the boss'). The others in the group support the speaker while s/he is telling the story. When s/he is finished, another speaker tells a story on the same topic: but it must out-do the first speaker's story, i.e. the story must be even more dramatic than the previous tale. When the second storyteller has finished, the third should take up the topic, and tell a third story, and so on until everyone in the group has contributed.
(5) *Language exponents*: the storyteller will use past-tense narrative; the listeners will use supporting moves, particularly evaluations (e.g. 'That's *terrible*', 'Good for you!' and so on).
(6) *Opportunity for reflection*: after a second-story sequence has finished, learners can reflect on the way each story-teller's tale related to the opening topic, and how successfully each member 'capped' the previous story. They can also reflect on the distribution of types of story by gender in the target culture and (if appropriate) their own: do males tend to tell stories in which they solve problems, and elicit admiration, and do women tend to tell stories that elicit sympathy and laughter?

By slightly modifying story-telling activities so that they become second-storying activities, their cultural purpose becomes much more evident to learners. Second-storying is a staple of fictional discourse: Monty Python's 'Four Yorkshiremen' sketch takes the genre to extremes by having four old friends, at a reunion, tell ever more absurd stories of the hardships they endured in their childhood. In *Jaws*, the shark-hunter and the marine biologist, who are initially antagonistic, eventually bond by telling escalating stories about how they acquired their scars. The film comedy, *Notting Hill*, also has a second-storying sequence: Julia Roberts plays a Hollywood star invited to an 'ordinary' English dinner party, where the guests compete for the last piece of dessert by telling stories of their failures in life. By being successful, Julia Roberts' character is excluded from the group, so she bids for the dessert (and, indirectly, for group membership) by arguing that her life too can be seen as a failure. In this scene, the function of the stories in creating group solidarity, and also their competitive function, are clear.

Gossiping activities

The last task is another complex one – a gossiping activity. The function of gossip, following the narrow definition in Eggins and Slade (1997), is to negotiate and reinforce group norms by describing and discussing behaviour that falls outside the accepted norms of the culture. By choosing an absent target, participants can safely draw, redraw and confirm the limits of acceptable behaviour in their small groups. The activity summarised below obviously focuses on a fictional situation. In 'real life' the malicious potential of gossip is often defused by discussing the behaviour of fictional characters such as those in television dramas and soap operas.

Gossiping

(1) *Participant roles*: a group of close friends.
(2) *Conversational focus*: a discussion of whether the behaviour of an absent friend is acceptable or not. The behaviour is described and evaluated, and the evaluation is then confirmed or challenged. Gossip ends with some kind of consensus or compromise.
(3) *Cultural purpose*: by gossiping, groups of friends establish and reconfirm what they regard as acceptable behaviour more generally in their culture.
(4) *Procedure*: Friends at a party are discussing the behaviour of an absent friend at a previous dinner party. The friend has insulted the host and caused an argument. The speakers have to decide whether or not to condemn the absentee friend's behaviour.
(5) *Language exponents*: language of evaluation, statements and challenges, requests for clarification, checking, support and/or compromise. There is often a particular emphasis on the use of modal auxiliary verbs, especially those to do with social obligation, such as *should*, and *ought to*.
(6) *Opportunity for reflection*: topics for reflection might include the following: (1) the morality of gossiping: is it fair on the absent friend? (2) the pleasures and social function of gossiping, (3) gossiping about celebrities, (4) do both men and women gossip, and if so, do they gossip about the same things?

The skeleton given above can be fleshed out with role-play cards that give different information to different speakers: one might be prompted to tell the story of the absent friend's bad behaviour to his host at a party. The other role cards might give information about why the absent friend might have behaved in such a fashion (perhaps, for example, the host had earlier refused to give him a loan that would have allowed him to repay some gambling debts). This particular role-play allows the learners to display their attitudes to a number of topics, for example, gambling, and acceptable etiquette at social occasions. As with other examples of this kind of activity, the role-play can be recorded, and the ways in which participants contributed to the discussion can be analysed, and alternatives suggested. The learners can also debate the consequences for group solidarity of coming, or failing to come, to a compromise about their attitudes to the 'transgressive' behaviour.

The function of gossip within and across cultures is further discussed in Blum-Kulka (2000), Hall (1993) and Tannen (1986). Like the other conversational skills and genres discussed here, gossip is open to intercultural reflection. Patterns of interaction in the home culture can be observed, discussed and compared with the patterns suggested here. In doing so, the learner comes to a richer, more complex understanding of how superficially trivial conversational interactions can have deeper cultural implications.

Conclusion

This chapter has considered ways of integrating an intercultural perspective with language activities that practise one of the most popular and yet elusive types of 'general' English, namely casual conversation. I have argued that one of the issues that has made the teaching of conversation difficult is that the communicative approach has tended to neglect the interactional function of speech and focused instead on its transactional function, namely, the exchange of information. The learner has been taught to understand and give, for example, facts, commands, advice and suggestions, but has not been taught how these are used to negotiate an individual and group identity within the target and home cultures. What is required to redress the balance is a shift in emphasis, rather than wholesale rejection of earlier models and activities. The activities sketched out in this chapter are not dissimilar to familiar communicative activities (indeed, some build on already published materials); however, the focus here is on recent research into the cultural functions of conversation, particularly by Eggins and Slade (1997). Such research forms the basis of practical classroom activities that in turn can provide a framework for further ethnographic analysis of discourse drawn from both the target and home cultures.

The intercultural approach raises some thorny ethical questions. The avoidance of a cultural perspective by some earlier communicative materials was not always an accident, but sometimes a principled stance. Ethical issues are evident when we look at, for example, the descriptions of roles that men and women take in mixed-gender conversations in 'Western' culture. Research in America, Britain and Australia suggests consistently that men tend to initiate and challenge, while women monitor, back-channel and respond – unless the group is composed of very good friends, where roles can be more evenly distributed. This, some argue, is indicative of women's role in a culture that is still deeply patriarchal, where men's power and women's subservience continues to be played out in the patterns of everyday conversational interaction.

Accepting that such a description is indeed a valid representation of actual conversational behaviour (which is arguable), how do we respond to it as materials writers, syllabus designers and teachers? Should, for example, Japanese or Argentinian teachers of English tell their female students that they should avoid opening conversational exchanges in mixed company unless with friends – but they should do a lot of *mmm-ing* and *wow-ing* to encourage male participants to develop their conversational topics? In other words, should teachers encourage learners to submerge their first-culture identity in an assumed, and almost certainly stereotypical, second-culture identity?

This question is too large to address adequately here (see FitzGerald, 2003 for an extensive discussion of intercultural talk), but a provisional, if somewhat glib, response is that teachers and materials designers should build into cultural activities genuine *opportunities for reflection*. Reflection should allow a critique of both home and target cultures, and the exploration of how learners position themselves in each. Active reflection should develop intercultural awareness (cf. Byram & Fleming, 1998; Kramsch, 1993). Obviously, as educators, we must expect learners' behaviour to change – after all, that is the purpose of education – but that change should be a result of choices that the learner controls, not a result of values imposed by a teacher, syllabus or institutional authority. An intercultural perspective is therefore a rich and powerful learning resource, which satisfies not just language-learning goals but the goals of a wider humanistic curriculum.

Chapter 4

Culture and Written Genres

This chapter moves from the discussion of conversational English to address issues in reading and writing. Topics addressed include:

- *Culture, genre and English for Specific Purposes (ESP).*
- *The meanings of 'genre' in different disciplines.*
- *The concept of the 'discourse community'.*
- *Shifting from genre to genre.*
- *Genre in the intercultural classroom.*
- *Tasks for reading and writing generic discourse.*

English for General and Specific Purposes

It is no accident that a concern for culture in ELT has been found mostly in the teaching of English as a second language (ESL, that is, the teaching of English to immigrants in anglophone countries) and English for specific purposes, especially English for academic purposes (EAP). In ESL and EAP contexts, teachers must deal with the fact that their learners have to learn more than the language of the target culture. In ESL courses, the students learn English as part of a process of acculturation, or integration into the host culture (Roberts *et al*., 1992), while in EAP courses, the process of learning English has increasingly been seen as part of the wider process of socialisation into a new academic community (see, for example, Swales, 1990). In these contexts, teachers and students have had to face more urgently than 'general' English teachers the issue of relating language use to patterns of cultural beliefs and expectations. In this chapter, the focus is on exploring writing from a cultural and intercultural perspective. The examples are taken mainly from scientific writing, though the principles can be applied to a more diverse range of genres.

It might not be immediately apparent why there should be an intercultural component to ESP teaching, particularly in the area of scientific English. Scientific and professional contexts might indeed be viewed as arenas in which participants primarily transfer information from one to another. Certainly, in the 1970s, when ESP experienced a remarkable growth in courses and textbooks, it seemed that all English teachers needed to do was to explain how particular surface features expressed universal processes. Contents of ESP textbooks of the 1970s and early 1980s focus on expressions used to articulate notions such as 'cyclical and linear processes', 'structures of classification', and 'defining technical terms'. The assumption that scientific English is the surface manifestation of universal procedures underlies H.G. Widdowson and J.P.B. Allen's approach to teaching scientific English in higher education in their series *English in Focus* (Widdowson & Allen, 1974, reprinted in Swales, 1985: 75):

> We will suppose that we are to design an English course for students of science in the first year of higher education. We make two basic assumptions. Firstly, we assume that in spite of the shortcomings of secondary school English teaching, the students have acquired considerable dormant competence in the manipulation of the language system. Secondly, we assume that they already have knowledge of basic science. Hitherto, these two kinds of knowledge have existed in separation: our task is to relate them.

The *English in Focus* series was popular and influential in the 1970s, and Widdowson is, of course, regarded as one of the main theorists of a communicative methodology. It is interesting to note that his concern with the communication of 'basic science' implies that it is unaffected by matters of cultural relativity: the scientific culture of the L2 learners is regarded as identical to that of their native-speaker science teachers. More precisely, the communicative activities engaged in by scientists are regarded as constant across cultures and levels of professional qualification. More recent work in the philosophy, sociology and discourse analysis of scientific texts has called this assumption into question. Any communicative activity implies a cultural context, which must be drawn upon to make sense of it: if the cultural context is changed, then the meaning of the communication changes too. This is true even of scientific and professional English.

Connor (1996) surveys developments in the discipline of contrastive rhetoric in the last three decades of the 20th century, and cites various studies of cultural difference in scientific and professional writing. There are, for example, many differences in the degree of explicitness and certainty with which a suggestion or a claim to knowledge is expressed across cultures. Connor reports a study that argues that Japanese business managers are more tentative when making recommendations than their American counterparts (Connor, 1988, 1996: 141–2). Other writers suggest that Anglo-American scientists are more tentative than their continental counterparts when reporting results of experimental research in peer-review journals (cf. Myers, 1989).

Some at least of the difficulties faced by learners moving into new academic contexts may arise from clashes in the various cultures to which they are affiliated or aspire: national, educational and professional. Students are socialised into ways of writing by their national educational curricula, which might value assignment structures and styles that are accorded less credit in the target culture. For example, Bickner and Peyasantiwong (1988; cited in Connor, 1996: 131) compared Thai and American schoolchildren's responses to essay tasks that prompted the students to reflect upon topics such as why older and younger people find it difficult to communicate. Bickner and Peyasantiwong's results suggest that Thai students are trained to take an impersonal view of the topic and seek counter-arguments, whereas the American students were more likely to express a teenager's point of view and use a more colloquial style. Such general differences may be traced back to the societal pressure on the Thai education system to stress community rather than individual values, while the US education system fosters writing as the expression of the individual's personality. Furthermore, at undergraduate level, Western and Eastern approaches to student assignments again seem to differ: in general, Asian university teachers expect students to treat published texts with reverence. Rather than explicitly express a point-of-view that contradicts that found in a published article or book, Asian students are expected to construct a harmonious balance of arguments for and against a proposition, and to defer to the teacher's authority to choose between them. In contrast, Western university teachers often expect published findings to be explicitly challenged, and usually expect their students to construct an argument in which their own point-of-view is clearly stated and justified (Ballard & Clancy, 1991; cited in Connor, 1996: 171–2). Students transferring their preferred writing styles across cultures are therefore likely to encounter problems: Western students writing in an Asian context may well be perceived as arrogant and disrespectful, while Asians writing in a Western context might be perceived as vague and unwilling to commit to an opinion.

Even within a discipline there can be cultural clashes. As noted in Chapter 2, Casanave (1992) describes the problems experienced by 'Virginia', a Hispanic sociology graduate who dropped out of a postgraduate degree course, partly because of her dawning realisation that the expectations of her theoretically inclined professors were not relevant to her own interests as a female member of an ethnic community who hoped to make practical use of her research in that community. While the professors demanded a high degree of abstraction and a grounding in quantitative theory, her own needs would possibly have been better served by a qualitative approach to the subject. Casanave concludes that, in intercultural communication, both sides of the divide should move towards each other – it is unreasonable simply to expect the person with least power in the situation (the immigrant, or the non-native student) to bear all the responsibility for managing the cultural shift. Similar conclusions are reached by Roberts *et al*. (1992) in a discussion of the problems facing immigrants who have to survive in an L2 culture whose expectations they do not necessarily share. However, the ideal of ongoing cultural sensitivity on the part of host institutions is, as Casanave implies, often dependent on the risk of breaking with a tradition from which many members of the institutions themselves construct their professional identities. In established academic subjects, a culture that is different is often regarded as a culture that is invalid, or, at best, suspect. Often, then, it falls to English teachers to take an intercultural approach, by making explicit the cultural norms and expectations governing contexts such as the academic discipline that learners find themselves in, and showing how those norms and expectations constrain the forms of communication and the type of language used in the discipline. In this task, genre analysis has been found to be a useful tool.

Genre analysis can be more widely applied in an intercultural approach to teaching – particularly the teaching of writing skills. An analysis of language from a generic perspective assumes that the form of the text, written or spoken, has evolved as it has in order to meet the cultural needs of the 'discourse community', that is, the group of people characterised by their use of particular types of text, from university assignments, to business presentations, to teen magazines.

Genres and Cultures

The word 'genre' has various definitions, within and outside discourse analysis. In literary and film studies, genres are usually considered to be text types with recurrent characteristics, themes or topics – the epic and romance are genres, and the western and *film noir* are genres. In these disciplines, generic texts can be analysed and evaluated by comparing how they integrate convention with originality. In linguistics, however genres are analysed, they are considered as texts that share a common set of cultural *purposes.* In other words, generic texts are designed to accomplish similar goals within the culture that has developed them.

A systemic-functional approach to genre

Within linguistics, there are three general traditions of genre analysis: systemic-functional, applied linguistic, and new rhetorical (cf. Connor,

1996; Hyon, 1996; Reynolds, 1998). Systemic-functional linguists argue that cultural purpose is a constraining factor upon text organisation, and that the structure of texts can therefore be in part accounted for by referring to their cultural purpose. Genres are conceived of as 'staged goal-oriented social processes' (Halliday & Martin, 1993: 36). To analyse a generic text, the systemic-functional analyst breaks it down into stages, each of which contributes to the overall cultural goal. For example, the discourse structure of entries in travel guides might be broken down into stages giving information about, say, location of destination, things to see there, shopping, eating, accommodation, and environs. These stages are determined by the fact that a tourist industry has developed over the last few centuries catering to a market which expects to do certain things on holiday, for example, lying on a beach, gazing at architecture or landscape, eating 'typical' local food, buying souvenirs, and moving on. The guidebooks themselves will target certain tourist subcultures: some will target the budget traveller and others, perhaps, wealthier sophisticates. The content, organisation and staging of the sections of the guidebook will vary according to the perceived needs of the readership that is being addressed – and the style of guidebooks will change over time as the market and its cultural expectations develop. Such texts can be compared and contrasted to show the 'generic structure potential' of this type of text – that is, which stages are compulsory, which are optional, and the order in which they are likely to occur. A range of generic text-types can therefore be analysed and presented to L2 learners as 'formulae', with certain components marked as compulsory and others as optional.

Applied linguistic approaches to genre

The systemic-functional approach assumes that culture is 'within' the text; in other words, that by examining the organisation of the text, the analyst can reveal the cultural expectations and values of the readers and writers. Despite some similarities to the systemic-functional approach, an applied linguistic method of text analysis draws more on ethnography and sociolinguistics. Associated particularly with the work of ESP researchers and teachers such as Bex (1996), Bhatia (1993), Candlin and Hyland (1999), Hyland (2000), Swales (1990), this type of genre analysis looks beyond the text to the social organisation of the community that it serves. Like the systemic-functional approach, the applied linguistic approach looks to social purpose as a factor which constrains text organisation and content, but unlike the systemic-functional approach, it supplements linguistic observation with other research techniques, such as interviews to elicit from 'expert' users their views about the social purposes served by the texts. One example of the use of this kind of technique would be to consider the different uses of citations in an undergraduate assignment and a research article. In undergraduate assignments, citations might display to the assessor that the student is familiar with the prescribed reading on the course and can integrate it appropriately into a coherent argument. In research articles, researchers use citations to indicate to their peers how they are positioning themselves with respect to a research tradition: which branch of research they are affiliating with and which they are challenging or disputing (cf. Swales, 1990: 148–51). Citations act as a kind of 'family tree' for researchers: they use them to establish intellectual kinship. If asked why they cite other people's work in their assignments or articles, students and researchers will usually offer quite different reasons. Knowing why a certain community uses aspects of text like citations can obviously help L2 learners to choose appropriate content and present it according to the cultural expectations of their readers.

A 'new rhetorical' approach to genre

The third school of genre analysis is the North American 'new rhetorical' approach which, as its name suggests, is concerned mainly with how persuasive texts accomplish their social goals. Since the late 1950s 'new rhetoricians' have sought to account for the persuasive quality of argumentative texts by drawing on 'recent studies in the psychology and sociology of communication' (Fogarty, 1959: 130) as well as linguistic observation of how *knowledge claims* were justified and supported within and across disciplines (Toulmin, 1958; Toulmin *et al.*, 1979). Perelman (1982) draws on classical rhetoric in an investigation of how informal argument is directed towards different audiences (cf. Connor, 1996: 69–70), and Bazerman (1988) considers in depth how knowledge comes to be 'shaped' through the evolution of the scientific article (cf. Halliday & Martin, 1993, for a systemic-functional explanation). What unites these 'new rhetoricians' is an interest in texts that result from particular social interactions in which an individual or group seeks to persuade another that its claims to knowledge are valid. As Hyland (2000: 7) observes:

> The importance of social factors in transforming research activities into academic knowledge is perhaps most clearly illustrated by the sociohistorical variability of rhetorical practices. The conventional linguistic means for securing support for scientific knowledge are not defined by a timeless idea, but developed in response to particular rhetorical situations.

There are considerable similarities between the three approaches to genre analysis outlined above, as well as some differences in methodology, particularly in the status (or lack of it) assigned to evidence beyond that of the text itself. The genres considered, too, vary. The systemic-functional approach tends to conceive of genres in broad terms; for example, Martin (1985) focuses on the 'hortatory' or 'expository' genres found in the writing of schoolchildren. The applied linguistic approach has conceived of genres much more specifically, to the extent that Swales (1990) devotes considerable space to the genre of requests for academics to provide reprints of their articles, and Bhatia (1993) to that of job application letters. 'New rhetoricians', such as Bazerman (1988) look at topics such as the way academic research articles evolve as a result of developments in the social organisation of the discipline. Each approach has something to offer the intercultural language teacher. Systemic-functionalism encourages a close analysis of textual features while the applied linguistic approach takes a more ethnographic stance that pays attention to very specific text-types, and the 'new rhetoricians' encourage a broader sociohistorical perspective.

Discourse Communities

Genres serve 'discourse communities', which are effectively subcultural communities characterised principally by having common goals and interests. The concept of the discourse community has already gone through several transformations in the literature. Swales (1990, 1998) introduced the concept, drawing on the sociolinguistic concept of the 'speech community', that is, a group whose accent and dialect distinguish them as having a common identity. Swales' earlier formulations of the discourse community were relatively rigid and included the following defining characteristics (Swales 1990: 24–7):

(1) A discourse community has a broadly agreed set of common public goals.
(2) A discourse community has mechanisms of intercommunication among its members.
(3) A discourse community uses its participatory mechanisms primarily to provide information and feedback.
(4) A discourse community utilizes and hence possesses one or more genres in the communicative furtherance of its aims.
(5) In addition to owning genres, a discourse community has acquired some specific lexis.
(6) A discourse community has a threshold level of members with a suitable degree of relevant content and discoursal expertise.

The origins of these characteristics in academic writing are immediately evident; indeed, Swales (1990) suggests that 'Special Interest Groups' (SIGs) run by members of English teachers' organisations such as IATEFL and TESOL are typical examples of discourse communities. A SIG will often have an agreed set of public goals (sometimes advertised in membership forms); it will have a newsletter and conferences which are its primary methods of intercommunication among members; the main reason for membership of a SIG is to obtain current information and ideas about teaching practices; genres used by a SIG will include lectures, workshops, newsletter reports and articles, and tips for teaching; each SIG will develop its own lexis (those interested in computer-assisted learning will be familiar with the technical as well as the everyday meanings of 'platform' and 'mouse'); and, to continue functioning, a SIG will require a critical mass of interested members, who can draw upon available expertise. These characteristics certainly define one kind of discourse community, in which many members participate actively (by subscribing to the newsletter and attending events), and which can readily identify its expert members. However, the existence of such discourse communities cannot account for all available genres. They might account for academic and professional journals and newsletters, but they have more difficulty in accounting for popularisations and mass media texts. What is the discourse community that accounts for, say, a tabloid editorial or even an article in a popular science magazine?

Barton (1994: 57; cited in Bex, 1996: 65) offers a less rigid description of a discourse community:

> A discourse community is a group of people who have texts and practices in common, whether it is a group of academics or the readers of teenage magazines. In fact, discourse community can refer to several overlapping groups of people: it can refer to the people a text is aimed at; it can be the people who read a text; or it can refer to the people who participate in a set of discourse practices both by reading and by writing.

Barton thus brings out the different orientations each individual has to the discourse communities to which he or she belongs. We can imagine a novice teacher joining a SIG, receiving the newsletter and actively participating in scheduled workshops. She may in time lose interest and drift away from the SIG, only receiving and occasionally reading the newsletter. Let us say that she then decides to undertake a further training course and her interest is rekindled. She starts attending workshops again, and even begins writing for the newsletter, and is elected to the organising committee. She contributes to the shaping of policy and leads some workshops herself. This notional teacher, then, moves to and from the centre of the discourse community at different periods of her life. Presumably she also has other interests, domestic and public, which simultaneously involve her to similarly different degrees in other discourse communities. She, like all of us, is moving within and across different subcultural groupings over time.

Not all discourse communities will, of course, have the participatory structure of a SIG. A teenage magazine will have fewer participatory structures: few of the readers will ever become writers, and the readership itself will always be transient and renewed. Bex (1996: 66–7) adapts a further concept from sociolinguistics to capture the fuzzy and variable nature of discourse communities: that of loosely-knit and close-knit social networks (cf. Milroy, 1987). Milroy's work on dialect preservation and change resulted in a characterisation of the speech community as more or less closely knit. Where members interact within a community in a variety of roles (e.g. at work and socially) then the network is close-knit and can often be identified by its maintenance of dialect forms. Where, on the other hand, members of a speech community socialise and work with different people, and have a range of 'outsiders' with whom they interact, they are 'weakly or loosely tied' to their community, and more open to language innovation.

It is easy to see the parallels with the discourse community. The teacher who is an active member of the SIG, both reading and writing articles, and attending and leading workshops, would be closely tied to the discourse community, and more familiar with its conventions and its generic modes of communication than a 'loosely-tied' teacher who only reads the newsletter on occasion. Readers of a teenage magazine would generally not move beyond a loose affiliation with a fairly diverse discourse community. The nature of the discourse community and the strength of the individual's involvement with it are therefore both variable. Bex (1996: 66–7) stresses the dynamic nature of discourse communities:

> What I am proposing then is a complex interrelationship between social discourses, discourse communities, text production and text reception. The model I have in mind is entirely dynamic. Individuals either produce, or produce interpretations of, texts according to the norms of the discourse community and the functions which the text is intended to serve within that discourse community. These are then verified by the group as meaningful, or challenged and refined. Such groups may develop highly characteristic modes of expression that remain internal to the group. However, these modes of expression are always situated historically, in that they develop from earlier 'ways of saying', and socially, in that they interact with and take on (some) of the meanings of the larger social groups of which they are part.

Bex's model reinforces the view that 'culture' is heterogeneous and always in the process of negotiation and development. This view is further affirmed by Hyland (2000: 11) in his discussion of 'disciplinary cultures', that is, the cultures of academic disciplines:

> Communities are frequently pluralities of practices and beliefs which accommodate disagreement and allow subgroups and individuals to innovate within the margins of its practices in ways that do not weaken its ability to engage in common actions. Seeing disciplines as cultures helps to account for what and how issues can be discussed and for the understandings which are the basis for cooperative action and knowledge-creation. It is not important that everyone agrees but members should be able to engage with each others' ideas and analyses in agreed ways. Disciplines are the contexts in which disagreement can be deliberated.

The concept of the discourse community is a powerful explanation of how and why genres develop. It does not in itself suggest how genres can be taught, although a clear description of genres and the discourse communities they serve can suggest some ways of selecting and organising teaching materials. For example, if we accept Bex's model of variable membership of different kinds of close-knit and loosely-knit discourse communities, we can actively seek texts which exemplify a shift in genre, in order to demonstrate the importance of contextualising writing in relation to the goals of different cultural groupings.

Shifting Genres

One of the recommendations in Kay and Dudley-Evans (1998) is to immerse learners in different examples from a given genre. This section offers a detailed example of a complementary 'immersion' strategy – a consideration of how generic texts shift around a relatively constant topic. This phenomenon is particularly marked when an active member of a close-knit discourse community (such as professional scientists) rewrites his or her research for a more popular audience. Much attention has been paid to popularisations (e.g. Myers, 1990) precisely because they exhibit the linguistic consequences of a shift in genre. The readers of a popular science magazine like *New Scientist* are only linked to the scientific community by virtue of a general interest, and so the authors of popular articles on science have a different set of goals when they write for a popular rather than a peer-group readership. Myers (1990) goes so far as to argue that the views of science implicated in peer-group and popular articles are incompatible, at least in the field of biology: whereas research articles construct a 'narrative of science' around a discussion about the validity of scientific procedures, popular articles construct a 'narrative of nature' which focuses on the natural world itself. In other words, whereas a popular article will tell a story about the natural world, its more academic counterpart will construct an argument about the validity of the methods used to research the natural world. This change alters the ways that scientists are represented, the way that scientific activity is represented, and, obviously, the organisation of the content, and the formality of the language used. The English teacher can therefore explore these changes by looking systematically at the changes that occur when a writer directs his or her work to others *within* the immediate discourse community, and then *outside* the discourse community. Teachers can also supplement these perspectives by looking at how writers outside the discourse community represent those within the discourse community. In short, the following questions can be asked:

- How do the members of a discourse community – a subculture – represent themselves to themselves?
- How do the same members represent themselves to people outside the discourse community?
- How do people from outside the discourse community represent people who are inside that community?

These questions can be used to guide text selection across a range of discourse communities. Youth subcultures, for example, can be explored by looking at 'fanzines' (fans' magazines) written by subcultural members largely for consumption by other members; interviews in other media can be used to show how they present themselves to other social groups; and newspaper and television articles about them can show the representations given to them by 'mainstream' society. There will, of course, as Bex observes above, be an ongoing negotiation across these three dimensions, as perhaps the subculture persuades other groups to accept its norms and values, or mainstream norms and values impinge upon those of the groups. An example of this negotiation can be seen by searching websites about skinheads, and the, often explicit, refutation on such sites that this particular subculture should be linked to a fascist ideology. The ideological tension within the discourse community, about what being a skinhead means, here interacts with stereotypical assumptions from outside the community, to generate challenges and denials from subcultural members, directed both at themselves and the vaguely defined readership that browses the web.

From subculture to mainstream

A more detailed examination of the shift in genres is now given, with reference to the discourse community of biologists working on DNA (cf.

Corbett, 1997). The sections deal in turn with generic texts which explain subcultural activity to a general, or 'mainstream', audience; present subcultural activity to others within the subculture; and portray subcultural activity from outside its own boundaries, in other words, give a view from the outside looking in. Consider first the opening of an article in *New Scientist* ('All About Eve' by Joanna Poulton, 14 May 1987):

> 'And Adam called his wife's name Eve; because she was the mother of all living' (Genesis 3, 20). Eve hit the papers in the first week of 1987, following an article in *Nature* which suggested that a common maternal ancestor of all living humans had lived 200 000 years ago in Africa. 'Super Eve' must have lived in East Africa' said the *Daily Telegraph*. What is the story really about?
>
> Rebecca Cann, Mark Stoneking and Allan Wilson, of the University of California at Berkeley, present evidence for evolutionary relationships between different racial groups and then estimate the date of the point at which these lineages diverge. The common ancestor of all the lineages may represent one woman living at that time, 'Eve'.

A popular view of science constrains the language of this extract: it alludes in its title to a well-known mass-media text, the 1950s Hollywood film, *All About Eve*, and in its first sentence quotes from the Book of Genesis, an even more influential mass media text. The allusions link this text to works in the popular domain – common ground is raised, in the case of the title possibly gratuitously, since in fact it has nothing to do with the Hollywood film. This popular science text employs a simple question-answer discourse structure, and focuses on the results of the experiment – the tracing of DNA lineages to find a common ancestor, the mother of all humans alive today. The methodology is mentioned only to confirm its reliability – DNA analysis has superseded morphological analysis in evolutionary studies. The real focus of concern here is the sensational result – the mother of humankind has been scientifically dated. The article also uses occasional colloquial expressions ('hit the headlines') among the more formal and technical descriptions. The grammar and vocabulary thus exhibit the tension between the specialised content and the wider public at which it is aimed.

Within the subculture

Poulton's text, then, is an example of how scientists and scientific activity are presented from 'inside' the discourse community to 'outsiders'. The view of scientific culture as one in which an authoritative observer looks at and explains external natural phenomena is rather different from that presented in genres in which scientists communicate with other scientists; in other words, from a perspective 'within the subculture'. This is evident if we compare Poulton's *New Scientist* article with opening paragraphs of the professional text on which it is based, ('Mitochondrial DNA and Human Evolution', by Rebecca L. Cann, Mark Stoneking and Allan C. Wilson, in *Nature*, Vol. 325: 1 January 1987):

> Molecular biology is now a major source of quantitative and objective information about the evolutionary history of the human species. It has provided new insights into our genetic divergence from apes,[1–8] and into the way in which humans are related to one another genetically.[9–14] Our picture of genetic evolution within the human species is clouded, however, because it is based mainly on comparisons of genes in the nucleus. Mutations accumulate slowly in nuclear genes. In addition, nuclear genes are inherited from both parents and mix in every generation. This mixing obscures the history of individuals and allows recombinations to occur. Recombination makes it hard to trace the history of particular segments of DNA unless tightly linked sites within them are considered.
>
> Our world-wide survey of mitochondrial DNA (mtDNA) adds to our knowledge of the history of the human gene pool in three ways. First, mtDNA gives a magnified view of the diversity present in the human gene pool, because mutations accumulate in this DNA several times faster than in the nucleus.[15] Second, because mtDNA is inherited maternally and does not recombine,[16] it is a tool for relating individuals to one another. Third, there are about 10^{16} mtDNA molecules within a typical human and they are usually identical to one another.[17–19] Typical mammalian females consequently behave as haploids, owing to a bottleneck in the genetically effective size of the population of mtDNA molecules within each oocyte.[20] This maternal and haploid inheritance means that mtDNA is more sensitive than nuclear DNA to severe reductions in the number of individuals in a population of organisms.[15] A pair of breeding individuals can transmit only one type of mtDNA but carry four haploid sets of nuclear genes, all of which are transmissible to offspring. The fast evolution and peculiar mode of inheritance of mtDNA provide new perspectives on how, where and when the human gene pool arose and grew.

This research article introduction follows the now-familiar generic moves identified by Swales (1981, 1990): in brief, the centrality of the topic is identified, past research is summarised (the sources are referenced via endnotes, indicated by the superscript numbers), a gap in the research is indicated, and the findings of the research previewed. This kind of analysis has proved useful and popular in teaching EAP, but it obviously has cultural implications too. The professional scientist takes care to situate himself or herself within the scientific community, using citations to construct a professional 'genealogy' for the research. The issues raised by professional scientific articles focus on research methodology, on procedures rather than results – since only by persuading us of the validity of the procedures will the results seem credible. The scientist in this picture is a team player rather than a lone individual, and the writer or writers of the articles are deferential to the authority of the community as a whole. The article is structured usually as a rational problem-solving process, even when lab notes of the experimental chronology sometimes suggest that chance plays a larger role than most professional science articles would admit. The dramatic impact of chance is usually visible only in the narratives of popular science.

The grammar and vocabulary of this article make no concessions to a potential popular audience: colloquial expressions are avoided and there is a high density of abstract, nominalised expressions ('comparisons', 'recombination', 'mutations', etc.). The abundance of these nominalisations, which contributes to the reading difficulty of the extract, is typical of scientific texts. Nominalisation in this genre functions to turn processes in the natural world into objects of study. As Halliday and Martin (1993: 15) observe:

> Where the everyday 'mother tongue' of commonsense knowledge construes reality as a balanced tension between things and processes, the elaborated register of scientific knowledge reconstrues it as an edifice of things. It holds reality still, to be held under observation and experimented with; and in so doing, interprets it not as changing with time but as persisting – or rather, persistence – through time, which is the mode of being a noun.

We must be careful not to jump too quickly to premature conclusions here. While it is true that the research article has a high proportion of nominalisations, the popular article also has its share. Both describe the acts of observing and experimenting. Nominalisation is also evident in genres other than professional scientific writing, although Halliday and Martin further suggest that there it 'is largely a ritual feature, engendering only prestige and bureaucratic power' (ibid.). The surface linguistic features of learned science can thus 'cross borders' and be borrowed as a persuasive strategy by other genres (cf. Fairclough, 1995).

It is important to remember that professional scientific writing is a rhetorical construct. Scientific activity is a culturally specific set of discursive practices which are articulated through generic writings. The brief letter to the journal *Nature*, written by James Watson and Francis Crick (reprinted in Bazerman, 1988: 49–50), proposing a double helix structure for DNA, confirms this. The article 'suggests' a structure for DNA and in the short letter the tentative vocabulary of perception and belief – 'appears', 'in our opinion', 'we believe' – figure largely. Generous credit is given to fellow researchers in different institutions, many who have 'kindly' given access to unpublished research; and the main claim to knowledge – that the proposed structure of DNA solves the problem of how genetic material is reproduced – is couched in the modest phrase 'it has not escaped our notice'. It is a triumphalist modesty, given that the article reports one of the major scientific discoveries of all time, but modesty it is: the rhetorical conventions of professional science demand that face-threatening claims are avoided, and that due deference is paid to the scientific community as a whole (cf. Myers, 1989, 1990). The community itself is represented as an altruistic, sharing group of rational colleagues. This is not necessarily the view presented in other genres that represent scientific activity.

The mainstream's view of the subculture

The final point of triangulation in our survey of shifting generic representations of a subculture, is the perspective of the mainstream. So far the representations of science and scientific activity have come largely from within that disciplinary subculture. An alternative representation of scientists and scientific culture can be seen in the mass media, where the popular stereotype of the obsessive, absent-minded, even mad, professor, engaged in crazy and dangerous schemes, is more likely to emerge. In some ways the popular stereotype of the scientist and of scientific activity is similar to those representations in which scientists attempt to explain themselves to society at large – the dedicated loner, concentrating on results rather than a rather vague set of procedures. The boundaries between fact and fiction can blur in media representations, as can be seen in *Life Story*, a BBC dramatisation of Watson and Crick's scientific partnership. Here we have the 'true' story of the discovery of the double helix. Instead of the generous community of rational colleagues, we find two scientists racing against better-informed and experienced competition to guess the structure of DNA, and eventually triumphing. It is significant that James Watson, the American in the partnership, who eventually shares the Nobel Prize with Francis Crick and Maurice Wilkins (and on whose popular account the film is partly based), is played in the dramatisation by Jeff Goldblum. Goldblum reprises his 'obsessive scientist' characterisation from *The Fly* (a remake of a 1950s horror film) in which he plays a mad scientist whose DNA is spliced with that of a common housefly, with nauseating results. Goldblum has, indeed, made a career out of portraying quirky scientists in further science fiction blockbusters, such as *Independence Day, Jurassic Park* and *The Lost World. Life Story* dramatises a variety of issues, including the popular versus the professional views of science. One of the most poignant features of the film is Juliet Stevenson's portrayal of Rosalind Franklin, 'the dark lady of DNA'. The drama presents her as a woman stifled by the cosy patri- archal nature of the British scientific community. While her collection of data is crucial to the discovery of the double helical structure of DNA, she refuses to indulge in the guesswork that clinches it. The personal and meth- odological tensions are evident in the following dramatised exchanges, first between Franklin and her research assistant, Raymond, and then between her and her colleague, Maurice Wilkins:

Franklin: You know what I like about our kind of work? You can be happy or unhappy, it makes no difference. It doesn't matter whether you like what you find or hate it. You look at it and say, *So that's how it is.* It doesn't sound much when I say it.

Raymond: It sounds like it's much to you.

Franklin: Sometimes I feel like an archaeologist, breaking into a sealed tomb. I don't want to touch anything, I just want to look.

Rosalind Franklin is presented here, as in many popular representations of sci- entists, as the archetypal observer, content to look, to study and thus to know. Her impersonality, even coldness, also corresponds to one popular image of the scientist: she is devoted to her work to the exclusion of 'normal' emotions and relationships. She later condemns the activity of 'guesswork' in gendered terms as 'boys' games', and she further dismisses it in a heated exchange with Wilkins, whom she catches discussing her work with her lab assistant, Raymond:

Wilkins: These are very good, Raymond, very good. I'm impressed with the amount of detail you're getting. What's the humidity range?

Raymond: Seventy to eighty percent, for the crystalline state. She's using concentrated salt solutions to control the humidity. The dif- ferent forms are showing up much more clearly. She's calling them A and B forms.

Wilkins: Look at that, Raymond. Wouldn't you say that was a helix? I said all along it would turn out to have a helical structure.

Franklin (*Entering*): I wonder why we bother to do experiments.

Wilkins: What? Rosalind, I – I must congratulate you. What you have here, surely it could be helical, couldn't it?

Franklin: So what do you conclude from that? Because it's possible it must exist?

Wilkins: Wha . . . well, I'm just throwing out ideas.
Franklin: Guesses.
Wilkins: Well, informed guesses, I hope.
Franklin: Look, you may be guessing right and you may not. We won't know till we've done the work, and when we've done the work we won't need the guesses because we'll know the answer. So what's the point of the guesses? Being able to say later you were right all along.
Wilkins: No I don't think that at all.
Franklin: I really would appreciate it if you'd restrict your guesses to your own experimental work.
Wilkins: Very well, I'll be on my way, Raymond. *(Leaves)*
Franklin: Raymond, I am not Maurice Wilkins' research assistant. If there's anything he wants to know about our work, please tell him to ask me.

The dramatic irony is that although Franklin best fulfils the popular stereotype of the dispassionate, observing scientist, her adherence to this code denies her the public recognition given to her male colleagues – she died of cancer before the Nobel Prize was awarded to Watson, Crick and Wilkins. This popular dramatisation portrays science as essentially a social activity – competitive, accidental, and driven by a range of human desires and impulses. The philosophy of science itself is gendered and dramatised, as Franklin acts out the role of the dispassionate inductivist, that is, she waits for her accumulating data to 'suggest' a theory. In the meantime, Watson and Crick play the 'boys' game' of falsificationism, testing their many different hypotheses against newly available data (Chalmers, 1982 gives a clear survey of the different ideologies underlying scientific method).

By selecting texts systematically according to their relation to the discourse community, it is possible to illustrate that the content and language are contingent on the purposes that the texts serve. The representations of science and scientists vary systematically according to the origin and audience of the text, and, as Myers notes, these representations may even be in conflict. The popular image of the obsessive loner uncovering facts about nature may be similar to scientists' broad presentation of themselves as dispassionate observers of the physical universe, but these two stereotypes contrast with scientists' self-representation in their peer-group articles as generous team workers, concerned principally with validating research procedures.

However, it is necessary to exercise caution when making generalisations about the structure and content of generic texts. Research traditions vary both within a discipline and over time, and there are obviously different methods of practice in what I have rather sweepingly referred to as 'science'. Swales' (1981, 1990) analysis of research article introductions focused on the sciences and social sciences, and found broadly similar discourse patterns. However, Connor (1996: 40, 134) reviews research which suggests that corresponding disciplines in different national cultures employ variations of Swales' model; furthermore, a cursory analysis of research articles in the humanities shows very different introductory styles. The differing patterns of communication across the humanities and sciences are discussed in Becher (1989). Given that little detailed work has so far been accomplished on describing texts in relation to whether they are the products of close-knit or loosely-knit discourse communities, it is up to the materials designer and the teacher to select texts appropriate to their students' goals and linguistic level. An 'intercultural' perspective on texts produced by a subcultural group (whether scientists, business people, football fans, or followers of a musical fashion) involves the 'triangulation' of texts according to whether they are produced by the subculture for wider consumption, by the subculture for peer-group consumption, or by 'outsiders' about the subculture. Given the potential for 'lurking' on electronic discussion groups (i.e. registering in order to see what members write, but never actually contributing to any discussion), it is now probably easier than ever to gather data in order to triangulate perceptions of discourse communities in this way. As suggested earlier, youth subcultures such as 'skinheads' or 'goths', which can be characterised partly through fashion options and music choice, will often post websites to celebrate or negotiate their identities among themselves, but also to show a 'public face' to the world. The ideologies and values of the subculture will be negotiated largely between members of the subculture through media such as specialised fanzines or electronic discussion groups. Meanwhile, the press and other mass media will characterise the members from the perspective of the wider community. Texts from all three points of the triangle are necessary if a wider understanding of the discourse community and its textual products is to be achieved.

Clearly, work on genre and the nature of discourse communities calls into question the very labels 'general English' and 'English for Specific Purposes' (ESP). The former has always been a vacuous expression, no doubt coined as a response to the rise in popularity of ESP. It may in fact be better to rethink texts (especially written ones) as always being for 'specific purposes', and characterised by their functions in different types of discourse community. The modes of writing usually characterised as ESP (namely, essays, articles, business letters, reports, etc.) can be viewed as the products of well-defined discourse communities in which those people reading are likely also to be those people writing publicly sanctioned text-types. The modes of writing sometimes characterised as 'general' English (journals and diaries, personal letters, reflective writing, and so forth) can be considered as the products of more diffuse communities whose membership and goals are less easily defined. Diaries, after all, may be written primarily for oneself, but learner diaries are also written for the teacher, and a politician's diary might always be written with future publication, and public self-justification, in mind. Furthermore, 'personal' letters might be written with a strictly limited readership in mind, for the purpose of simply maintaining social contact with family or friends – to this extent such letters have goals, and possibly content, that is similar to speech genres (cf. Chapter 3 on the cultural functions of gossip and story-telling). Even so, such letters might eventually find a larger readership than originally intended – they might be passed around the family, and, in special cases, might even be published. From this perspective, it is clear that there is no such thing as 'general' English: there are only texts that serve different kinds of functions for individuals variously positioned in different kinds of discourse community.

Genres in the Intercultural Language Classroom

Despite the interest in genres, linguists have only just begun the task of investigating and describing the many possible genres available in a culture. Describing them all is an unrealisable goal, since the genres used by a culture are constantly changing, but even if it could be realised, the issue of what the teacher should do with knowledge of genres must still be addressed. In a survey of ESP teachers' attitudes to genre-based approaches to reading and writing, Kay and Dudley-Evans (1998) found that they were ambivalent. On the positive side, the teachers surveyed felt that exploring genres enabled students to 'enter a particular discourse community, and discover how writers organize texts' (p. 310); while, more negatively, some teachers felt that 'the 'rigidity of formula-type teaching disempowers rather than empowers' – and that a genre-based approach may give an 'imposed rather than responsive notion of text' (p. 311). In short, teachers were understandably enthusiastic about an approach that linked the teaching of reading and writing to identifiable social purpose, but they were equally wary about an approach that potentially reduced reading and writing to the identification and reproduction of generic formulae.

Kay and Dudley-Evans (1998: 311–12) suggest ways of fostering the positive aspects of genre-based approaches in the English classroom by:

- allowing for variations due to cultural and ideological factors;
- contextualising a text by considering its purpose, audience, institutional expectations, values, etc.;
- immersing students in a variety of typical and non-typical texts from the chosen genre;
- making the examples authentic;
- promoting learner interaction;
- using genre as part of a process-based approach to writing.

Clearly the analysis of genre itself does not impose a methodology upon the English language teacher. Genre analysis makes explicit the conventions governing typical examples of a text type, written or spoken, and attempts to account for these conventions by relating them to cultural goals. The conventions and explanations can be taught as immutable rules, or through discovery procedures, as suggested above.

As Connor (1996: 168) observes, there has been a 'paradigm shift' in the teaching of second language writing over the past few decades:

> The emphasis is no longer on the product. Instead, writing is taught as a process, in which each stage – prewriting, composing, and editing – is important. In addition, writing is not considered a solitary act; it involves teachers, peers, and other readers. The responses of other readers are a vital part of writing considered as a social construction of meaning. The second language teacher who is familiar with the teaching of writing as a process does not teach her students to write through model compositions. Instead, she focuses on helping students make revisions in students' drafts from the beginning to the final editing.

Process-based writing has examined anew the status of the 'product', that is, the model that in earlier approaches guided second-language composition. A genre approach, which focuses on the constraints that a discourse community places on the writer, seems at first glance to conflict with a process-based methodology, since a genre approach once again presents a 'model', or at least a generic 'formula' such as Swales' four-move introduction to research articles, for learners to follow. This apparent conflict explains the reservations expressed by language teachers about teaching genres, as reported in Kay and Dudley-Evans (1998), cited earlier in this chapter. It also helps us to understand Martin's (1985: 61) criticism of the use of process-based writing in the teaching of English as a first language in

Australia. Martin argues that process-based writing, at its most extreme, dislocates language use from a cultural context, and no amount of groupwork, or 'conferencing' can make up for this loss:

> With its stress on ownership and voice, its preoccupation with children selecting their own topics, its reluctance to intervene positively and constructively during conferencing, and its complete mystification of what has to be learned for children to produce effective written products, [process writing] is currently promoting a situation in which only the brightest middle-class children can possibly learn what is needed. Conferencing is not used to teach but to obscure.

There is clearly a balance to be sought between imposing a rigid model for imitation, and the denial of any kind of explicit instruction about products at all. A possible solution to the problem lies in the construction of writing tasks that vary the ways that generic models are integrated into the language-learning process. White (1988) brings together a collection of useful case studies and suggestions for effective process-based writing. In the comparison of product and process approaches shown in Table 4.1, it is evident that imitation has been replaced by the communicative task, and the model has been re-introduced but in a less imposing way at a later stage in the drafting of the student's writing:

Table 4.1 Product and process approached

Product-based approach	Process-based approach
(attempt to mimic model: more predictable outcome)	(ask, discover, adapt: less predictable outcome)
1. Study the model.	1. Study the task requirements.
2. Manipulate the components.	2. Communicate as far as possible.
3. Produce a parallel text.	3. Study a model if necessary, or obtain advice elsewhere.
	4. Practise new language as necessary.
	5. Redraft.

In his introduction to the same book, White suggests five main stages in the training of writers: identifying goals, brainstorming, organising ideas, directing towards an audience, and redrafting. Clearly, in the process-based approach, models are guides to effective writing, but should not necessarily be slavishly imitated. Each writing task is different, after all, and the writing task given might well demand a degree of originality. Generic models can be introduced at different stages in the writing process – to

sensitise writers to different audiences, perhaps, or at the redrafting stage –
to present possibilities, but not to determine outcomes.

Identifying and Comparing Genres

An explicit overview of the steps to be used in process writing is useful
because it can structure an otherwise mystifying experience and make it
comprehensible to students. Such an overview can also help focus task
design on reading and writing subskills that contribute to the overall
composing process. Three general tasks might be considered as *identifying
genres, comparing genres* and *rewriting genres*. Examples of genre shift, such
as the popularisation of scientific articles, can be used to raise students'
awareness of the link between written texts and the discourse community
from which they originate. A simple task would be to ask students to
identify the intended readership of given extracts. For example, the
excerpts given below are from a description of an experiment to determine
the impact of predators on brittlestars, a type of starfish, or, more technically, ophiuroid. Both excerpts were written or co-written by the same
biologist, Richard Aronson, but for different audiences: a readership of
professional scientists, and a more popular readership. Can you (1) identify
the excerpt from the professional and the popular article, and (2) describe
the linguistic changes that have taken place as the article has been rewritten
for the popular audience?

Text A
To measure predation directly, I tied *Ophiothrix* to small weights and
set them out as 'bait' at Bay Stacka. For comparison, I did the same
experiment on a rocky reef just outside Port Erin Bay. Here brittlestars
are much more sparse and we find them only under rocks and in
crevices.

Nothing much happened at Bay Stacka. Starfish consumed bits of a few
tethered brittlestars, but most of them survived. At Port Erin, on the
other hand, ballan wrasses and flatfish ate most of my experimental
animals. I repeated the experiment at the Millport Marine Station on
the Isle of Cumbrae. *Ophiocomina nigra* forms a dense bed in 10 metres
of water, just offshore of the laboratory. The results were identical:
predation pressure is low in brittlestar beds.

Text B
When assemblages of ophiuroids comparable in density to those in
Sweetings Pond were exposed in open arenas (from which they could
not escape) at a coastal site off Eleuthera, the brittlestars were com-

pletely consumed within 48 hours. No significant ophiuroid mortality occurred in similar arenas in the lake. Gut content and fecal analyses of all possible Sweetings Pond predators of *Ophiothrix*, including the large majid crab *Mithrax spinosissimus* confirmed the virtual absence of predation. Through observation and experimentation, Aronson and Harms (1987) demonstrated that density variations within the lake are determined by variations in the degree of small-scale topographical heterogeneity, not by variations in predation pressure. In stark contrast to coastal conspecifics, Sweetings Pond brittlestars expose themselves day and night. This behavioral difference is causally related to the difference in predatory activity by fishes (Aronson, 1987).

It is not difficult to realise that the second extract is from the professional text. What is perhaps more surprising is that both extracts give almost exactly the same information. Once students have identified the different genres, they can compare the language used in each text and relate it to the relevant discourse community. One notable feature here is the way Aronson refers to himself: in the popular article he uses the pronoun 'I' in combination with verbs of action: 'I tied', 'I did the same experiment', 'I repeated the experiment'. Here the scientist is a lone investigator. The title of this popularisation 'A Murder Mystery from the Mesozoic' reinforces the image of the scientist as a private detective, searching for clues to account for the deaths of communities of this kind of starfish. In contrast, the professional article downplays the scientist's individual effort: passives are used to delete the agent ('assemblages were exposed') and even references to the author are couched in the third person, through the reference to his earlier publications, and team effort is acknowledged. As Myers (1989, 1990) observes, the code of politeness in academic writing means that the academic community should take priority over the lone researcher, and so examples of first-person reference are few. In popular writing, however, the lay reader wishes to identify with a protagonist, and so the scientist is represented in this role.

Elsewhere in the articles, there are examples of changes in vocabulary and grammar as the genre shifts from professional to popular article. Examples include:

Text A	Text B
Nothing much happened . . .	No significant ophiuroid mortality occurred . . .
ballan wrasses and flatfish ate most of my experimental animals	the brittlestars were completely consumed
The results were identical: predation pressure is low	Gut content and fecal analyses . . . confirmed the virtual absence of predation

Here we see some further examples of the typical language of science – nominalisation is used in both extracts but to a greater degree in Text B. The process which can be paraphrased as *no brittlestars died* is nominalised as the phrase 'ophiuroid mortality' in Text B, whereas Text A uses the informal pronoun expression, 'nothing much', in a full clause: 'nothing much happened'. *Nothing ate the brittlestars* is nominalised as low 'predation pressure' in Text A, and as 'the absence of predation' in Text B. Text A dramatises the results through an organisation of the text that previews the findings up front, and then gives details of them, while Text B carefully specifies the methodology used to obtain the results. In sum, the 'scientific' language of Text B is designed to objectify processes and subject them to experimentation, and also to specify and foreground the *procedures* that ensure that the experiments achieve valid results. The more 'popular' language of Text A retains some nominalisation but has a higher proportion of 'action' verbs like 'happened' and it foregrounds the *results* of the research rather than the methodology used to obtain them. Identification and comparison of the genres shows how the language of each article is adapted to the purposes and interests of the discourse community it serves.

Rewriting genres

A useful advanced writing task is to recast one genre into another. Transformation tasks, of the type 'rewrite active sentences as passive sentences', are usually associated with 'product-based' approaches, and yet they can represent 'authentic' scientific practice in so far as there are often situations in which writers do have to adapt a given text (written by themselves or others) for a different discourse community. An advanced class could therefore be divided in two and given the task of rewriting extracts from one genre into another. The student products could then be compared with the originals and writing options discussed. For example, the following tasks can be used with the texts discussed in the previous section:

Group A
You are writing an article for a professional biology journal. Your fieldnotes contain the following information about the ancient and modern living environments of brittlestars, a type of starfish (known more technically as 'ophiuroids'). You are aware that the style is not 'academic' enough for your audience. How would you rewrite it for the professional journal?

The top carnivores in Sweetings Pond are octopuses. They eat the small crustaceans and clams that live in the lake but leave brittlestars alone. Octopuses are relatives of the shelled cephalopods, Nautilus, for example, that were important predators before the Mesozoic marine revolution. A cephalopod at the top of the food chain makes the analogy between Sweetings Pond and ancient communities all the more plausible.

Group B
You are writing an article for a popular science journal, based on a report you have read in a professional journal. The journal contains the following information about the ancient and modern living environments of ophiuroids, a type of starfish (known more broadly as 'brittlestars'). You are aware that the style is not 'popular' enough for your audience. How would you rewrite it for the magazine?

It is not unreasonable to imagine that cephalopods were common predators in some ancient ophiuroid-dominated communities, as they are in Sweetings Pond. . . . Based on data from Sweetings Pond we suspect that many cephalopods in Paleozoic and Mesozoic communities did not consume brittlestars, even when the latter were extremely abundant. To our knowledge, the only living cephaolopod that preys on ophiuroids is the deep-dwelling Bathypolypus arcticus (O'Dor and MacAlester, 1983). In the absence of fish, crustacean and cephalopod durophagy, then, dense populations of ophiuroids could thrive in 'Paleozoic' communities.

Here, generic models (based on Aronson, 1987 and Aronson & Harms, 1987) are used as a stimulus to rewriting activities, in order to raise students' awareness of the implications of shifting from one discourse community to another. Obviously, Groups A and B will not produce versions of the other group's 'model text' but the choice of writing strategies they use – hedging or stating directly, using more or fewer nominalisations, focusing on events or methodology – should be directed towards their chosen readership, and prepare them for tasks where no 'model text' is provided. Through tasks such as these the writer can become culturally aware of the norms of the target discourse community, and learn – as all writers have to learn – how to position their own texts within the fuzzy and shifting space of different genres.

Conclusion

In its discussion of cultural aspects of written English, this chapter largely focuses on the teaching of writing for academic purposes, specifically within the discipline of science. This focus is limited, but the combination of genre analysis and process writing advocated above has implications beyond the disciplinary boundaries used here for illustration. A genre-based approach to language learning and teaching (whichever 'school' of genre analysis is favoured) accepts that language use takes place in social contexts and serves cultural purposes. Discourse communities can effectively be viewed as subcultural groupings of different types – professional and social, transitory and enduring – in which individuals with shared social goals develop conventional means of intercommunication to further those goals. The goals may vary from knowledge-generation and career progression within a professional discipline, to making and keeping friends. The conventional means of communication – the genres – are also ways of linguistically structuring the social values and experiences of the discourse community. The learning of a language should recognise how language use identifies the individual as a participant to varying degrees in overlapping and differently structured discourse communities. Facility in reading and writing the genres that serve the communities is often an index of the degree of membership of the group, especially if the group is a professional one. Genres can be spoken, written, or, indeed, spoken-to-be-written (e.g. dictated letters) or written-to-be-spoken (prepared speeches, newscasts, playscripts, etc.).

Writing itself is a special activity, since it has to be taught formally to native speakers as well as to second-language learners. Current teaching methodology favours a process approach, in which learners discover, through trial-and-error, and with appropriate feedback from peers and tutor, the appropriate language to accomplish a given task. The combination of process writing with a genre-based approach helps define the nature of certain tasks (e.g. identifying, comparing, rewriting or even parodying genres) and promotes effective intervention at the feedback and redrafting stages, to help shape students' writing in relation to the cultural norms of the target discourse communities.

Chapter 5

Ethnographic Approaches to Culture and Language

This chapter turns from a 'skills-based' focus on intercultural language education, to consider in more depth insights from ethnography. The topics addressed in this chapter are:

- *What is ethnography?*
- *The role of ethnography in different research disciplines.*
- *The role of ethnography in language education.*
- *Ethnographic activities in the language classroom.*
- *Devising larger-scale ethnographic projects for intercultural language development.*

What is Ethnography?

English language teaching has long drawn on the discipline of linguistics, to the point where English language teaching theory has practically become synonymous with the expression 'applied linguistics'. However, as we saw in Chapter 1, ELT can benefit from the application of other disciplines. Over the past few decades the term 'ethnography' has gained currency in the literature of both cultural studies and language learning (e.g. Byram *et al.*, 1994; Byram & Fleming, 1998; Damen, 1987; Holliday, 1994; Nightingale, 1989; Radway, 1988; Roberts *et al.*, 1992; Roberts *et al.*, 2001). Ethnographic practices, in a variety of forms, are becoming increasingly central to intercultural approaches to language teaching and learning. This chapter looks first at how ethnography is understood as a research methodology in different disciplines (anthropology, sociolinguistics, cultural studies and media research) and then considers more specifically what the practice of ethnography across these disciplines can offer the English language teacher and learner. In EFL contexts, direct contact with anglophone cultures is usually more limited – comparatively few learners can take advantage of overseas trips, or even a study year abroad – however, many of the techniques used to stimulate the 'ethnographic imagination' are still valid and applicable.

Ethnographic Research

The academic end of the ethnographic spectrum involves several related disciplines, which can be briefly classified as follows.

Ethnology

Ethnography originates in the anthropological study of cultures. In anthropology the general term given to the study of living and recent cultures is 'ethnology'. There are various aspects of ethnology, including ethnography, ethnomethodology and microethnography. All these terms are related, although they are not strictly synonymous. 'Ethnology' originally referred to the study of 'primitive' (i.e. non-industrialised) societies, by the detailed observation of the workings of those societies by anthropologists ('ethnologists'), usually living near or among them. One popular textbook, *Contemporary Cultural Anthropology* (Howard, 1989), for example, includes essays on living among the Nasioi tribe of New Guinea, communication problems in the southern Philippines, patterns of subsistence in the Aleutian Islands, and marriage customs of the Mapuche Indians, on the Chilean island of Huapi. 'Ethnography', technically, is what ethnologists produce; that is, it refers to the descriptions produced of such societies (Damen, 1987: 57; Howard, 1989: 16–17). However, over time 'ethnography' has tended to overtake 'ethnology' as the general term used for using fieldwork to accomplish the systematic study of cultural practices.

Ethnography, then, developed within the discipline of anthropology in the early years of the 20th century, falling out of favour somewhat in mid-century, outside the bounds of anthropology, as more 'scientific' means of research dominated the human sciences (Saville-Troike, 1989: 7). However, as social scientists became disenchanted with the inadequacy of experimental methods to capture the complexity of social life, ethnography regained a wider popularity in the last decades of the century, and the meaning of the term broadened considerably. Later ethnographers, like Heath (1983), differed from her earlier counterparts by immersing herself in the society that she studied. She became what is known as a 'participant-observer' by taking a role within the target community. The community in question was also different: rather than an 'exotic' non-industrial society, Heath chose to observe two ethnically distinct working-class communities of mill-workers in the southern United States. Heath lived with the communities as a participant-observer, and observed them over a 10-year period. Her description of the two communities is therefore the result of years of detailed, systematic observation – including fieldnotes and tape-recordings. Over a full decade, she attempted to explore the question of how one's cultural environment impacts on the learning of the language structures and functions required for success at school and in the workplace. The validity of this kind of ethnography as a language research procedure, and its relevance to language teaching, is discussed by Nunan (1992: 64–8).

Contemporary ethnography, then, ideally immerses the trained field-worker in the target culture for a lengthy period of time, with the goal of relating social context and behaviour, particularly linguistic behaviour. As Saville-Troike (1989: 7) puts it:

> Observed behaviour is now recognized as a manifestation of a deeper set of codes and rules, and the task of ethnography is seen as the discovery and explication of the rules for contextually appropriate behaviour in a community or group; in other words, culture is what the individual needs to know to be a functional member of the community.

Here again we see the current notion of 'culture' as types of knowledge, often implicit, that in turn govern different types of behaviour which take place in concrete situations. By looking systematically at behaviour in context, the researcher can eventually work back to an account of the deeper 'rules' that govern the behaviour. This account is an ethnographic description of the culture. The construction of ethnographic accounts of cultures is clearly a job for highly trained, dedicated, professional research-ers. However, advocates of an intercultural approach to language learning argue that some training in ethnographic techniques can benefit the language learner (e.g. Byram *et al.*, 1994; Roberts *et al.*, 2001). Later in this chapter, we shall look at ways in which language learners can be taught to 'think ethnographically'.

Ethnomethodology and microethnography

The influence of ethnography on the intercultural approach goes beyond the general observation of a target culture. Some research into behaviour in context has concentrated much more specifically on how participants in conversations interact to construct meaning jointly. This particular focus on communicative events is the substance of ethno-methodology (Garfinkel, 1967; Gumperz, 1977, 1984; Saville-Troike, 1989: 130–3). Ethnomethodologists argue that meaning arises out of the interaction between individuals in a specific context, the individuals bringing to their encounter social knowledge and prior experiences that are used to interpret the utterances of the other participants. Communication through dialogue therefore arises out of a complex, ongoing negotiation about what utterances mean. The idea that meaning is 'dialogic' (i.e. negotiated through interaction between participants in a context) rather than 'mono-logic' (arising, say, from an individual's wish to express him or herself) echoes the Russian philosopher Mikhail Bakhtin's writing in the 1920s. Bakhtin's work was suppressed by the Stalinist regime, however, and so his writings did not filter through to the West for a number of decades, and then only in translation and under assumed names (e.g. Vološinov, 1973). However, now that his ideas are more widely accessible, Bakhtin can be recognised as a precursor of much that is considered 'new' in language research from a sociocultural perspective, and his ideas have influenced much recent work on culture and language teaching (e.g. Kramsch, 1993).

The detailed description of how particular conversations work is termed 'microethnography' or 'ethnographic microanalysis' (e.g. Erickson, 1996). The assumption is that meaning is dialogic, and so the model of 'active speaker and passive listener' is discarded in favour of 'active-speaker and active listener'. As one participant speaks, the listener actively processes the message, perhaps offering back-channelling sounds (e.g. 'uh-uh', 'yeah, 'mmm'), or perhaps overlapping in speech by interrupting, clarify-ing, paraphrasing, and so on. A concrete situation is also important to microethnographic analysis insofar as it affects the way participants present themselves to each other. An individual will present him or herself in different ways, depending on whether he or she is conversing with, say, a parent, a potential employer or a close friend. Where ethnography considers the whole life of the community, then, microethnography focuses on the 'ebb and flow' of particular conversations, using the context only to elucidate the ways in which participants present themselves and negotiate meanings. Microethnography has influenced the kind of descrip-tion of casual conversation already discussed in Chapter 3, and it also influences detailed discourse analyses of intercultural communication, such as Scollon and Scollon (2001).

The kinds of ethnographic research so far considered range from the anthropologist's general interest in providing a detailed account of the practices and beliefs of whole communities, to the specific issue of how meaning is constructed through dialogue between members of a community. As noted above, however, ethnography has regained popular-ity beyond the discipline of anthropology. It has also been adopted and modified in the relatively newer disciplines of cultural and media studies. The kinds of ethnographic techniques practised within these disciplines, and their core concerns, have also influenced intercultural language teaching.

Ethnographic research in cultural studies

An important influence on the intercultural approach is cultural studies, a discipline that overlaps with, but is nevertheless distinct from, anthropology. Cultural studies combines elements of anthropology, sociology, history, literary and media studies in diverse and interdisciplinary interpretations of contemporary cultural groups, movements and practices. Cultural studies usually focuses on and even celebrates the marginalised practices of politically powerless groups in society, such as the working class, youth, women and ethnic minorities (Gray & McGuigan, 1997; Turner, 1990).

Ethnography has a central position – albeit a controversial one – in the methodological techniques of cultural studies. A central text in the British tradition is Willis' (1977) *Learning to Labour: How Working Class Kids Get Working Class Jobs*, the result of three-years' observation of 12 'anti-academic', working-class school-leavers, both at school and as they began careers in unskilled jobs. Willis' description of this group of friends (the 'lads') is based on observation, diaries, group discussions and informal interviews. The resulting analysis is in part descriptive, in part theoretical, and informed by an analysis of their socioeconomic context, and partly by an analysis of their *style*, that is, how they present themselves through their dress, and through the social 'rituals' they perform. Willis, like other researchers into youth cultures (e.g. Cohen, 1980; Hebdige, 1979; Widdecombe & Wooffit, 1995), sees style as an important resource in the construction of group identity. For example, he interprets the lads' smoking as a sign of their rejection of school values and their adoption of adult working-class behaviour (Turner, 1990: 175; Willis, 1979: 19). In other words, a social practice is considered as a kind of 'text' through which certain meanings are produced and interpreted. Willis also claims that his group rejects the ethos of mainstream education because at some level of consciousness they recognise that its promises are a sham. Their class position effectively restricts them to certain modes of employment.

Ethnographic studies are not without their critics. As Nunan notes (1992: 65), long-term ethnographic analyses are immensely rich in data, and their reporting therefore requires selection and interpretation. Since the data gathered by ethnographic researchers is unique and complex, it is impossible for other researchers to check it or replicate it, and so the interpretations and conclusions of ethnographic researchers must be taken on trust. Even despite the richness of ethnographic data, the selection made by researchers can lead to obvious gaps. McRobbie (1981) points out that Willis' study of his 'lads' makes practically no mention of the women in their lives, whether mothers or girlfriends. This at least raises the question of whether women indeed figure little in the boys' lives, or whether the researcher has only chosen to discuss data that supports his thesis that the 'lads' construct a vigorous male working-class identity for themselves. Ethnographic research in general is always open to the criticism of subjectivity, a charge intensified when the observer is drawn to a subculture because of previous (or current) involvement and empathy. In such cases ethnographic reports can recall the old description of sports journalists as 'fans with typewriters'.

A further theoretical issue is the status accorded in ethnography to empirical evidence and its interpretation. Hebdige's influential *Subculture: The Meaning of Style* (1979: 116–17) notoriously interprets punks' use of the swastika as an empty symbol designed only to shock, divorced from its Nazi associations. Although he had obviously observed this subculture's use of the swastika, and notes a newspaper report on one punk's reason for its use, he obviously did not ask any young people why they adopted it. His confidence in his authority as a semiotician, that is, as an expert in interpreting visual signs, allows him to dispense with the strategy of checking his own interpretation against that of a subcultural member. However, it might fairly be asked whether the reasons given by punks as to why they adopted this symbol should be any more authoritative than Hebdige's. The key issue, ultimately, is that the strength of ethnography is in its detailed observation and the richness of its data, but data is not itself an explanation. At some point, someone has to organise the data according to a theory, and a simple acceptance of the accounts of those observed can be read as an avoidance of academic responsibility by the researcher.

The question remains, however, on what authority and by what criteria the ethnographic researcher comes to his or her conclusions and interpretations. As Turner (1990: 178) warns: 'When we read ethnographic studies, there is always a point at which we need to ask who is speaking, and for whom.' Lecompte and Goetz identify some steps that can be taken to safeguard the reliability of ethnographic studies, by making explicit 'the status of the researcher, the choice of informants, the social situations and conditions, the analytical constructs and premises, and the methods of data collection and analysis' (cited in Nunan, 1992: 59–64). In short, reliable ethnographic research should clearly state the following:

(a) what is the relationship of the researcher to the community being described? Is s/he, for example, a visiting observer, a participant-observer, a working member of the community, etc.?
(b) why were the informants chosen? If they are considered typical of some subcultural grouping, on what grounds are they to be considered representative? If they are chosen as random samples of a culture, what procedures were used to select them?

(c) what were the social situation and conditions pertaining to the research? Details of the class, ethnicity, gender, educational background, etc., of informants need to be clearly stated.

(d) what were the methods of analysis? Were multiple observers used to limit individual subjectivity? Was the kind of behaviour observed easy to agree upon (i.e. does it demand inferencing on the part of the observer?) For example, it would be easy to agree whether a learner volunteered answers in class or not. It would be less easy to agree that a relatively quiet student 'lacked interest' or 'showed signs of boredom'.

(e) what were the methods of data analysis and collection? Were observation schedules used to give consistency in the description of routine behaviours? Was behaviour recorded in sound or vision, and/or written down in field notes? If the latter, were the field notes written during the event, immediately afterwards, or some time later?

Even if ethnographic research can probably never be satisfactorily replicated – too many factors are unique to each piece of research – the findings and conclusions of good ethnographic research can be persuasive if the above factors are made explicit. The safeguards suggested by Lecompte and Goetz are useful to bear in mind when reading ethnographic research in preparation for a class project, and also when preparing learners to undertake ethnographic projects of their own. Again, it is unlikely that most learners will undertake an ethnographic project on the scale of a professional researcher; however, similar critical criteria can guide the 'practical' or 'amateur' ethnographer, when he or she comes to reflect on what has been learned.

Ethnographic research in media studies

A final branch of ethnographic research – at least in name – can be found in media studies. Certain kinds of media research have certainly evolved from ethnography, and indeed also serve as useful models for the kind of 'practical' ethnography advocated by the intercultural approach. For example, media researchers might observe audiences watching certain programmes, note their responses, and elicit further, more detailed reactions. Media researchers also take the theoretical position that meanings are not encoded only in the television programmes but are dialogically constructed in the interaction between viewers and the 'text'. Consequently, we may assume that different groups of viewers construct meanings in different ways. Media researchers are therefore interested in how different social groupings 'decode' the messages broadcast to them via television. Finally, the broad political questions which interest researchers in cultural studies equally interest media researchers; principally, how might certain subcultural groupings 'resist' the dominant viewing positions assumed by mainstream television programmes? Such viewers, in the tradition of Willis' rebellious schoolboys, can be seen as operating strategies to construct identities in opposition to those offered to them by the media institutions that create the programmes. In other words, they devise strategies of resistance to the social forces that are attempts to persuade them to accept their subordinate positions in society.

Examples of ethnographic media research include Morley's (1980) *The Nationwide Audience,* an attempt to discover how groups that were differentiated by class variously interpreted a popular early-evening current affairs programme of the 1970s. Collections of key articles on media studies typically include ethnographic research of different kinds; for example, Marris and Thornham's (1996) anthology includes short studies of housewives' choices of viewing, and gendered uses of the video-recorder, as well as critiques of the methodology and assumptions of ethnographic research. Media ethnography is usually very different in depth from studies such as Heath's (1983). Whereas Heath observed patterns of interaction in two entire communities for a decade, Hobson (1980; reprinted in Marris and Thornham, 1996: 307–12), concentrated on one particular group, namely housewives, and explored a single research question, their preferred television viewing. Nightingale (1989) questions whether such small-scale research, interesting though it is, can be termed 'ethnographic' at all – a question echoed by Turner (1990: 158–67). One problem with such small-scale studies is that by focusing on, say, one group of viewers, you lose the complexity or 'thickness' of description valued by broader ethnographic studies. For example, by focusing on male-versus-female uses of the video-recorder, the researcher is in danger of losing insight into wider male/ female uses of leisure time or wider patterns of gender relationships that could illuminate the behaviour under consideration.

Small-scale ethnographic studies in media research share some of the advantages and disadvantages of broader ethnographic research. They share the political curiosity of ethnographic research in cultural studies, and assume, like all ethnographic research, that meaning derives from interactions (between participants or viewers and texts) concretely situated in social contexts. They share the great attraction of being able to point to 'real data' to support an argument: for instance, instead of speculating about what an utterance might mean out of context, you observe carefully, and describe the negotiation and production of meanings in real-life interactions. This attraction can become seductive and the availability of a wealth of 'real data' can obscure the necessary subjectivity involved in the interpretation of interactions by the researcher and his or her informants.

The various branches of ethnographic research, outlined above, seek to uncover the cultural knowledge which governs social behaviour in context, by observing communities discreetly over a lengthy period of time. Ethnomethodology and microethnography in particular seek models for the way participants in interactions actively construct meanings through negotiation in concrete situations. Ethnography in cultural and media studies often focuses on marginalised groups and attempts to raise their status by treating their social practices as complex and meaningful. However, research agendas are not necessarily pedagogical agendas. The methodological techniques adopted by the research community must be adapted to serve the interests of the intercultural curriculum, where the goals are (1) increased language competence, and (2) increased ability to understand and mediate between different cultural practices. The sections that follow turn to the value of ethnographic strategies to different aspects of language teaching and learning.

Ethnography and Language Education

Ethnography has influenced language education in a variety of different ways (see for example, the 'Case Studies' section in Richards & Nunan, 1990). Outside the immediate classroom, it has influenced curriculum planners and materials designers, particularly in English as a Second Language (ESL) teaching.

Ethnography and curriculum change

For many schools and educational institutions, the adoption of an intercultural approach demands some form of teacher development and curricular change – for example, it demands a new way of thinking about how language works, and a new set of goals for the learner to achieve. The very act of implementing an intercultural approach, then, demands a change in the established learning culture of ELT schools, a change that has to be negotiated and managed. At this level of language education, ethnography can support more effective innovation.

Holliday (1994) observes that cross-cultural encounters occur every time a teacher meets a new group of students, and every time a curriculum planner enters a new institution. He argues that curriculum planners and teachers should use ethnographic skills to come to understand the 'deep action' of colleagues and students, that is, the 'hidden agendas' and wider life objectives that lie behind the adoption or rejection of curricular innovations and styles of teaching and learning. The introduction of 'discovery' teaching strategies favoured by the commercial ELT sector into more conservative state institutions (whether in Europe, the US or elsewhere) can give rise to cross-cultural tensions. For example, Holliday reports that university lecturers in Egypt who attempted to substitute group-work and task-based discovery procedures instead of traditional lectures sometimes lost the respect of students who valued the traditional lecturer's authority. He argues that curriculum consultants who disregard the educational culture they are trying to change will fail. Innovation must take into consideration the way in which established practices accord status to members of the educational community.

Attention must therefore be paid to the, usually unarticulated, expectations and social relationships that any innovation is almost bound to challenge. In any staff room there is likely to be rivalry for status, sometimes promotion, and some teachers might visibly adopt institutionally favoured innovations in order to further their own careers, rather than out of a conviction that the innovation is worthwhile (although the two are not, of course, necessarily incompatible). Established teachers, however, might see the introduction of innovations as a threat to their hard-won status, and reject it on those grounds. Ethnographic analysis of the institutions undergoing curriculum change therefore demands sensitivity to the self-image of teachers and students in the institution, and an understanding and respect for established teaching practices. Ethnographic analysis seeks to observe, understand and describe preferred patterns of teacher–learner, learner–learner and teacher–teacher interaction before trying to impose changes that might be perceived by the target group as inappropriate and unnecessary. Curriculum planning which involves a period of ethnographic exploration is more likely to result in curriculum planners, teachers and learners finding more than token agreement on strategies for educational improvement. Only if the planners' colleagues and their students 'own' the innovations worked out with the curriculum planners – only if they see that innovations are in their own and their students' best interests – will they actually continue to develop them when the planners have left.

The intercultural approach outlined in this book, accordingly, seeks to build on practices that will be familiar to most EFL teachers. In particular, the suggested tasks are based on the kinds of activities that are already used successfully in communicative classrooms: role-plays, projects, and other co-operative goal-directed activities. However, as the intercultural approach spells out, the view of language and the goals of the intercultural curriculum are substantially different from mainstream EFL courses, in that a greater emphasis is given to the role of language in the construction of identities, and great importance is given to the understanding and mediation of cultural differences. While this book seeks to persuade teachers to adopt an intercultural approach to language learning, it also acknowledges that that different institutions and teachers will necessarily respond according to their own perceived needs and priorities.

Ethnography and ESL

Given adequate resources, in-depth ethnographic research in second language teaching has been shown to be both possible and desirable. Roberts *et al.* (1992: 171–244) report on the ethnographic investigations that were made possible by UK government funding for the Industrial Language Training service (ILT) in the 1970s and 1980s. This service was set up to investigate the language needs of ethnic minority workers, and provide training that would meet these needs in English workplaces. An enlightened local education policy allowed the ILT service to conduct detailed research into the communications used on the shop floors. As Roberts *et al.* (1992: 171) observe, this research was viewed as necessary, rather than as a luxury, because they wished (1) to convince employers that training would meet their actual requirements, (2) to document and counter explicit racial hostility encountered in the workplace, and (3) to provide input for training materials. As part of their ethnographic research, which also included factual data collection and interviews with ethnic-minority workers, the ILT team undertook participant observation in the workplace, to 'record the nature of work, patterns of social and work contact and examples of interaction (often recorded on audiotape)' (1992: 172). Even so, Roberts *et al.* – like Holliday (1994) – distinguish between 'practical' or 'applied' ethnography and 'full' or 'pure' ethnographic research. They do so, first, because applied ethnographers do not seek a comprehensive account of a community, only of part of one; secondly, in the case of the ILT, because they submitted the data to a more detailed discourse analysis than most earlier ethnographies; and, finally, because applied ethnography has a practical outcome rather than an academic one. The ILT team were committed to effective training as a practical means of challenging workplace racism and improving equal opportunities (1992: 180–1), while Holliday was committed to finding a way of ensuring that curricular innovation was acceptable to the host institution and therefore more likely to be adopted by its teachers and students.

Roberts *et al.*'s (1992) report on the work of the ILT makes illuminating reading, and the procedures used by the service are spelled out as a suggested model for other projects to follow. There are clear descriptions of methods of participant observation; for example, trainers were taken on as employees in the client firms, and expected to work alongside other workers whose patterns of socialisation and communication they observed and wrote up (see pp. 185–93 for examples of reports, recordings and analysis). In this situation, the use of ethnography has clear practical benefits: in many cases it convinced employers that not only did their ethnic minority workers require language training, but their native-speaker employees did, too – not because their language was 'deficient' but because their cultural assumptions about communication patterns were often discriminatory, however unconsciously. A vivid illustration of this fact is given in accounts of 'gatekeeping' interactions, such as interviews for jobs or promotions (see further, Chapter 6). The advantage of an ethnographic approach to such communicative events is that it perceives meaning as arising from the *interaction* between participants. The ILT team therefore used the information gathered in their ethnographic surveys to devise communication training both for ethnic minority workers *and* their native-speaking employers, workmates and 'gatekeepers'.

Ethnographic Activities in the Intercultural Classroom

Roberts, Davies and Jupp's (1992) report is a detailed account of the benefits and difficulties of using ethnography in such a wide-scale programme of workplace language training. However, it is true that most EFL teachers, as opposed to teachers of ESL, are working with learners who have little or no daily contact with native speakers. Neither do they have the extensive opportunity to observe native speakers interacting among themselves that the trainers in the ILT programmes enjoyed. What relevance, then, does ethnography have for EFL teachers, teacher-trainers and course co-ordinators? Sercu (1998) describes in detail a programme of inservice training for Belgian teachers of modern languages. Developed to increase teachers' awareness of intercultural competence, the course Sercu describes involves textual interpretation (of items like cartoons and photographs), discussion of intercultural competence training versus the nature of more traditional 'Landeskunde' classes (whose emphasis was more on factual information), and a degree of participant observation and 'empathy-building' activities. The training course also covered topics such as prejudices and stereotypes, and the evaluation of course materials. Ideally, course materials should not simply provide models for good language use; they should also encourage the exploration of cultural practices (e.g. what kind of body language accompanies basic exchanges such as greetings; when handshakes or kisses are acceptable or unacceptable). If the course materials themselves do not contain 'ethnographic' activities then teachers and curriculum designers need to supplement them with activities that develop the ethnographic skills of systematic observation.

The idea of teaching learners ethnographic skills is not a new one. For example, Damen (1987) draws upon a wealth of cross-cultural training techniques and anthropological writing in the USA in her detailed exploration of 'culture learning' in the language classroom. Like those involved in the ILT projects described in the above section, Damen is concerned largely with learners who are immigrants, although the contexts of learning are different. Damen's language classrooms are not in the workplace, and the ultimate goal of language and culture learning for her is 'acculturation', which she defines as 'the continuous process in which the immigrant adapts to and acquires the host culture, so as to be directed towards ultimate assimilation' (1987: 141; see also 228–30). Although Damen grants that the degree of assimilation attained is a matter for the learners to decide, the goal of 'culture learning' for her is markedly different from those of the 'intercultural learner' as formulated by such as Kramsch (1993) or Byram (1997b). For Damen, the observation and understanding of the kinds of knowledge and assumptions that guide different cultural behaviours should lead ultimately to the adoption of that knowledge and behaviour to some degree. In the intercultural classroom, the learner is not expected or required to assimilate but to mediate. The target behaviour does not need to be simulated exactly, but an understanding of the behaviour of native speakers might lead to some adaptation of the learner's usual behaviour, in order to 'manage' an intercultural encounter. For example, a Moslem learner might be presented with an invitation to dinner by a non-Moslem friend or colleague. He or she might wish to refuse because of concerns about the preparation of the food. Repeated conventional refusals, no matter how polite, can put a strain on friendship. Presumably, an 'accultur-ated' learner would finally agree to the invitation, because acculturation implies assimilation into the norms of the target community. An inter-cultural learner, however, would recognise the conventions of friendship and religious belief that were in conflict and try to manage a resolution – for instance, by explaining politely that Islam demands strict conditions about the preparation of food, and he or she therefore cannot accept invitations of this kind. The learner might add that he or she does not wish to seem unfriendly or give offence, and could actively seek an alternative way of socialising.

On the other hand, even in intercultural classrooms, there may well be students who do wish to imitate the customs and behaviours of the target culture. Many EFL learners do have a strong 'integrative' motivation for learning the second language, and they should therefore be given a chance to 'think their way into' the target culture. A general distinction can therefore be made in the aims of ethnographic activities devised for learners: those which promote observation and understanding of the target culture, with intercultural mediation as a goal, and those activities which encourage learners to 'think' like those in the target culture, and to reproduce their cultural behaviour. Care should be taken, when the latter type of activities is used, to make explicit that the activities are largely exercises in 'decentring' the conventional attitudes of the home culture; they are not meant to deny or substitute the patterns of thought of the home culture or to imply that one way of thinking is better than another. A key part of any complete activity would be a period of reflection and discussion: what assumptions were at the root of the behaviours? Would such assumptions hold, and would such behaviour be acceptable in the learner's home culture?

Given these qualifications, then, cultural awareness activities can involve the following: systematic observation and understanding, followed by intercultural mediation, and/or imitation. Some practical activities illustrating these elements are given below. They are adapted from a range of textbooks, such as Damen (1987: 279–97); Fantini (1997); Sercu (1998); and Tomalin & Stempleski (1993).

Concept training

Concept training (cf. Sercu, 1998: 264–5; Anderson *et al.*, 1997) is a small-scale activity designed to develop systematic observation. A possible procedure is for trainees (that is, either teacher-trainees or learners themselves) to be assigned an everyday situation or event to observe. This may be a religious service, a school lesson, or even something as apparently 'ordinary' as people browsing or buying books in a bookshop. The activity tries to 'decentre' the observer's sense of the ordinary by contemplating the concept and devising questions to ask and answer. In the case of a bookshop, questions to ask might include:

Is this a specialised bookshop or a 'general' one? Where is it situated? What are the opening hours? What kind of customers are likely to visit this location? Are the books new, second-hand, antiquarian, remaindered, or a mixture of these?

How are the books organised? What is the proportion of books to each section? What does this indicate about the reading tastes of the customers?

Are the customers allowed to handle the books? If not, how do they obtain further information about the contents and pricing, etc.? Is there any space where they can sit and read before they decide whether or not to buy? Are refreshments available? If so, what kind?

What is the process of actually purchasing the book? What are the methods of payment: cash, credit card, cheque, store card? Are there preferred methods?

How typical of local bookshops is the one under observation? Is it a family business, a large organisation or a chain? What is its history? How have bookshops developed in the target culture? What is their social and economic history? What other products and services do they provide?

Bookshops (or 'bookstores' in North America) obviously vary from place to place, and the 'cultural frames' associated with them vary accordingly. While living in Moscow in the late 1980s, I found customers were usually physically separated from the books and had to call on assistants if they wished to handle a copy. If the customer wished to purchase a book, the assistant gave the price, which the customer then conveyed to the cashier, who, in turn, issued a receipt. The customer then took the receipt to the assistant, who surrendered the book. In contrast, in the USA, and more recently in the UK, some bookshops try to cultivate a social atmosphere, offering coffee shops or comfortable reading areas, where customers can take a book to look over, before purchasing. This is also true of larger chain stores in Brazil. There, as I found during a period of residence in the 1990s, information about prices can be obtained by passing the book in front of a computerised scanner, and checking the readout.

Detailed observation and contemplation of an ordinary 'concept', such as a bookshop, can lead to cultural insights and speculations. In the 1980s, in late communist Russia, the authorities still strictly regulated the flow of information, and a socialist, rather than a capitalist, ideology favoured the labour-intensive use of many shop assistants, who acted almost as a barrier between customers and books. In the USA, by comparison, the capitalist ethos promotes consumption as a leisure and social activity. The view of book-buying as a leisure and social event led some bookstores to encourage the use of the store as a place to meet friends and chat, and comfortable chairs and coffee were provided to encourage this. In Brazil, the use of computer scanners to give prices can be seen as a consequence of that country's history of economic instability: prices, especially of imported goods, can more easily be changed by a computerised system than by manually tagging each individual item. The ethnographic observer by careful observation of an everyday situation can start to work towards larger cultural generalisations that can later be checked against interviews and library research. In addition, teacher-observers can try to think themselves into the place of learners, and the culture-specific problems they might have in a given situation (e.g. unauthorised handling of books in Moscow; or knowing how to take advantage of leisurely browsing in the USA; or finding a price in Brazil when there is no indication on the book and the scanners are unobtrusively located). 'Concept Training' can function as a preliminary to larger-scale ethnographic study. It trains observers to realise that the ordinary is culturally constructed, and helps them begin to realise the kind of questions ethnographers ask.

Cultural associations

This activity (based on Damen, 1987: 285) is another small-scale activity to foster intercultural awareness. In this case, a specific subject is chosen and learners find out as much as they can about it, comparing information across cultures. One such 'cluster' of associations might involve food with particular cultural significance. Table 5.1 charts what might be found if learners investigated food from Brazil, Scotland and the USA.

Such 'association charts' are necessarily simplifications, even stereotypes: feijoada, haggis and hot dogs are all eaten outside the times and places specified, but there is an association in people's minds with set times, dates and places. Many Brazilian restaurants only serve feijoada on Wednesdays and Saturdays; haggis is associated with the birthday of the Scottish poet, Robert Burns, who immortalised it in verse; and although hot dogs are one of many common American fast foods, they have a particular association with sports. Seeking, learning and knowing this kind of information can help one to understand cultural allusions and jokes in the target

Table 5.1 Foods of cultural significance

	Brazil	*Scotland*	*USA*
food	feijoada	haggis	hot dogs
ingredients	salt pork, pork sausage, ham, salted tongue, pig's knuckle and trotters, black beans, onion, parsley, tomatoes, garlic	sheep's stomach, heart, liver, lungs and windpipe; onions, suet, oatmeal, salt, herbs	frankfurter sausage (beef or beef and pork), long, oval-shaped bun, optional mustard, ketchup, pickle
meal/snack?	meal	meal	snack
where or when eaten?	Weds & Sats	c. Jan 25th	sports games
accompanied by?	rice, mandioca flour, sliced kale, sliced orange; hot pepper sauce	mashed potatoes and turnips	nothing
origins	peasant food	peasant food	convenience food at sports games, etc
things to do afterwards	lie down; doze; chat sleepily	dance; listen to speeches, songs, poems	go back to watching the game

culture. It also casts light on cross-cultural similarities, such as the rise of lowly haggis and feijoada from the status of peasant staple to 'national dish'. In the case of haggis, as Burns' poem shows, the elevation of this form of offal in Scotland's affections is linked to a desire to present the nation as honest, straightforward, down-to-earth and free of pretensions.

Like 'Concept Training', charting 'Cultural Associations' can be a useful first step in perceiving ordinary phenomena as culturally significant. In this, it helps develop an ethnographic turn of mind.

Negative etiquette

If the previous two activities help learners and trainees to 'decentre', the final three examples suggest ways of helping students recognise and manage tricky intercultural encounters. As Roberts *et al.* (1992: 168–9) observe, one humorous way to raise consciousness of cultural patterns of behaviour is to devise rules of 'how not to behave' in certain situations – effectively, a guide to 'negative etiquette'. They offer a list showing 'How to Make Sure A Candidate Fails Your Interview', a list of 17 items including:

> Misuse or mispronounce the candidate's name.
> Be jokey and informal.
> Do not explain the reasons behind lines of questioning.
> Ignore what the candidate says and change the topic.
> To show your humour / cynicism / solidarity, say the opposite of what you mean.

The list is directed not at learners but at native-speaking interviewers, pointing out modes of behaviour that disadvantage ethnic minority candidates. However, it could also be used to indicate to learners how native speakers behave. The 'how not to' format has the advantage of using humour to identify areas that, perhaps, native speakers should modify, and, more likely, non-native interviewees should expect. The final example is a good case in point – to demonstrate wit, or even solidarity, a native speaker often says the opposite of what he or she means, signalling the irony by intonation. If a learner does not catch the intonation shift, the ironic signal might be lost.

Similarly, in a textbook about Scotland, targeted at EFL learners, David Maule includes the following list of 'seven ways to annoy the Scots' (Maule, 1989: 26–7):

(1) Use *England* instead of *Britain*, or *English* instead of *British*.
(2) Use *British* instead of *Scottish*.
(3) Use *Scotch* to refer to the people.
(4) Pretend never to have heard of Robert Burns.

(5) Say it would be better if the UK had one football team instead of four.

(6) Talk about men wearing skirts.

(7) Imitate the local accent.

A list like this can give interesting cultural insights into the Scottish mentality: the sensitivity about its relation with its larger southern partner in the Union underlies the first two items. As members of a small nation, the Scots are sometimes anxious that their individuality will be subsumed within that of England, or in a larger British conglomerate. Items 3–6 focus on concrete symbols of the national identity: national drink, national poet, national football team and national dress. The selection of items here speaks to a range of issues, such as the stereotypes of drunkenness and masculinity which pervade Scottish culture, and the role sport plays for small nations which are politically relatively powerless. The final item is about the difficulties faced by an 'outsider' imitating an 'insider's accent – is this to be interpreted by an insider as flattery (= I wish to be identified with you) or ridicule (= You talk in a strange and funny way)?

Lists explaining 'how not to behave' can be drawn up for a range of situations and groups, based on observation and/or interviews with native speakers (simply by asking questions like 'what annoys you?'). Lists for one's home culture can also be drawn up and discussed.

Critical incidents

The final sample activity to be considered here suggests more 'realistic' incidences of problems that can arise from differences in communication patterns. Various cultural training textbooks use 'critical incidents' in different ways (e.g. Barnak, 1979: 134; Bosher, 1997; Damen, 1987: 282–3; Roberts *et al.*, 1992; Tomalin and Stempleski, 1993: 84–8). In general, however, learners are invited to consider an incident (fabricated or from personal experience) in which (1) a conflict about values, goals or meaning arises; (2) the solution to the conflict is not immediately apparent, or it is controversial; and (3) the cultural context of the conflict is clearly and concisely presented. Learners are invited to discuss possible reasons for the conflict. A similar technique, the 'cultural assimilator' (Damen, 1987: 283–5), offers different interpretations of the cause of the conflict and invites learners to choose from among them. Examples of critical incidents, based on the literature cited, include the following:

(1) A female English supervisor works in a factory alongside a multicultural workforce. Last week, a male Bangladeshi employee came to ask her if he could have extended unpaid leave to visit his family in Bangladesh. You told him you were doubtful but you would see what you

could do. Later, after checking the work schedules, you decided that you cannot afford anyone to be absent for a long time. You made your decision known to your employee. Yesterday, you discovered that the employee has gone over your head to ask your line manager directly for unpaid leave. Your manager has passed the request back to you, since this is supposed to be your responsibility. You call the employee to your office to explain why he is challenging your decision.

(2)   An American teacher on a short multicultural summer course decided to give a party to her students, so she invited them to her house. The Japanese arrived at 8 pm and ate much of the food; however, they left at 10 pm just as the Italians were arriving. At around midnight the Latin Americans arrived, by which time the food was finished, but they stayed, singing and dancing, until about four. The Saudis did not turn up at all. Should she ever hold a party again?

Critical incidents are simple, but often effective, ways of investigating cultural differences which cause communicational misfires. There is a danger that they encourage stereotyping by making unwarranted generalisations about cultural behaviour (such as all Latin Americans sing and dance). Given that qualification, they are useful in dealing with some fairly general patterns of cultural behaviour and expectation. In the first example, the critical incident arises probably from the different conceptions of a supervisor by the Englishwoman and the Bangladeshi. The supervisor regards it as her responsibility to make decisions, and she expects those decisions to be respected. She does not like her decisions to be ignored, or to lose face with her own line manager. The Bangladeshi, on the other hand, might see the supervisor's position as a mediator between him and higher authorities. When she fails 'to see what she can do', he feels it is legitimate to approach someone who can grant his request. Neither individual in this situation is 'right' or 'wrong' – each has a culturally influenced way of perceiving the obligations of the other. An intercultural mediator would attempt to resolve the situation by making each aware of the other's position.

The second situation is based on the slightly different cultural expectations of 'partying'. Cultural differences can arise regarding the time parties occur, and what happens during them (eating, drinking, dancing). The Japanese tend to function in groups, and the Saudis would probably avoid attending anything which might involve alcohol and non-halal food. If the Latin Americans had not been told a specific time, they would not have arrived either: in Brazil, the utterance, 'You must come round sometime' often functions as a simple indicator of friendship, unless it is accompanied by a date and time. An American, however, might regard this expression as a more definite invitation.

Like the other activities described in this section, 'Critical Incidents' should be understood as a way of training learners to think ethnographically, to 'decentre' from their everyday habits of thought, and to realise that the ordinary is culturally constructed. This kind of activity can therefore lead up to fuller ethnographic projects as described in the following section.

Devising Larger-scale Ethnographic Projects

An increasing volume of literature on the intercultural approach (e.g. Barro *et al.*, 1998; Roberts *et al.*, 2001) encourages learners to undertake larger-scale ethnographic projects, preferably as part of a visit to the target culture. Damen (1987) advises teachers to undertake a more extended ethnographic project, although she is as hesitant as Roberts *et al.* (1992) to identify classroom ethnography with the kind of research outlined earlier in this chapter. Damen calls such projects 'pragmatic ethnography', noting:

> This designation has been chosen in order to remind all of us that the procedures used are to serve personal and practical purposes and not to provide scientific data and theory. (Damen, 1987: 63)

Although pragmatic ethnography is not scientific, it is systematic, and Damen suggests seven steps towards an individual ethnographic project for teachers (1987: 64–9). These are summarised, with some minor adaptations, below:

(1) Choose a target group
(2) Choose informant(s) able to represent this group
(3) Do library research on the group, if possible
(4) Interview the informant(s), remembering:
　　(a) not to identify the informant by name unless you have his/her permission;
　　(b) do not make evaluative comments during the interview. The informant's views should be elicited, not judged;
　　(c) request permission to make notes or to record the interview in some other way.
(5) Analyse the data and form a cultural hypothesis.
(6) Reflect upon your own frames of reference; and seek to understand the limitations of the evidence used to make the hypothesis formed in (5).
(7) Use the insights from your research to inform your teaching materials.

For example, a project might look at the experience of schoolchildren in the culture under consideration. Available informants would have to be chosen. Is it possible for the teacher to visit a school in the target community? If not, is there anyone within the target community accessible by mail or email? Would an expatriate, native-speaker colleague or acquaintance be appropriate as an informant? Background research on the education system in the target culture would be used to devise interview questions – teachers might seek educational documents or newspaper reports, or (if they have access) seek out relevant documents on the World Wide Web.

The interview stage is an important one, and the questions to be asked should balance general and more specific information. Interviews can be analysed for content, but the discourse structure of the interview can also be analysed to reveal cultural presuppositions (see further, Chapter 6). Step 6 is a necessary corrective to the researcher's over-enthusiasm. It explores the limitations of the investigative process by considering first what the interview has shown about the cultural presuppositions of the interviewers. Their frame of reference should be clear from the very topics they have chosen to dwell on – say, forms of school discipline, the goals of the English curriculum, or even whether or not pupils wear uniforms. The reliability of the informant(s) should also be reconsidered. For example, how much can an informant who is an expatriate teacher, perhaps educated at a comprehensive school in Scotland in the 1970s, tell us about British education as whole today? Scotland and England have long had separate educational systems, and since the establishment of a devolved parliament in Scotland in the late 1990s, the Scottish system has developed under the governance of the Scottish Executive. To make generalisations about 'British' education, then, the researcher would require a number of informants from different parts of the UK, who might have very different experiences of education, both state and private.

The seventh step is one in which Damen suggests that teachers use their ethnographic investigations to help select, and supplement, their course materials. Another possibility, obviously, is to use these guidelines to structure learners' own ethnographic investigations. More support would need to be given to learners at different stages, for example, the background reading might be partly pre-selected by the teacher, and learners might be prepared for interviewing by role-plays in which they have to formulate questions, ask for clarification, and express interest without being judgemental. Instead of step seven, the learners can present and discuss their findings in the classroom, and the learners' reports can inform further debates and topics on related issues, such as means of enforcing discipline in school.

Ethnographic projects for learners can be more or less developed than those that strictly follow the guidelines that Damen suggests. A less detailed ethnographic project might follow the tradition of media research, and take the form of, say, a small-scale survey of how a group of non-native speakers watch and respond to a US sitcom, shown locally on cable television. Again, the observation would be systematic, and take into consideration the way the audience 'interacts' with the programme: e.g. do they comment on anyone, or anything, while the programme is being shown, at what points do they laugh or groan (and for how long), and what is their opinion of the characters and situations? If the learners have access to native speakers, a cross-cultural comparison of audience response can be built up.

A much more detailed course in ethnographic learner-training is described in Barro *et al.* (1998) and Roberts *et al.* (2001). Lecturers at Thames Valley University in Ealing, England, developed a course to prepare modern languages students for ethnographic fieldwork during their 'year abroad', that part of their studies in which they live in the country whose language they are learning. The Ealing Ethnography programme was developed over three years in three distinct stages: (1) an introduction to ethnography during the second year of a BA programme, (2) fieldwork conducted during their year abroad, and (3) a written project, completed in the final year of the degree programme, based on the fieldwork undertaken. The project had to be written in the target language. The introductory programme in ethnography covered such skills as participant observation, interviewing, conversation analysis, recording and analysing 'naturally occurring' events, as well as topics such as non-verbal communication, family structures, gender relations, education, national and local identities, politics and belief structures (Barro *et al.*, 1998: 82). This programme was taught 'experientially' through fieldwork in the home culture, in the expectation that ethnographic skills thus developed would transfer to investigation of the target culture later. However, there was also background reading, mainly of academic texts in the discipline of ethnography. Although the Ealing Ethnographic project is elaborate and integrated fully into the degree programme at Thames Valley University, it is still distinguished by the course team from 'real' ethnographic research. They conclude (Barro *et al.*, 1998: 97):

> The students are not intending to become specialists in social anthro-
> pology. They are language students who, we hope, will become even
> better language students as a result of living the ethnographic life . . .
> They need the cultural tools for making sense of new intercultural
> contacts and experiences rather than positivistic facts about other

countries, structures and systems which are, despite the text-books' attempts to freeze-dry them and turn them into fresh-looking, digestible items of information, constantly in a process of contestation and change.

From the limited to the elaborate, then, there is a range of ways in which learners can be encouraged to 'live the ethnographic life'. Much depends upon the context of learning and the resources available to teachers and students; however, the basic materials for 'pragmatic ethnography' (i.e. someone to talk to and some events to observe) are available to different learners to some degree. At one extreme is a course like the Ealing Ethnography programme, which benefits from academic integration, legitimacy and funding. At the other extreme, home-based EFL learners are restricted to more limited access to native speakers and target culture products through media input, and communication at a distance. Even so, as we have seen, ethnographic skills can be developed through 'decentring' activities that analyse the home culture, and imaginative use of whatever target language speakers and products are available. Morgan (2001) reports on an 'international partnership project' through which schoolchildren in France and England learnt more of each other's culture by creating and sending by post materials on specific topics, such as law and order. Byram (1997b: 81–6) considers the materials available to teach French on the east coast of the USA, where connections with France (and even francophone Canada) are limited. In this case, there is indeed a greater dependence on media sources, supplemented by access to any native speakers in the community, and occasional help from educational agencies such as the Alliance Française and the French Embassy. For English, the British Council has long been a source of information and materials in educational situations where resources are limited. Electronic communication and the World Wide Web are also becoming increasingly available and offer exciting opportunities to bridge the distances between language classrooms across cultures and facilitate joint ethnographic projects. Dodd (2001) reports on an email-based project to teach language and culture to English and French schoolboys who hitherto had little motivation. Carel (2001) reports on a project that trains learners to be 'virtual ethnographers' using a combination of video, computer software, and classroom investigation.

Ethnography, then, is clearly a core feature of the intercultural approach. First of all, learners acquire observational skills that will stand them in good stead when they encounter unfamiliar cultures first-hand. Their ethnographic observations can be linked to ways of managing intercultural clashes, and the fostering of mediation skills. However, perhaps the most useful application of ethnography in ELT is to the systematic observation of how people from different cultures – whether national cultures, professional cultures, ethnic cultures, or others – communicate. By training learners to pay attention to the significance of the ways people from different cultural backgrounds choose to communicate, we can equip them to be independent, practical ethnographers and more efficient language learners. Since interviewing informants and analysing their responses is a key part of ethnographic training, Chapter 6 concentrates on ways of exploiting interviews in the intercultural classroom.

Chapter 6

Exploring Culture Through Interviews

In this chapter, the ethnographic theme is further developed by focusing on the key tool of the interview. Topics addressed are:

- *The interview as a speech genre.*
- *Interviewing strategies.*
- *The presentation of the self in interviews.*
- *Interviews as interaction.*
- *Using interviews to collect cultural information.*
- *Preparing learners to be interviewers.*

The Interview as a Speech Genre

In this chapter we shall consider how interviews can be treated from an intercultural perspective. In particular, the focus will be on how to conduct interviews as part of small and large-scale ethnographic research, and how to analyse the data collected from interviews. Interviews might seem a very specific topic to be allocated a full chapter in this book; however, they are important for an intercultural approach to ELT for two reasons. First of all, interviews seem at first glance to be a speech genre that exists mainly to exchange information – an interviewer asks a question, and the interviewee responds. In communicative language textbooks, interviews are often used in listening passages as examples of information gaps being bridged. However, as we shall see, the content and form of questions and responses in interviews also incidentally give *cultural* information, about the participants' social and geographical identities, and about their values, assumptions and attitudes. This aspect of interviews is often neglected. Commenting on the use of interviews in anthropological research, Roberts *et al.* (2001: 142–3) observe:

> The conclusions drawn from data collected in interviews are not unproblematic facts. The questions are asked in particular ways and construct and constrain the answers. A different question would produce a different response and so different data. So any interview

data is jointly produced and is as much a product of the interviewers'
social world as it is of the informants'.

Despite these misgivings, however, interviews are still a major way in
which learners, particularly in an ELT situation, can conduct practical
ethnographic research – for example, they can make contact with English
speakers and ask them about aspects of the target culture. What must be
remembered and anticipated is that the responses they elicit might not be
entirely straightforward, and both the questions and the answers will
probably require careful analysis to shed light on the 'joint production' of
social reality. This chapter gives some guidance in how to analyse interviews from a cultural perspective, by using examples from linguistic and
social research, as well as data collected by L2 learners.

Chapter 3 argued that conversations and interviews are different types
of speech genre. Casual conversation has been problematic in ELT because
its cultural function is not primarily to exchange information, but to
establish or maintain social identity by sharing experiences and negotiating or affirming the values and norms of the group. An understanding of
the cultural function of conversation can lend purpose to the familiar characteristics of conversation – turn-taking, holding the floor, second-
storying, and so on – and help teachers and students prepare for the difficulties inherent in this speech genre. At first glance, interviews should be a
much easier genre to cope with in a classroom with a focus on information
exchange. In interviews, at least superficially, content is primary: they are
ostensibly a genre in which an information gap is bridged. A brief excerpt
from a tape script from an ESP course book *Business Venture 1* (Barnard &
Cady, 1992: 86) illustrates a typical exchange of information:

A: Could you tell me something about IKEA?
B: Yes, we're a big international furniture company. We have 89
         stores in 21 countries.
A: How do you operate?
B: Well, first we do market research; that's very important. We ask
         people what they want and, using this information, we design a
         new piece of furniture.
A: And what's the next stage?
B: After that, we ask the suppliers to manufacture the furniture.
         Then, they pack it, and send it to our stores.
A: And then the customers buy it.
B: Yes. They visit our stores and see the furniture. They decide what
         they want and buy it.

The interview is evidently constructed in part to demonstrate the use of sequencers (*first, after that, then*), and partly to offer a simple model of interview structure. 'A' asks a question, or probes with a statement, and 'B' either gives a minimal response ('Yes'), or sometimes elaborates with further information ('We have 89 stores . . . '), and sometimes offers an evaluation ('that's very important'). Over the course of the interview, 'A' learns new information about the company. However, in 'real' interviews, even information exchange of this kind occurs within cultural 'frames' that vary from speaker to speaker. These 'frames' contextualise the speech event, allowing the speaker to assess the significance of the information exchanged, and to understand implicit meanings which underlie the explicit questions asked. Successful communication in interviews depends on the sharing of cultural frames of reference.

The uses of interviews, moreover, are varied. The example above is contextualised briefly in the course book as an exchange between a journalist and an IKEA manager – the type of journalistic end-product of the interview is not made clear, but we can imagine that it would be some kind of business feature or public relations exercise. The participants in the interview are on relatively equal terms professionally, and treat each other co-operatively, and with respect. Similar relationships would normally be found in interviews that are for research purposes – whether market research, sociolinguistic research or other types of research conducted by professionals upon strangers. Other types of interview are more complex and problematic. Some interviews, such as those on television 'chat shows', are as much about performance as about genuine information exchange, and they will be dealt with separately in Chapter 8. Many interviews, like those with personnel officers, social services or promotion panels, involve unequal relationships between applicants and 'gatekeepers' to resources or power. In such interviews, the questions asked are not as straightforward as the IKEA example, and the applicants' responses will determine whether or not they are granted access to employment, services or a promoted post. It has been shown that in gatekeeping interviews with ESL speakers, not knowing the 'cultural game' of anglophone interviewing style can put applicants at a severe disadvantage. Roberts *et al.* (1992: 47) give the example of a job interview in which an ethnic minority candidate ('B') was asked about his driving experience:

N: You obviously don't drive in the job you're doing. What sort of driving experience have you had?

B: In this country?

N: Um hum.

B: I've got um light goods vehicle driving licence and I've . . . I don't think done nothing wrong.

As Roberts *et al.* observe, the applicant here puts himself at a disadvantage by giving what appears to be a defensive and only tangentially relevant answer to 'N's question. 'N' is indirectly offering the applicant an opportunity to present his skills and experience, according to the cultural conventions of anglophone job interviews. However, 'B', who comes from a culture where interviews are more closely akin to tests where weaknesses are probed, interprets the question as an attempt to find fault, and answers in the light of his own cultural assumptions. In his own terms, he is being relevant, but both 'N' and 'B' have different assumptions about the cultural function of the question, and therefore different expectations about the kind of information that is to be exchanged.

This example is a vivid illustration that even 'straight' information exchange is culturally conditioned, not least by the participants' presuppositions about what kind of information is important, and why it is being exchanged. This chapter considers the way that culture impacts upon interview situations, examines the way that meaning is constructed interactively by participants in interviews, and suggests ways in which interviews can be exploited more fully from an intercultural perspective in the ELT classroom.

Interview Techniques

Interviewing is only one way of gaining cultural information. Ethnographers currently tend to avoid formal interviews, preferring covert observation, or 'focused conversation'. Roberts *et al.* (2001: 141) comment in their description of the Thames Valley University ethnography programme that:

> One of the most difficult aspects of the methods element of the course is to help students unlearn their preconceptions about the interview as a research method. They have to replace their image of the white coat and the clipboard with something that is much closer to a focused conversation. This does not mean that ethnographic interviews are unstructured, unprepared encounters.

A structured guide to interview technique is given in Spradley (1979). Key points to consider include:

- Try, if possible, to interview the respondent more than once, over time.
- Decide in advance which general themes or topics you wish to cover in the first interview.
- Listen to the interviewee's responses to establish further topics to follow up later, in more focused interviews.

- Decide in advance how you will record the responses (notes taken during or immediately after the interview, audio or video-recordings?). This will depend in part on the location of the research and the relationship with the respondents.
- Avoid 'leading questions' of the kind, 'How do you show that you are proud to be Scottish?' This assumes that the respondent *is* proud to be Scottish.
- Elicit information with as little evaluation as possible. Back-channelling, or repeating what the respondent has just said, often encourages the respondent to elaborate. Alternatively, probe the interviewee's responses by asking questions like, 'What do you mean by –?'.
- Encourage interviewees to elaborate on topics. Do not be in a hurry to hasten them on to new topics by asking a new direct question after they have given a brief response to an earlier question.

Ethnographic interviewing in a foreign language is not as difficult as might be supposed. Roberts *et al.* introduced their students to ethnographic interviewing first by practising in their mother tongue, and then by role-playing in the target language. They found that their students' anxieties were ill-founded (2001: 145):

> Interestingly, the fears about their own competence in interviewing in the foreign language are quickly laid to rest. They find that ethnographic interviewing requires relatively little productive competence because the whole point is to give the informant control of the interview and because questions so often use the informants' own language.

After the data has been recorded, the interviews should be transcribed, in whole or part. Different conventions are used in published interviews to mark hesitations, pauses, overlaps, non-verbal features such as laughs and gestures, and characteristics such as volume, intonation and whispering. How interviews are transcribed depends in large part on what the research identifies as important. If two interviewees are talking, and one interrupts or overlaps with the other, this should be shown, particularly if the learner is interested in why they are interrupting and overlapping. If an interviewee changes his or her voice quality to dramatise certain incidents in the interview, this should be coded in order to be shown systematically. The interviews transcribed below illustrate some of the differences in the conventions governing the presentation of speech in writing

Finally, the transcribed data has to be analysed. As noted above, this is not a transparent process, and it involves the learner reflecting on the usefulness of his or her questions, and the assumptions underlying both the questions and the answers. The following sections suggest, first of all, different ways in which interview data can be analysed, according to a range of cultural perspectives to do with topics such as class, gender, and subcultural group membership. Finally, more practical, 'classroom' examples of data collection and analysis are presented.

The Presentation of the Self in Interviews

People respond to interviews in different ways. This fact itself has been the subject of discussion in sociolinguistics for over three decades, since Bernstein (Bernstein, 1971) investigated the speech styles of children in interviews, and controversially correlated those styles to their working-class and middle-class status, that is, their 'social formations'. In brief, Bernstein argued that working-class children grew up in a social environment in which individuals fitted into a fairly rigid and uncontested hierarchy. In traditional working-class communities, in other words, people knew their place within the social structure. Working-class communities were stable and promoted solidarity and well-defined social roles. Middle-class children, in contrast, grew up in an environment in which there was more scope for negotiation – social roles (e.g. of males and females) were less 'fixed', and the community itself was less well-defined. The contrasting social formations led to a disposition to use language in different ways: working-class speakers use language to affirm their identity as part of a collective; while middle-class speakers use language to affirm their identity as a negotiating individual. As Montgomery (1986) puts it:

> The contrast between the two social formations could be summed up in terms of the relative bias of each toward the collectivity or the individual. The first raises the 'we' over the 'I'; the second raises the 'I' over the 'we'. In doing so, each formation – with its characteristic role systems – develops a distinctive orientation towards communication. (Montgomery, 1986; reprinted in Montgomery & Reid-Thomas, 1994: 60)

Bernstein's view of the relationship between language use and social class was hotly criticised in the 1970s – some of the findings were, for example, interpreted as suggesting that working-class speakers were unable to form arguments, and that they were linguistically 'deprived'. Their use of a 'restricted code' that favoured collective narrative over individual argument was sometimes contrasted unfavourably with middle-class speakers' mastery of an 'elaborated code'. Such arguments demonstrate the dangers of over-generalising from limited data. As Montgomery observes, most sociolinguists today would not consider 'orientations towards communication' as completely determining the way working-class or middle-class speakers use language – they are simply 'orientations'. Any speaker can move along a continuum between individual-oriented and community-oriented speech styles, depending on personal inclination, speech situation, and the relationship between participants. However, in given speech genres, such as interviews, general patterns of preference can be correlated with social classes, or 'formations'. In other words, working-class and middle-class speakers tended to view interviews in systematically different ways, and construct a relationship with the interviewers in accordance with these varying perceptions.

The realisation of communicative orientations can frequently be observed in interviews, particularly those favoured by sociolinguists, which probe for personal information as a way of putting the interviewee at ease. Macaulay (1991) elicited the following data when interviewing middle-class and working-class speakers from Ayr in Scotland. The transcripts are organised in lines, each of which is a phrase that contains a single verb. Both speakers are reminiscing about their past, but they present themselves in quite different ways. Extract A shows a middle-class speaker presenting himself in terms of likes and dislikes. He constructs an argument to justify his preferences, and explicitly draws attention to the status of one of his statements as a 'generalisation'. At one point he even appeals to the written mode ('put normal in inverted commas'), which serves to underline the fact that his presentation of himself takes the form of an argument – a negotiating position.

> *Extract A*
> well I quite like this environment
> I like the people here
> and I like the countryside
> and I like the attitudes of people
> because I found
> one – one problem with say Germany or Oxford was
> that there was a certain amount of [.] unreality in Oxford
> in that the academics were really a bit isolated from the
> rest of the community
> and many of them felt
> that this was the whole point of living
> to solve their own particular research problems
> and nothing else was really all that important
> and they tend
> to live in this sort of ivory tower atmosphere
> although obviously with a generalization like that you know
> there were many exceptions
> and there were many sort of – sort of normal people
> put normal in inverted commas

In contrast, the working-class speaker below presents herself not as someone who negotiates, but as someone who narrates. In other words, she reveals herself through stories rather than argumentation. As Macaulay points out (Macaulay 1991, 1995/6), this style of self-presentation is no less sophisticated than the middle-class style, requiring as it does a command of pacing, suspense, and a control of dramatised direct speech, used at moments of crisis. The spelling of the working-class transcript represents some features of a working-class Ayrshire accent and dialect (e.g. 'oot', *out*; 'telt', *told*) and these also, obviously, indicate the social and geographical origins of the speaker. The middle-class speaker above would also have an Ayrshire accent, but his dialect is closer to that of written standard English, and so it is more difficult to represent in writing. (For a further discussion of non-standard varieties in the intercultural classroom, see Corbett, 2000.)

Extract B [talking about her mother]
she watched you like a hawk
so I goes oot this night
it was my first husband
I'd made arrangements
to meet him – away at Tam's Brig
away from the Prestwick Road to the Tam's Brig
and somebody had telt her
they had seen me
so we'd made arrangements
we'd meet at Tam's Brig
he would go his road
and I would go mine
and then naebody would see us
walking hame
however whoever spouted on me
had telt her
where I was and aw the rest of it
so she –
I come to Tam's Brig this night
and I'm just coming ower Tam's Brig
and I stopped dead
Bertie says to me
"What's up with you?"
I says
"Oh don't luck the noo
there's my mother"
he says

"It is nut"
I says
"It is"
"Well come on
and we'll face her"
I says
"You may
but I won't"
says I
"You'd better stop there
and I'll go on"
he stopped
as I telt him
and I went on
well she hammered me fae the Tam's Brig tae the
Prestwick Road
and everybody watching me
and I was eighteen

The content of the anecdote here is directly concerned with social roles in working-class communities in the speaker's youth – by courting without her parents' permission, the speaker had violated the norms of the community, and her mother makes a public example of her. Both she and her boyfriend seem aware of the social conventions they have violated and although the man appears willing to 'face' the mother and negotiate, the speaker is not, and accepts her public punishment without resisting. The speaker seems to be saying that, as a young woman, she accepted the roles and constraints of traditional working-class communities more readily than she would now. The working-class speaker here presents herself not through explicit argument, but by way of a narrative that dramatises key social issues, but does so implicitly, in a way that the interviewer is supposed to understand and appreciate. As a means of self-presentation, the narrative is no less sophisticated than the argument of the middle-class speaker, though in educational contexts it may well be less valued.

These examples illustrate the fact that even in interview situations, the exchange of information is influenced – though not completely determined – by cultural factors like class and ethnicity. Gender, too, may play a part in the way that information is selected and communicated. Certainly in one real-life case study of a classic ELT situation – buying tickets at a railway station – researchers discovered that women asked more questions than men, especially when the ticket-seller was male (Brouwer *et al.*, 1979, cited in Montgomery & Reid-Thomas, 1994: 32). This difference in gender behaviour can be interpreted in various ways but it does at least suggest once more that information exchange is culturally shaped.

The educational implications of this insight are considerable. In native-speaker education it has long been argued that in oral assessments, working-class speakers can be disadvantaged because their speech-styles do not conform to the middle-class expectations of the education system. In the USA, in particular, there are long-standing debates about the assessment of sociolinguistic competence of African-American Vernacular English (AAVE) speakers (e.g. Rickford, 1987). In ELT, of course, the situation is different but analogous: as we have observed, there are some gatekeeping encounters (e.g. oral examinations, and job interviews) in which speakers from different cultural backgrounds might be disadvantaged, though one would hope that in the former, the training of ELT examiners would encourage them to compensate for varying speech styles. From an intercultural perspective, it is necessary for learners (and their assessors) to be aware that even in apparently 'objective' situations of information transfer – typically in interview situations – background and communicative orientation will predispose individuals to select and structure information in systematically different ways. The remainder of this chapter looks at the construction of meaning during the process of interviews, and considers ways of raising awareness of cultural differences in information-exchange.

Interviews as Interaction

The interviews found in ELT coursebooks often share a problem with simulated conversations: a stiltedness that becomes even more apparent if learners are asked to read dialogues aloud. Erickson (1996: 292) pinpoints the source of this recurring inauthenticity in the absence of 'the on-line mutual influence that we experience in naturally occurring conversation, the dynamic ebb and flow of listening and speaking relations' and 'the fluidity of social identification that can occur as real people converse face to face'. There may be other good reasons for reading dialogues aloud, of course, but they do not offer learners the opportunity to cope with real-life interaction, which, as Erickson observes, demands a degree of spontaneity and the ability to cope with the unexpected. One simple strategy for leading learners from the controlled ritual of a textbook dialogue to the relative unpredictability of spontaneous speech is to devise a role-play based on the dialogue. One such role-play was devised by Sheila Cogill and Denise Gubbay for ESL learners in industrial contexts (cited in Roberts *et al*. 1992: 267). It begins with the telephone dialogue:

Teacher: Westwide plumbing.
Student: I need a plumber. My tap is leaking.
Teacher: Name please.
Student: [supplies]
Teacher: Address?
Student: [supplies]
Teacher: OK. I'll come this afternoon.
Student: What time?
Teacher: Between twelve and five. I can't be exact.
Student: That's alright. Thanks.

Once students have practised this, the teacher begins to give unpredicted and largely unwanted responses, such as:

(wrong number):	'No plumber here. This is a private house.'
(plumber ill):	'We're not taking orders. Mr Jones is ill.'
(plumber busy):	'We can't do anything for a week.'
(request for direction):	'Where can I find you?'

Within the familiar framework of the known dialogue, then, a 'controlled element of unpredictability' is introduced. The learner does not need to process the whole situation in order to deal with the unfamiliar elements, and can focus on producing something more akin to the 'dynamic ebb and flow' of an authentic exchange of information, where he or she has to negotiate a successful conclusion to the interaction.

However, as Erickson observes, spontaneity and dealing with unpredictability is only part of what makes spoken interactions 'authentic'. There is a cultural element, namely the 'fluidity of social identification' that can occur as speakers interact. Again this fluidity of identification is as pertinent to interviews as it is to casual conversation. Erickson (1996: 292–3) gives the fictional example of an interview between a supervisor and a new employee, a young, female Puerto Rican of African ancestry, who happens also to be a college graduate in business, a former track star, a lesbian, a mother of small children, and an active member of the local Protestant church. Her identity is multifaceted, as are all our identities, and in the interaction with her supervisor, she may choose to select one topic in preference to another. Thus, as Erickson (1996: 293) sums up:

> Different badges for attributes of identity could be made more salient at one moment in the encounter than at other moments. Thus, which attributes of identity would be emphasized as central to the conduct of interaction might vary for a given individual, not from one social situation to the next but within a given situation.

Such a 'fluidity of social identification' explains the responses of members of 'spectacular' youth subcultures (i.e. goths, punks, rockers and hippies), when interviewed by social scientists investigating subcultural affiliations (Widdiecombe and Wooffitt, 1995). The researchers hoped that their interviews with subculture members would cast light on their need for group affiliation; while, in fact, in the interviews, respondents typically avoided categorising themselves and instead stressed their 'ordinariness' and individuality. One interview with two 'goths' (R1 and R2) makes this point clearly (Widdiecombe and Wooffitt, 1995: 106–7; presentation adapted):

I: right, so as a said I'm doing stuff on style and appearance can you tell me something about yourselves the- the way you look

R1:   w-wu-wh't d'you mean like . . . what do you mean . . . about ourselves's a bit general huhh

I: well . . . how would you describe what you're wearing

R1:   ehm . . . what I feel . . . be(hh)st in hhuh . . . what I feel is sort'f myself . . .

I: what about you

R2:   uhm . . .

        [Alarm goes off in backround]

R2:   I just find it really offensive when people . . .

I: sorry

R2:   I just find it really offensive when people try to label . . . what you look like and so . . .

I: yeah

R2:   then go away and write a magazine article and say oh they're gothic . . . or they're hippy or something

Here, as the researchers comment, the interviewer seeks what seems to be unproblematic information about the visual style adopted by two 'goths', that is, members of a subculture that typically dresses in funereal black, uses deathly pale make-up, and listens to rock bands that dwell on morbid themes. Both interviewees resist the interviewer's categorisation of them, however, the first by seeking clarification of the question and then, in her response, emphasising personal choice rather than affiliation with other goths. The second respondent 'forcibly protests about the kind of self-identification which the interviewer's first turn was designed to achieve' (Widdiecombe & Wooffitt, 1995: 107). Information, here, is not exchanged in the straightforward way that the interviewer originally intended: the respondents choose to downplay visually explicit markers of their group affiliation, and protest against the easy assumptions of a 'straight' mainstream interviewer.

Widdiecombe and Wooffitt argue (1995: 75n) that they did not look like 'prototypical market researchers', and did not look 'out of place in the festivals we attended' and so their informal interviews should be regarded as equivalent to conversations. However, this is in fact a difficult claim to justify. As we saw in Chapter 3, participants in casual conversation are typically engaged in an implicit negotiation of values to construct a shared identity – if those negotiations break down, the group can also fragment. By contrast, in Widdiecombe and Wooffitt's interviews, an outsider (no matter how inoffensive) is asking for information about the group affiliations of individuals – the purpose is different and so the speech genre is different from that of everyday conversation. In their interviews, the youths are implicitly being asked to explain or justify their dress style, which is assumed to be a badge of their subcultural membership. The first respondent's request for clarification can be interpreted as a strategy to make the interviewer 'come clean' about the intent of the question; the second respondent's complaint can be interpreted as a rejection of the assumptions that might lead the interviewer to categorise them as one thing or another. It is important to note that the interview progresses on the basis of one participant's interpretation of the intent *behind* the utterances of the other participants. The second respondent assumes that the social researcher is a journalist, hoping to write a stereotypical magazine piece on teen styles, and her complaint can be read partly as a protest about being misunderstood, and partly about being exploited.

The downplaying of what may seem to be obvious badges of social identity was a common (but not universal) feature of Widdiecombe and Wooffitt's interviews exploring subcultural identities, and this fact is a cautionary warning to anyone conducting ethnographic projects on the topic of identity. The way that identity is constructed is not straightforward, and the question-answer structure of interviews may not be the best way to elicit it. Even when the respondents are being co-operative, the answers to the questions may not be direct, although they are sometimes surprisingly systematic. When Widdiecombe and Wooffit asked various subcultural members, 'Is being a punk / hippy / rocker important to you', they received very similar answers, although none of them directly addressed the benefits of subcultural affiliation (1995: 168–76; presentation adapted):

I: is being a punk very important to you?
R: yeah, very indeed
        I couldn't imagine myself being straight at all . . .
        like dressing neatly in tidy nice clothes an' having
        my hair down and all that hh
        . . .

I: is it very important to you . . . being a hippy?

R: er . . . I dunno, y'know, I – well I wouldn't like to be anything else – put it that way – I wouldn't like to be 'orrible trendy smelly yellow shirts an' things like that . . .
      . . .

I: is being a rocker very important to you?

R: er . . . ahha aye . . . it's jus the way I am er . . . couldn't imagine life . . . of er . . . of say I lived wi' . . . I dunno . . . bu' . . . I remember the Royal Family you know having a go at these people as er you know an' er going about wearing suits an' everything . . . going to all these functions and do's an' that er . . . driving about in a Ferrari . . . I jus couldn't see it . . . I mean . . .

I: mmhm

R: it's easier being being the way I am . . . it's jus . . . jus comes natural ken?

Here, instead of saying something like 'it's important / not important to me because . . . ' the respondents construct their answers in terms of what Widdiecombe and Wooffitt call 'a rejection of alternatives'. Those who are rejected are those who conform (are 'straight'), are fashionable ('trendy'), or, in the third case, are business people ('suits') or the epitomes of the establishment ('the Royal Family'). Respondents 'address and affirm the importance of membership of a subcultural group without actually referring, say, to the lifestyle, beliefs or activities associated with that subculture' (ibid.: 174). In short, when asked about their identities, respondents tend to construct themselves by referring to what they are not – what is sometimes called in cultural studies, the 'Other'. By describing and rejecting the Other (here, 'straight' middle-class or even aristocratic people), the respondents are indirectly describing themselves.

The interviews discussed immediately above are significant from several perspectives. First, they again demonstrate what is meant by speech progressing through interaction, even in interview situations, when the focus might be expected to be on the 'objective' information exchange. In other words, the oppositional position of some subcultural styles is communicated not by the explicit statement of a position, but implicitly, by strategies such as seeking clarification, rejecting the inferred basis for the question, and rejecting alternatives rather than supporting preferences. As the ethnic minority interviewee also discovered during the job interview referred to earlier, much successful question-and-answering activity in another language depends on co-operation and in having a cultural frame in common which will allow participants to infer the implicit purpose behind what is often indirect questioning. Secondly, the final example shows the kind of difficulties that a researcher – even a professional researcher – can run into when trying to describe an interesting cultural phenomenon. Interviewing members of 'spectacular' youth subcultures, in order to glean information about group affiliation and perceived benefits, can be difficult since the interviewer will likely be treated as an 'outsider', and his or her motives may be questioned. Moreover, the inferences that inform the interviewer's line of questioning might be denied by the interviewees in a series of interactional strategies through which, if they answer the question at all, they answer it only indirectly.

Using Interviews to Collect Cultural Data

It will be clear from the foregoing discussion that interviews can be approached from two perspectives in an intercultural English language course. Learners who have direct access to native speakers can be encouraged to interview them about some aspect of their lives. For more advanced learners, transcripts of interviews in textbooks such as Montgomery and Reid-Thomas (1994) might be used. In the analysis of the interview both the content and the interactive speech style are worth considering. In other words, as well as paying attention to what is said, learners should also pay attention to how it was said; for example:

(1) Setting
(a)   Where did the interview take place?
(b)   How comfortable would the interviewee feel there?
(c)   How well did the participants know each other before the interview?
(d)   What was the purpose of the interview? Did the interviewee know of its purpose beforehand?

(2) How were the interviewer's questions understood?
(a)   What points, if any, needed clarification?
(b)   Were any of the questions challenged?
(c)   Were any of the questions rephrased?
(d)   Did the interviewee give minimal or extensive responses?
(e)   Were difficult questions responded to by hesitation, false starts, changes of direction?
(f)   How explicitly did the interviewer articulate his/her questions? How far did s/he attempt to elicit information by *indirect* questioning?

(3) Presentation of the self/Relationship with interviewer
(a)   Did the interviewee mainly argue, describe or tell stories, etc?
(b)   Did s/he answer from an individual or a group perspective?

(c)   Was the language relatively formal or informal?
(d)   Did the interviewee interrupt the interviewer?
(e)   (If videoed) How did posture, gesture, eye movement, etc, contribute to the interaction?

To give examples of possible commentaries on interviews, we shall now consider in detail two interviews between a couple of advanced L2 speakers (one from Turkey and the other from Brazil) and two respondents they met in Glasgow Gallery of Modern Art. The interviews were conducted by participants on a cultural studies course, organised by the British Council in Glasgow. These interviews illustrate the kind of project work that can be done with advanced non-native speakers who have access to native-speaker respondents, here in a particular institutional setting. The two L2 speakers, one Brazilian and one Turkish, decided to interview visitors to the then newly opened Glasgow Museum of Modern Art, to gather information about their opinions about Glasgow's status as a 'city of culture'. For several decades the city has been promoted as a destination for cultural tourism, and in 1990 it was officially designated as 'European City of Culture'. The transcripts of two extracts are given below. The interviewers are A and B; C is an older woman, self-confessedly 'working-class', and D and E are a younger couple, who profess themselves to be 'ordinary'.

In the Art Gallery (1)

A: And you think that this idea of city of culture . . . come . . . is a new . . . new one?

C: It's a new thing. And I don't feel it's for the ordinary working class people you know

B: [mumbles]

C: I don't think so, I think they're going over the top as far as ordinary peop – ordinary people can't get to these things, you know what I mean.

A: mmm

C: They're so expensive. Even the new eh concert hall, now it's been built I think maybe it might be two years, maybe three, maybe even four, I have never been near it

B: ohh

C: and as I say because of all the – they've built a lot of nice – people go there – but things are so expensive they're really not for the ordinary person if you can understand. I'm sorry to go on like this but I really feel that that's what it's about you know, they're dealing – they're they're definitely going above theirself and people just can't afford these kind of things. If they'd get down to a lower level I feel that, em you know, it would be much better. But that's only my opinion. Thanks very much.

B: Thank you.

In the Art Gallery (2)

A: It's presented eh as a city of culture mainly and we we were wondering to eh what extent this idea is eh real and genuine and to what extent it is something constructed, created eh by the tourism industry maybe.

D: Yeah, the 1990 year of culture thing helped quite a lot

A: mmm

D: but I think a lot –

E: That was built upon.

D: Yeah, I think it's been built upon a lot since then and -

E: It I think it started off as em just sort of being created to help tourism or whatever and now they've built upon that em -

D: Yeah, I think the people of Glasgow have taken to their heart quite a lot to actually build on it quite a lot –

E: It means they've done a lot with theatre and you know constructing the art gallery and things like that and they've taken pride in their city being a city of culture –

A: yeh

E: and so it's developed from there.

A: When the word culture comes into one's mind is it high culture which is meant here in Glasgow or popular culture in general?

D: I think it's popular culture.

E: Yeah.

A: Popular culture.

D: It's very much a culture of the people, you know, it's it's a culture that [clears throat] that everyone can take part in, it's not a sort of hierarchy culture.

A: Ordinary people.

D: Yeah, uh huh, definitely, I mean there's here –

E: There's not there's not a great deal of snobbery in it.

D: No, no.

E: Em, you know it's just your everyday person what they believe culture is.

D: Yeah, everyone takes part –

A: Yeh.

D: very much so.

Normally, in projects like this, the students will gather a number of responses from different people – that is, pragmatic ethnography tends to yield a sample of diverse opinions. This kind of data collection is manifestly unsystematic and therefore unrepresentative, and learners must be cautioned against making easy over-generalisations based on such data. What ethnographic research seeks is the 'telling' example rather than the 'typical' example (cf. Mitchell, 1984: 239) – that is, while we cannot argue that the respondents in interviews like this represent the general population, the patterns of their responses do clarify certain illuminating principles.

The interviews can be exploited to show how the respondents construct their answers, and this tells us about the cultural frames of reference underlying their inferences and arguments. Despite the fact that the interviewees in the two extracts above have divergent opinions, they use almost identical strategies to justify them. To the invitation to comment on Glasgow as a city of culture, C chooses to complain that it is not for the 'ordinary' person: it is too expensive, and it is 'over their heads'. She backs this up with the observation that she has never been near the new concert hall. Her combination of personal evaluation, ('I think / feel'), general evaluation ('they're . . . going above theirself'), and anecdotal support shows the inadequacy of a polarised view of speech styles as *either* individual or community-oriented in the terms discussed earlier in this chapter. The respondent, who aligns herself with the working-class, is articulate in negotiating what she acknowledges is 'only her opinion', and draws upon elements of both Bernstein's 'restricted code' (in the narrative element) and 'elaborated' code (in the argumentative element) to do so.

The couple in the second extract are more individually-oriented in their argument: there are many generalisations, often hedged with 'I think . . . '. Even here though, as in the other interview, the 'I thinks' are balanced by the community-oriented discourse marker 'you know', the function of which is to raise 'common ground' between interviewer and respondent, that is, it appeals to shared community norms. It is often the place where the interviewer will back-channel with a nod or a supportive 'mmm' to show assent. There are no anecdotes to support the claims made, though E gives several examples chronicling the development of the artistic programme of the city, in defence of the repeated statement that its cultural reputation has been 'built upon'. What links the two divergent opinions is the common construction of the 'ordinary' person's perspective. Although consistently referred to in the third person (A: 'People just can't afford . . . '; E: 'It's just your everyday person, what they believe culture is.'), the 'ordinary / everyday person' is the position from which each of the respondents chooses to discuss Glasgow's cultural aspirations. The cultural construction of 'ordinariness' may vary according to age and social class, but it is clearly seen by all three respondents here as a powerful rhetorical position from which to advance one's opinions

This finding is not particularly original: when researching youth subcultures, Widdiecombe and Wooffit were surprised to find that members of youth subcultures, easily identifiable from their 'spectacular' modes of dress, make-up and hairstyle, clearly regarded themselves as representatives of 'ordinariness'. This is evident in an interview with a punk (Widdiecombe and Wooffit, 1995: 124; presentation adapted):

R: ah mean I know ah'm a punk know
            but I jus(t) . . . I just feel as though
            I'm the same as everyone else . . . I mean I dress
            diff'rently (h) but there again everyone
            dresses differently to everyone else
            so like
I: yeah
R: when people look at me as if I'm an alien,
            it sometimes . . . it gets me really annoyed because . . .
            you know, I'm just the same as everybody else

It is clear that, whatever their opinions, fashions or lifestyles, people wish to be considered 'ordinary'. The interesting thing to note in the 'art gallery' interviews is how 'ordinary people' are assumed to behave, and what values they are supposed to have. In the first of the interviews, the ordinary person is presupposed to have limited access to city centre venues, limited funds, and a common-sense understanding of art objects. The woman's criticism of the gallery is based on the argument that the city council is not making art accessible – economically or intellectually – to the ordinary person thus conceived. The young couple constructs the 'ordinary' person as interested in culture, as taking a pride in the city and as being without pretension. Their 'ordinary person' is an active participant in cultural events, who has even hi-jacked the city council's agenda, which is seen as based on expanding tourism, by encouraging a more democratic participation in cultural events. Not unnaturally, their 'ordinary person' is much more positive about the new art gallery. The responses of C, D and E in these interviews can be seen as telling us much more about their cultural values than about their opinion of the art gallery itself – the responses can be seen as part of an ongoing cultural negotiation about what it is to be 'ordinary' and what values and behaviour represent ordinary people.

The interviews discussed so far have ranged from examples from sociolinguistic and ethnographic textbooks, to informal interviews eliciting personal opinions. In each case cultural content can be interpreted by (1) paying attention to the content of the interview, (2) observing to the way the interaction develops between interviewee and interviewer, and (3) analysing in detail the speech styles and discourse strategies used by the respondents, as they describe, narrate and argue their case.

Preparing Learners to be Interviewers

Interviewing respondents is an obvious way of encouraging learners to use their language skills 'ethnographically', to gather information about aspects of the target culture. As the sample interviews above show, a range of interviews can yield cultural data but not always – or only – because the content of the interview gives information about the aspect of culture being investigated. The speech styles and inferencing strategies used by the respondent can also be analysed to suggest the kind of presuppositions which allow him or her to interpret the interaction.

As shown earlier in the chapter, previously recorded interviews (or transcripts of them) can be used to alert learners to community oriented and individually oriented speech styles (cf. also Montgomery & Reid-Thomas, 1994: 52–64). Role-plays can also be used to sensitise learners to the ways in which presuppositions govern the kinds of question asked in interviews, and how the questions are answered. For example, the teacher can set up situations in which people from different cultures are interviewing each other about their lives, or people with different cultural assumptions about interviews are assessed during a 'gatekeeping' interview. An extreme variation of the first example might be to set up a role-play in which an 'alien' from another planet interviews the class about life on the planet Earth. The role-card given to the learner playing the alien would give information about life on the alien's home planet; for instance, the alien might be a form of asexual vegetation, it might receive its education via implanted microchips, it might live to an advanced age, and so on. As the 'alien' asks questions about life on Earth, the class can be invited to speculate what these questions tell us about life in the alien's culture.

Many role-plays can be devised using interviews (cf. also Roberts *et al.* 1992: 352–63). The example suggested above focuses on the interviewer's cultural frame, and on the shared / different assumptions of interviewee and interviewer. If recorded, the different strategies of the interviewers and interviewees can be examined in class in more detail, and perhaps improved upon. However, it is important not to be prescriptive about cultural frames and the resulting speech styles. As Roberts *et al.* (1992: 128–46) demonstrate, communication breakdown, and unfair assessment during gatekeeping interviews, often arise because the interview frames of the anglophone interviewers predispose them towards asking indirect questions, the purpose of which is not easily perceived by non-native speakers with different frames of expectation. Thus, if a job demands mobility, an interviewer might ask 'do you drive a car?', meaning 'have you currently got transport?'. A non-native speaker, expecting an orientation towards skills and tests, might answer, 'Yes, I passed my test first time' (1992: 130). The intercultural speaker should be aware of different cultural possibilities, even in information exchange, without necessarily privileging one mode above another. This should help learners to choose the speech style most suited to a given occasion, and, more pertinently, help them to request clarification and to adapt styles quickly if their hypotheses are proved incorrect.

Conclusion

This chapter has focused on interviews, since this type of interaction is common in communicative textbooks, where it is usually treated as a means of exchanging information. Interviews are also an obvious way of collecting data for ethnographic projects. As we have seen, smooth interviews depend on the participants sharing cultural frames of reference, and the questions and responses to interviews can tell us as much about the assumptions and attitudes of the interviewers as they do about the interviewees. Interviews are therefore valuable ways of exploring both the target culture *and* the learners' home culture. As we have also seen, the assumptions and attitudes of participants are not always directly articulated, and so interviews need to be carefully analysed in order to see how they indirectly present themselves, their values and their beliefs.

Chapter 7

Developing Visual Literacy

This chapter turns from ethnography and begins to consider other ways of 'decoding' a culture. First of all, we consider the visual representations of cultural information, and how to 'read' them critically. Topics addressed include:

- *Defining 'visual literacy'.*
- *Using images in the ELT classroom.*
- *Understanding visual composition.*
- *Understanding the grammar and vocabulary of visual images.*
- *Combining visual and textual information.*
- *The 'iconography' of English in non-anglophone countries.*

From Ethnography to Semiotics

The preceding two chapters illustrated how a cultural approach to language teaching draws on disciplines other than mainstream linguistics. Ethnography offers invaluable strategies for systematic observation of a culture, supplemented by data-gathering techniques, such as the interviewing of respondents. Practical ethnography, on a limited scale, can be practised by curriculum planners, materials writers, teachers, and, above all, learners. Given the constraints of practical ethnography, it is valuable to train learners to consider the different ways that participants interact in interviews. A close study of interviews reveals that they are not simply occasions for the exchange of information: they also are ways of constructing and presenting identities.

This chapter turns from ethnography to consider another discipline relevant to the cultural approach: 'visual literacy' or semiotics. 'Semiotics', the study of signs, can be a difficult discipline to understand and master (cf. Barthes, 1977; Eco, 1976). Nevertheless, semiotics has much to offer the culturally-oriented language teacher who wishes his or her students to develop skills not only in *understanding* but in *interpreting*. Most students live in an ever-changing world of visual data, and by paying attention to and developing a critical awareness of how this data communicates messages to them, they can also develop their verbal skills and intercultural competence. However, first of all, semiotics must, like ethnography, be made accessible in the classroom, and a number of recent textbooks and articles suggest ways of doing this (e.g. Bignell, 1997; Goodman, 1996; Kress & van Leeuwen, 1996; Rose, 2001). This chapter discusses recent developments in the analysis of visual images, and suggests how teachers and learners can develop a 'visual literacy' with which to explore their own and other cultures.

Using Images in the Classroom

There is, of course, a long-established history of using images, or 'visual aids', in the ELT classroom. The reasons for using images are good and obvious: they can be used at all levels of language learning, from beginners to advanced, and they can bring into the classroom those objects which would otherwise be forever outside it; for example, aeroplanes, beaches, and tourist locations in the target culture. Depending on the image, visual aids can be used to bring vocabulary to life, or to act as input into information-transfer activities (for example, one learner might have access to visual information and then have to describe it verbally to another learner). Communicative methodologists typically stress the value of images as prompts for language production; for example, Scrivener (1994: 167) comments on picture stories, that is, images sequenced to form a narrative:

> Traditionally, they have been used as a starting point for writing exercises, but they are also very useful for focusing on specific language points or as material for speaking and listening activities. Most picture stories seem inevitably to involve practice of the past simple and past continuous.

Photographs, drawings, cartoons and diagrams make EFL textbooks look attractive, but they also contextualise the language used in any given lesson, and they can even make a linguistic concept like 'tense' or 'aspect' easier to grasp by giving a visual image such as a 'time-line'. Oral examinations often use photographs as cues for speech: for instance, candidates can be asked to describe the content of the picture, and to speculate about what went before and what might come after the situation portrayed in the photograph.

Visual aids, then, are widely acknowledged as a rich resource in ELT, but what all the activities mentioned above share is a primary focus on *content* in order to promote language learning. Images tend to be exploited in diverse ways for their language-learning potential, but their cultural significance is comparatively neglected. The exploration of the images produced by different cultures is, however, a powerful way into intercultural studies in the ELT classroom – where the focus is on both images produced by the target culture and those produced by the home culture. The analysis of images can exploit pictures from a variety of sources, of which the following are only a few:

- newspaper and magazine reports and features;
- magazine and billboard advertising;
- political campaign literature;
- ELT textbooks;
- travel agents' literature;
- school / college textbook illustrations;
- compact disc covers;
- postcards;
- paintings in art galleries;
- pictures on websites (several of the images discussed in this chapter were obtained under licence from < scran.ac.uk >, an archive of thousands of images, film and audio recordings held in Scotland).

Pictures can be used as data for the exploration of social issues in the home and target cultures. Over time, learners may come up with their own ideas, prompted by their own observations and interests. However, in the initial stages they may well need guidance about themes that are likely to yield interesting results, for example:

- how are certain age groups (e.g. men, women, children, teenagers) represented in advertising?
- how are certain nationalities / ethnic groups represented?
- how is authority / lack of authority constructed visually, e.g. by politicians, or in advertising?
- what is it that a society considers visually attractive? Is this constant over all societies / periods of time?
- what do fashions tell us about the values of the social groups that adopt them?
- are the photographs or diagrams used in newspaper reports 'neutral' illustrations of the text?
- are the pictures used in travel agents' literature representative of the countries they are sending people to?
- what kind of information about Britain / the USA / etc. is given in EFL textbook illustrations?

- does the visual information in EFL textbooks correspond to that given about the country in geography textbooks?
- can you track the social history of an image (e.g. of a kilted Scotsman) over time, using art books, textbooks, advertising? Did the image always refer to exactly the same group? What values did it have at different times, and for whom (e.g. crude barbarian, exotic primitive, imperial soldier, comic miser, romantic warrior)?

In tackling these projects, students will need to develop what is referred to above as 'visual literacy'. In other words, they will need to develop a systematic means of looking at visual images and talking about the kinds of messages they convey. This chapter aims to give guidance on how learners might be encouraged to develop these skills. The sections below are intended to give the teacher suggestions about ways of approaching the analysis of images. These discursive sections are followed by a checklist that may be used or adapted for class projects.

Reading Images as Messages

If visual images are messages then it should be in principle possible to 'read' them. The titles of articles and books on the analysis of visual images often directly play on this supposition: Barthes' 'The rhetoric of the image' in *Image/Music/Text* (1977); Fiske and Hartley's *Reading Television* (1978) and Monaco's *How to Read a Film* (1981). The principal influences on this chapter, Kress and van Leewen's *Reading Images: The Grammar of Visual Design* (1996) and Goodman's 'Visual English' (1996), deliberately position themselves in this tradition, and, moreover, actively seek parallels between linguistic analysis and the analysis of visual images. For example, Kress and van Leeuwen (1996: 44) state that:

> What in language is realized by locative prepositions, is realized in pictures by the formal characteristics that create the contrast between foreground and background. This is not to say that all the relations that can be realized in language can also be realized in pictures, or vice versa, that all the relations that can be realized in pictures can also be realized in language. Rather, a given culture has a range of general, possible relations which is not tied to expression in any particular semiotic code, although some relations can only be realized in pictures and others only in words, or some more easily in pictures and others more easily in words.

Kress and van Leeuwen's argument is that if visual images are really a way of sending messages, then they should be subject to some kind of analysis along linguistic lines, bearing in mind the inherent differences in the nature of the 'semiotic codes', that is, the visual and the verbal message-bearing sign-systems (for a critical discussion of this claim, see Forceville, 1999). We can argue, for example, that visual images have a 'vocabulary' and a 'grammar'. The 'vocabulary' of visual images consists of their content, or what they represent. This may be, depending on the image, a soldier, a skinhead, a child, a beautiful woman, an empty landscape, a blueprint of a football stadium, or a map of the world.

Like vocabulary items, what is represented in images will have denotational and connotational meanings. These meanings are culturally situated and they can be compared and contrasted across different contexts. For example, political campaigns in different countries often use images of children. In 1997, shortly after it had won its first general election victory for over a decade the UK Labour Party's website showed a picture of a young girl dressed in a red T-shirt, on which was written the slogan 'Things Just Got Better'. She was looking at the viewer while punching the air in apparent joy. In Brazil the following year, an election billboard for candidate Mario Covas' campaign to be governor of the state of São Paulo also prominently featured a child (Figure 7.1).

It is interesting that both political campaigns used the image of a child. The connotations of the child were clearly useful to each party – in both cultures, they communicate associations of innocence and youthfulness (important to 'New Labour' as it re-invented itself after years out of government). Both the Brazilian and British campaigns alleged that their rivals were tainted by 'sleaze' and corruption – the slogan in the Brazilian poster translates as 'Father, do you think that lying is right?' The choice of a child as a visual 'vocabulary item' is relevant to the impression that each political

Figure 7.1 Billboard for 1998 Covas Campaign

campaign wished to convey: the images associated the parties' candidates with the freshness, vigour and innocence of youth.

Linguistic texts are not simply random assemblies of vocabulary items. For texts to make sense, the words have to be arranged in sequences according to linguistic conventions, or 'rules'. In the same way, the content of images has to be arranged in acceptable ways for the message to make sense. The 'grammar' of the image, then, is the relationship between those people or objects represented by the image. For example, is one person or object acting on another, as in a transitive clause? Or is there only one person or object represented, as in an intransitive clause? It is necessary to make clear what we are doing here. We are not saying that images *are* clause types, but that visual information can be used to convey similar messages to clauses. Therefore they can be subjected to a similar kind of analysis, an analysis that relates different types of form (in this case, visual forms) to meanings. The remainder of this chapter will focus mainly on presenting an elementary grammar of the image, based largely on the principles outlined in much more detail by Kress and van Leeuwen (1996). As they acknowledge, some of their grammar presupposes a Western orientation towards the image – for example, the fact that Western writing systems operate from left to right influences the composition of images. However, the tools of analysis that they provide can be adapted for radically different cultural positions, and they certainly highlight the nuances and shadings of different cultures within the West. The questions asked of images are summarised in a checklist at the end of this chapter, for ease of use in the intercultural classroom.

Understanding Composition

We shall begin our exploration of the grammar of images by considering the composition of the image as a whole; in other words, what is the relationship of the elements of the image to each other, and how are they placed in the overall image?

Single images

The single image can be considered in terms of the different areas that are available within the frame: left/right, centre/margins, top/bottom. The positioning of an element within one of these areas gives it a particular meaning. Obviously, a strong central presence might dominate a picture, indicating that the element within that position is important, the focus of our attention. In contrast, an element placed at the margins is more likely to be read as peripheral to the main message of the image – an observer, a by-product, or someone/thing affected by the central object or event. The rival

Figure 7.2 Billboard for 1998 Maluf Campaign

candidate to Mario Covas in the 1998 race to be governor of São Paulo was Paulo Maluf. His campaign team devised a billboard (Figure 7.2) in which he was featured prominently, slightly right-of-centre (a possible visual 'echo' of his political position).

The positioning of Maluf in this billboard emphasises his importance – he is shown alone, and near the centre, between the textual components. 'Ele faz' translates roughly as 'He gets it done'. (The interaction of text and image is further considered below.)

The left / right split that is found in many images is influenced by the fact that the sentence in western languages tends to be read from left to right. In English, the sentence can also be divided into two parts: the left-most constituent is the Theme, while the part to the right is called the Rheme. These technical terms refer to the conventional organisation of the English sentence as an utterance which moves from a point of orientation (the Theme) to the substance of the message (the Rheme). In spoken English, the intonation system tends to follow a parallel pattern: the sentence begins with Given information – what the listener can already be expected to know – and then ends, with a strong tonal shift, on New information, or what the listener is expected to find salient or important. Kress and van Leeuwen argue that the left / right distinction visually conveys similar meaning to the left / right distinction in the sentence. In other words, what is placed on the left-hand-side of most images can be read as Theme: the information which provides a context for the message. The elements placed to the right-hand-side constitute the Rheme: the new information, or the nub of the message. Many visual images that have no centre have a strong left-right movement: these images can therefore be read as messages proceeding from a given context to new information. The elements on the right should be read in relation to the elements to their left. The Covas billboard

(Figure 7.1) clearly has a left-right organisation. The image of the child on the left provides a context for the verbal text on the right: we therefore interpret this billboard as the child asking a question. The Maluf billboard, on the other hand, begins with text: 'Ele faz' ('He gets it done'). The obvious question is: 'Who are we talking about?' and the succeeding image of Maluf, and the text which follows the image, provide the new information, the answer to our question.

The final general distinction, top/bottom, conventionally expresses a sense of the ideal versus the real. Kress and van Leeuwen trace this division back to mediaeval religious art, where heaven, or paradise, is placed at the top of the picture, while earth (or hell) is placed below. A later, 15th century print that falls into this tradition is Albrecht Dürer's 'The Four Horsemen of the Apocalypse: Revelation of St John the Divine' (Figure 7.3). The woodcut shows four bringers of destruction, with the Grim Reaper on the left, then a strongly central Famine beside War, with Death on the far right, shooting

Figure 7.3 'The Four Horsemen of the Apocalypse'

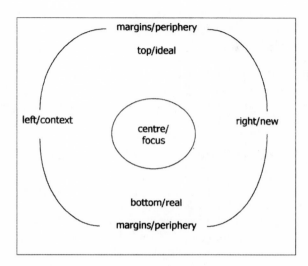

Figure 7.4 Summary of Composition of Image (adapted from Kress & van Leeuwen, 1996: 208)

an arrow. Above them all flies an angel, and below them poor sinners are swallowed up by the mouth of hell. The concept of 'up-ness' retains strong positive associations in Western culture, while being 'down' is still generally construed as negative. This dichotomy is even evident in idioms such as 'I'm feeling up today' versus 'I'm feeling really down'. Similarly, in pictures, what is positioned towards the top of the frame is considered to be the ideal, while what is positioned towards the bottom has a more realistic, or sometimes a negative connotation.

To summarise what has been said so far, the single image can be divided into the areas shown in Figure 7.4, each with its own meaning in relation to the others.

Within the image, certain features can be singled out for special attention. Elements in the foreground are nearer us, and therefore more eye-catching, than elements in the background. The relative sizes of elements signify their importance. They may be divided by a strong framing device – a shadow, a wall or some other feature that effectively puts them in 'separate boxes'. Alternatively, elements may be grouped together in equal sizes, at an equal distance, without frames, symbolising their communal identity. The four horsemen in Figure 7.3 overlap, and we view them as a single unit, charging from left to right, their eyes fixed on a goal that we cannot see.

Another means of establishing salience is through contrast in colour or differences in sharpness of focus. Near the beginning of many productions of Shakespeare's *Hamlet*, the hero is visually differentiated by the fact that he is wearing black, the colour of mourning, in opposition to the wedding gaiety of the rest of the court. The quality of focus can highlight a particular element in an image: it can be portrayed sharply against a soft-focus background, or (as is less frequently the case) in soft-focus against a sharply focused background.

The Grammar and Vocabulary of Visual Images

Positioning, framing and salience together provide the main resources for considering the composition of the image. In this section, we shall look more closely at particular combinations of the visual 'grammar' and 'vocabulary', and in particular how both relate to the viewer. First of all, we shall consider the portrayal of people in images, and then different types of object.

People

It is evident even from the images discussed above that the portrayal of people is one of the most powerful strategies for communication. Since we are social creatures, we respond to the sight of even an image of someone looking at us, or ignoring us. We make immediate and largely unconscious judgements based on the way someone looks, and we identify with images we find attractive, and disassociate ourselves from those we do not. What particular characteristics of images of people do we pay systematic attention to?

The gaze

One powerful factor in the representation of people (and animals, especially when they are given human-like qualities) is the direction of the gaze. Specifically, is the represented character in the image looking directly at you, the viewer, or at someone or something within the frame of the image, or elsewhere, beyond the frame? These different representations have different meanings. Eye-contact with the viewer can be interpreted as *demanding* some kind of response from the viewer. A smiling expression may demand social affiliation, a frown may demand that you back off. A more neutral expression may be interpreted as an enigmatic demand, and invitation to puzzle out what the represented character wants or thinks. Figure 7.5 is a print of a Scottish highland soldier in North America, published in 1790 as an advertisement for tobacco products. The soldier is taking snuff, while a slave is smoking a pipe in the background.

Figure 7.5 Advertisement for tobacco, featuring a Highland soldier and a slave

There is no eye contact between the soldier and the slave, nor between either of them and the viewer. Unlike the four horsemen, who are strongly grouped, we are presented with two separate individuals, linked only by the products they are using, and the elaborate feather head dress each displays. Both represent the 'exotic' to the tobacco-buying public of the 18th century. Highland regiments served in North America at the time, and, since the destruction of the clan system in the middle of that century, kilted highlanders were becoming strongly associated with romance and the fashionable concept of the 'noble savage'. These two exotic 'savages' are portrayed for our visual pleasure in their different states of fancy dress and undress. We look at them but they do not address us: compare the child's direct gaze at the viewer in Figure 7.1.

An absence of eye-contact with the viewer puts the viewer in a more distant, observational position. The viewer can dispassionately consider the relationship between the characters in the image who establish (or fail to establish) eye-contact, or we can puzzle about what it is, out-of-frame, that the characters are gazing at. Kress and van Leeuwen argue that when a character is gazing out-of-frame a strong feeling of empathy is induced in the viewer. They also argue that male characters (like the four horsemen) tend to gaze firmly at unseen goals or horizons, whereas female characters tend to be represented as staring blankly into the middle distance, 'as if they have mentally withdrawn from their immediate surroundings' (1996: 66). The two characters in the tobacco advertisement also seem to have withdrawn from their surroundings, presumably in this case under the influence of the narcotic.

Perspective and distance

Gaze is, of course, not the only factor in the representation of people. Perspective and distance interact with the gaze, and are important factors to consider more generally when seeking to understand images. As Kress and van Leeuwen (1996: 149) observe:

> One can, and perhaps should, always ask 'Who could see the scene in this way?' 'Where would one have to be to see this scene in this way, and what sort of person would one have to be to occupy this space?'

So, for example, if the image positions the viewer as looking down and meeting the gaze of a represented character looking up, the viewer is cast in the position of authority, and the represented character is in a subordinate position. Reverse the angle, and the authority-subordinate roles are also reversed: the represented character becomes someone the viewer owes respect and perhaps even obeisance to. Television newsreaders are often shot at a slightly elevated angle, to give their words more credibility. An eye-level representation puts character and viewer on an equal footing. A clear contrast of options here is shown in the two Brazilian political posters (Figures 7.1 and 7.2). The Maluf campaign shows the candidate in the typical posture of an editorialising newsreader: it is a 'head-and-shoulders' shot, slightly inclined away from the viewer. It is the archetypal posture of authority. The Covas campaign shows the child from above, so close that only part of his upper body is visible. The viewer stands over the child and close to him: both text and image position us quite explicitly as his father ('Pai') – other billboards in this particular campaign featured children addressing the viewer as 'mother' and asking similar moral questions. Each image constructs authority in a different way: the Maluf campaign invites the viewer to accept the authority of the candidate; the Covas campaign invests the viewer with parental authority, and demands moral action of a particular kind (namely, a vote for the preferred candidate).

Changes in perspective on the vertical axis are therefore related to

power. Changes on the horizontal axis are related to the viewer's involvement with or detachment from the image. If the viewer and character are
face-to-face on the same plane, there is a high degree of involvement. If the
character has turned away, or a scene is depicted from an oblique angle, the
viewer becomes more distant from it; the representation is no longer part of
his or her world. A character who meets the viewer's gaze but turns away
may be interpreted as coy, or inviting – there may be a tension between a
demanded response and a withdrawal to another plane, or an invitation to
join the character on the other plane.

The final factor to be considered here is distance between the character
and the viewer. Physical distance operates as an obvious metaphor for
social distance. A close-up shot has greater intimacy than a medium-shot.
A medium-shot in turn implies greater social affiliation than a long-shot,
which is the most impersonal of the options. By grading the degree of
physical distance in an image, one can grade the social distance between
character and viewer.

Fashion and style

If gaze, perspective, and distance are realisations of the grammar of the
image, fashion and style may be considered part of the vocabulary. The
very expression 'dress code' implies a set of behavioural rules governing
the clothes that people wear, a code that can be interpreted as a meaningful
system. Just as language can be formal or informal, so can clothes; just as
certain forms of address or particular words are appropriate to some
contexts and not others, so certain styles of clothing are 'formal' or 'casual'
and so more likely to be worn in some situations than others.

Our clothing is one way in which we give messages about the relationship between the individual and the wider community. Business people
dress in similar ways; men dress differently from women; the rigid hierar-
chical communities of the military are coded into the design of their
uniforms. Conventions, of course, change and vary – British school
uniforms today are more likely to comprise sweatshirt and jeans than
blazer, white shirt, tie, and grey flannel trousers or skirt. Most British bank
staff – especially women tellers – tend to wear uniforms, while in most
Brazilian banks, the staff is more diversely dressed. This apparently trivial
fact still perhaps gives an interesting insight into norms of corporate
culture in different countries.

Youth subcultures in particular are renowned for 'spectacular' styles –
partly because the adoption of such styles is consciously or unconsciously a
challenge to 'mainstream' society, that is, the culture organised and
governed by a minority of their elders. Hebdige (1979) charts the evolution
of British youth subcultures from teddy boys to punks, and in his survey

dress codes play a prominent part. Like others (e.g. Cohen, 1980) he draws attention to the exaggerated proletarianism of skinhead culture: the Doc Marten boots, jeans and braces, button-down shirts and shaved heads forming a caricature of the norms of working-class clothing. The xenophobic chauvinism of the skinhead stereotype is an extreme version of a more 'mainstream' working-class stereotype. Punks, on the other hand, constructed themselves according to a different visual code:

> Conventional ideas of prettiness were jettisoned along with the traditional feminine lore of cosmetics. Contrary to the advice of every woman's magazine, make-up for both boys and girls was worn to be seen. Faces became abstract portraits: sharply observed and meticulously studied portraits in alienation. Hair was obviously dyed (hay yellow, jet black, or bright orange with tufts of green or bleached in question marks), and T-shirts and trousers told the story of their own construction with multiple zips and outside seams clearly displayed. Similarly, fragments of school uniform (white bri-nylon shirts, school ties) were symbolically defiled (the shirts covered in graffiti, or fake blood; the ties left undone) and juxtaposed against leather drains or shocking pink mohair tops. The perverse and the abnormal were valued intrinsically. (Hebdige, 1979: 107)

If skinhead culture mocked the mainstream by taking some of its more reactionary elements to an extreme and aggressively championing them, then punk culture outraged the mainstream by taking its norms and trashing them. For Hebdige, however, part of the value of punk culture was that, by systematically debunking the mainstream norms, by giving intrinsic value to 'the perverse and abnormal', punk usefully demonstrated that mainstream values were themselves not 'natural', but rather the construction of a particular bourgeois culture. Punk style can be interpreted as an act of political subversion which challenged bourgeois ideology. How far punk succeeded in this aim is open to question. Youth subcultures are endlessly reinventing themselves, partly in response to corporate culture's commodification of its more commercially exploitable aspects. Punk moved fairly rapidly from the streets to the catwalks of high fashion, and, in music, from independent to multinational record labels.

The style adopted by characters in images, then, is a potent resource for telling the world which cultural group the character affiliates to. It may be the same group that the viewer affiliates to, it may be a group that challenges the viewer, or it may be a group that the viewer aspires to be a member of, whether overtly or secretly. Advertisements are particularly adept at using the styles of the characters represented to target particular client groups, and an analysis of the fashions and styles of advertisements can be revealing about cultural norms at any given time. It is no accident that the girl in the UK Labour Party image wears a red T-shirt – it is the traditional colour of socialism – but it is reinvested with new meaning by the slogan imprinted on it: 'Britain Just Got Better', referring both to the then-recent 1997 election victory, and to a popular song, 'Things Can Only Get Better', adopted as an anthem during that election campaign. New Labour sought to repackage its traditional values in a populist fashion. The right-wing Brazilian politician, Paulo Maluf, on the other hand, is represented in his billboard in suit and tie against a conservative blue background – the campaign portrays him as a traditional and trustworthy figure of authority (Figure 7.3). The Highland soldier in Figure 7.5 wears a kilt, a mode of dress that changed its signification in the 18th century, when this print was made. Before the Jacobite uprisings of 1715 and 1745, the kilted Highlander was generally considered a distant barbarian by the rest of Britain, including southern, or lowland, Scotland. After 1745, and the defeat of the Jacobites, the kilt was banned in Scotland for a long spell. It was only legally worn by soldiers serving in the British army, and so it began to be associated with the military. The kilt also began to symbolise the passing of a way of life, and was valued by those who saw it as a token of a more 'primitive' or 'natural' mode of existence. Today it has become a national icon, and it is now fashionable even for lowland Scots to wear the kilt at times of celebration, such as weddings and graduations.

Objects and settings

Obviously the range of non-human visual representations is too great to be able to give more than a few suggestions about how to understand and interpret them. Much of the foregoing discussion applies to things as much as to people: objects and settings can be regarded as given / new, ideal / real, central / marginal, and they can be seen from a direct, head-on perspective as part of our world, or situated obliquely as part of another plane. They can be portrayed in close-up, and sometimes so close as to be unavoidable or oppressive; or they can be shown at a distance, coolly, observationally. The grammar of the visual image applies to objects and settings as much as to people.

Like fashion and style, the vocabulary of visual objects and settings can have specific cultural associations that in turn can be interrogated. Something as apparently neutral as a car advertisement can be gendered, if the manufacturer perceives that the main market for the car is the woman driver. The way the car is designed, the choice of colours, the manner of its verbal description and visual representation, may all appeal to what a culture considers female rather than male tastes. This, in turn, applies only to cultures in which women are allowed to drive: in some countries – like

Saudi Arabia – custom and regulation would forbid most women from taking the wheel. This obviously affects what is visually represented as being normative.

Settings, too, have cultural connotations. An exploration of the way that the travel industry represents holiday destinations is an obvious means of investigating how a country is stereotyped, packaged and sold to people of other cultures. McCrone *et al.* (1995) observe that Scottish Tourist Board posters of Scotland airbrushed the people out of their images of mountains and lochs, in order to promote a tourist-friendly national image of Scotland as romantic wilderness. The fact that most of Scotland's population live in lowland towns and cities, not in highland villages and crofts, does not alter the power of the *imagined* landscape of Scotland to act both as a signifier of identity and as a commodity for consumption by tourists.

It will be clear from the above that images have a cultural history. Images of cars, specifically targeted at women, have resulted from the development of the market economy to the point at which the automobile industry sees its interests best served by identifying specialised niches (the family, the business traveller, the independent woman) and designing and promoting its products accordingly. The stereotypical landscape of Scotland results from several centuries in which national self-image was invested in a mythical Highlands of tartan-clad warriors, no matter that for much of that time the industry of Scotland was changing from agrarian to industrial, and its population from rural to (largely) urban.

Constructing 'the natural'

All visual representation is non-naturalistic. Even photographs are not 'mirrors of the world'. They use degrees of focus, colour saturation and tonal contrast to heighten or lower the degree of 'naturalism' conveyed by the image. As Kress and van Leeuwen demonstrate, the concept of the 'natural' in photography is socially constructed, and partly dependent on available technology, rather than on how the eye perceives colour. Too saturated an image seems 'hyper-real', as in the wish-fulfilling fantasy world of Hollywood's golden age. Rose (2001: 17–23) also points out that technological possibilities also contribute to our understanding of photographic images. Long exposure times in early photography meant that most subjects had to be posed in studios, often seated or holding on to some object for stability, whereas later cameras allowed outdoor 'snapshots' that better seemed to capture the spontaneous and 'natural'.

What is considered 'natural' also varies according to context. Long after photography in billboard advertising was 'naturally' in colour, the cost of technology restricted photographic reproduction in British newspapers to black-and-white. The first introduction of colour into newspapers was in the 'trivial' tabloids, rather than the 'heavyweight' broadsheets. As colour became the preferred mode in the tabloids, the broadsheets only slowly moved towards colour. What is natural in one format, seems unnatural in another. Monochrome images, though associated with 'serious' documentary realism, are in another context unreal – they do not represent the world as we actually see it (and can currently photograph it) and so black-and-white depiction is in fact an affectation, a pseudo-documentary pose.

In painting, what is considered 'natural' has shifted even more radically during the past century and a half. A crisis in representational art coincided with the invention of photography. Impressionism, pointillism and cubism, among other art movements, sought to challenge and reinvent the natural. Representational art no longer sought to give an illusion of documentary realism, but to explore the *impression* the world made on the senses, or to reproduce the way the world presents itself to us as *points* of light, or to schematise the world according to its underlying *geometric* design. Representational art is never a transparent, neutral, unproblematic medium for the transmission of information – not even photography, which is probably the visual equivalent of 'plain English'. All visual images interpret the world as we see it – if only by selecting items which are deemed worthy of note. There is no objective 'natural' way of doing this – the 'natural' is determined by available technology, habits of viewing, and individual expectations, all of which are culturally constructed and subject to negotiation and change.

Understanding Visual Narratives

So far, we have considered only what is in an image and how the various elements are positioned. In this section we shall consider what, if anything, the various elements are doing to each other. In other words, we shall consider whether and how the characters represented in an image 'do' things to each other. Kress and van Leewen (1996) discuss these questions in greater detail than is possible here. Their analogy for narrative and non-narrative images is transitive and intransitive clauses, that is, sentences like:

Transitive	*Intransitive*
1. Gary watched Clara.	3. Clara blushed.
2. Clara kissed Gary.	4. Gary turned red.

In transitive clauses, one character acts upon another through some kind of process. In (1) above, Gary acts upon Clara via a mental process: he is the senser, she the phenomenon. In (2) Clara acts upon Gary physically: in this case she can be termed the actor, he the goal of her action. The intransitive clauses are different in so far as they contain only one character. In each case our attention is fixed on that single character, who is the focus of the description.

We can consider images in similar ways by categorising them into *narrative* (transitive) images, in which characters act upon each other in some way, and *descriptive* (intransitive) images, in which a single character, or a set of characters who are nevertheless isolated from each other, is simply described.

Narrative images

Still images clearly do not have the resources of language to articulate processes. Instead of using verbs, still images use *vectors* to articulate action. A vector is a line, often diagonal, which leads the viewer's eye from one part of an image to another, often from represented character to character. It can be created and reinforced in a number of ways: by following the eye-line of one character to another, by gestures, pointing or poses, or by the angle of some kind of tool: e.g. a staff, walking-stick or rifle held by a character. In Figure 7.3, the angel's hands nearly connect with the sword carried by War, and the vector represented by the sword carries us down to the group of four. Here various vectors again serve to unite the group. The horses' heads form an arc leading down to the Grim Reaper and the fallen sinners. War's sword connects with Famine's head, and so establishes a vector that leads us out to his scales of justice, which themselves form an arc with the billowing cloak of the Reaper. Death's arrow points to that unseen target that the horsemen have fixed their eyes on, and which the angel is pointing to. The trampling forelegs of the horses echo each other, and their movement is completed by the Reaper's trident, which shovels the sinners into hell. The overall impression is of an unstoppable force bent on destruction.

Actions within the frame of the image can be unidirectional or bi-directional – characters may act mutually upon each other, or one upon the other. A vector may be 'non-transactional' in the terminology of Kress and van Leeuwen (1996: 74–5), in that it points out from one actor, but does not connect with another. This is the case with the soldier and the slave in Figure 7.5: both gaze, self-absorbed, in different directions. A character may be the goal of one process but the actor in another, as the angel and several of the sinners gaze at the horsemen in Figure 7.3, while the horsemen themselves gaze off into the distance. Varying these possibilities sets up a range of potential social relationships, which in turn may take place in a variety of settings.

Descriptive images

When no vector connects one character to another, the image is descrip-

Figure 7.6 Buddha

tive: the represented character, or a set of characters, is displayed for our contemplation and consideration. Such portrayals illustrate, celebrate, exemplify or commemorate. If the image is single, our attention is drawn to the attributes that make up the whole. An example of a single, descriptive image is obviously the meditating Buddha (Figure 7.6).

His eyes are closed, and his meditative pose constructs a closed circuit – no vectors point off elsewhere. He is literally at one with himself. If the image is a set of non-interacting characters, like the horsemen, we interpret them as a connected group and may seek (or be told) the criteria which categorises them: here they are all agents of destruction.

Some images, or elements of the image, may be symbolic: they are presented for our contemplation, either because they are particularly significant or because they have a conventional symbolic value. A portrait of an academic often shows a book as an accompaniment; a portrait of a musician will have a musical instrument. A portrayal of a man and woman alongside a bitten apple will prompt interpretations based on religious conventions. The bitten apple reappears as the logo of Apple computers, wittily suggesting a taste of the same forbidden knowledge as the religious symbol does – but also demonstrating the secularisation of Christian art in Western culture. Often in an image, the symbolic element will be lit specially, or pointed at, or presented in the foreground of the picture. On my computer screen, the apple icon appears at top left: marginal, but in the ideal/given position, a position of power from which all else on the screen proceeds.

Alternatively a symbolic 'atmosphere' can be given to an image by softening the focus, controlling the colour or shading – giving, for example, a cold blue tone to an institutional setting, or a warm, rosy glow to a domestic setting. In classic Hollywood films and some television soap operas, certain characters, usually women, are portrayed in soft-focus at key moments. In films such as *Casablanca*, the leading actress is shown in soft-focus to signify moments of heightened romantic interest; while in the 1980s television soap *Dallas*, the same technique was used on Barbara Bel Geddes, who played the matriarch, Miss Ellie. In this case the symbolic softening indicated not romantic interest but the mediating maternal values which acted as a counterbalance to the ruthless materialism of her offspring and their generation.

The example of soft-focus serves to remind us that visual images do not have a fixed, pre-determined meaning – they suggest through conventions assigned to them by a culture, and they are amenable to change and adaptation. When considering the cultural significance of an image, we have to pay attention to its context and the purpose for which it is being used.

Visuals and Text

The 'language' of visual images is generally less specific than that of verbal language. Unless the images have been developed into a complex system of grammatical signification, such as are found in Sign languages, the viewer has to interact considerably with the image in order to construct meanings. This process is usually below the level of consciousness – if anything, we pay attention to the 'what' of the image, rather than 'how' it gets its messages across. Interpretation depends largely on implicit knowledge of conventions and the ability to deduce from context. However, there are times when the image is presented in conjunction with language – when words guide us in how to interpret the image, or reinforce a message that might be obvious. Moreover, there are times when language becomes part of the image.

The combination of image and language is perhaps most evident in comic strips and cartoons, which show us the thoughts and spoken words of characters. Facial expressions that would otherwise remain enigmatic become comprehensible. Headlines and captions similarly narrow down the options for interpretation, in a way that can be questionable, particularly when used with photographs in advertisements, political propaganda or allegedly 'neutral' newspaper reports.

If language is used in combination with visual data, it is important not to see one medium as simply illustrating the other: both media construct messages independently, and what is ultimately communicated will depend on the interaction between them. It is therefore important to consider the way that the verbal and visual elements are presented. To return to the two Brazilian campaign billboards (Figs. 7.1 and 7.2), the positioning of text and visual are different. As we have seen, in the Covas poster, the image of the child contextualises the verbal message; while in the Maluf campaign the verbal message comes first and is 'anchored' or explained by the portrait of the candidate.

It is also useful to consider whether the text is separated from the image, as headlines and captions are separated from photographs; or whether text and image are framed separately; or whether they intrude, overlap or are superimposed. The choices made here will determine the degree of 'connectedness' of text and image (cf. Kress and van Leeuwen, 1996: 214–18). Text superimposed on an image signifies a harmony between them, whereas if an image is set apart by framing, offset, or tilted on a separate plane, it will signify a relative lack of connection – a disjunction between text and image, or between the world of the message and the world of the viewer. The politician in Figure 7.2 also looks askance and down upon the lowly viewer, from a different and slightly more exalted plane. It is a posture through which he simultaneously reinforces his authority and offers himself as an intermediary between worlds.

The interaction of text and language is therefore not a simple matter, with one element illustrating or explaining the other. Rather, the positioning of text with respect to image becomes part of the message.

The Iconography of English

A final point of relevance to the intercultural classroom, particularly those situated in non-anglophone countries, is the visual significance of the English language itself. The line between using a written alphabet as part of the communicative practice of a literate culture, and using that alphabet for its pictorial qualities can become blurred. Mediaeval manuscripts illuminated the initial letters, particularly of religious manuscripts – the image and the letter became united in manuscripts like *The Book of Kells*. In Islamic art, readings from the Qu'ran form the basis of near abstract designs of beauty and complexity. Letters themselves are images, after all, and languages evolve a range of styles of handwriting and font designs for those letters. When combined into words, the letters stand for the English language in a metonymic (part-whole) relation: they therefore can be used both decoratively, and to signify the connotations that English has as a whole, as the language of global economic, political, industrial and techno-logical power.

In non-anglophone cultures, learners can investigate if or where English is used in public images. In some cultures, English may be used to challenge, or subvert Anglo-American dominance; for instance, Iranian stamps used to carry anti-American slogans in English. In cultures aligned to the West, English is often used to glamorise a product or service being sold to the public. The English that is used in such contexts need not be 'idi-omatic' to the eyes and ears of a native speaker (cf. Neelankavil *et al.*, 1996). It may even be ungrammatical: there is a children's shop in São Paulo that is called 'Shoes' Kids.' Presumably the misused apostrophe is intended to indicate something like 'shoes *for* kids.' The Japanese soft drink 'Pocari Sweat' was so named because the concept of 'sweat' in Japanese has conno-tations of health and hard work. However, when the drink was marketed in the United States, the English word in its brand name, ironically, had to be dropped (Taylor, 1992). The point is not that a foreign word in a brand name or advertisement should communicate a message, but that it should communicate a cultural affiliation: English is the language of power, wealth, science, glamour, and youth culture. Depending on the context, images employing English, or pseudo-English words in a non-anglophone setting serve to orient the viewer towards or away from Anglo-American culture. The use of English overseas in advertisements for products such as *Pond's* face cream connote the scientific credibility and the glamour of anglophone culture. In Britain, ironically, beauty products would probably use French to convey a similar sense of glamour.

Checklist: Using Images in the Intercultural Classroom

The sections above illustrate how the rules of 'visual discourse' can be made explicit and then used in the interpretation of visual images. These rules can be reformulated as a checklist of questions that learners can use to probe the cultural meanings of visual texts. The checklist below is designed as a practical guide which teachers and learners can use to 'interrogate' an image. Not all the questions apply to every image; however, the questions are a good place to start when beginning to understand the images that permeate our own and other cultures.

A.   *Images of people*
What kind of person/people are shown (policeman, model, child, etc.)?

What kind of _values_ do the people shown represent (kindness, physical beauty, honesty, or miserliness, ugliness, corruption, etc)?

B.   _Who or what are the characters looking at?_
Are they looking at each other or not looking at each other? What does this tell you about how they feel about each other? Are they looking at something else, an object or a place? How do they feel about it?
Are they looking at you, the viewer? How are you expected to feel about them? Do you in fact feel this way?
Are they looking at something else, out of the frame of the picture? What might it be? Can you tell? How do the characters feel about this unseen presence?

C.   _How close are the characters to you?_
Are the people in close-up, medium-shot or long-shot? How does their distance from you make them seem to you – intimate, friendly or distant? Why do you think they have been shown this way?
Are the characters facing you, or angled away from you? How does this affect the way you feel about them? Are they distanced from you or are they inviting you to join them?
Are you looking up at the characters, looking down at them, or are they at eye-level with you? How does this affect the way you feel about them? Do you feel respect for them, superior to them, or are you equals?

D.   _Fashion and style_
How are the people in the image dressed? What does their style of clothing suggest about them – e.g. about their age, class, gender, nationality, ethnicity, profession? Are they up-to-date or out-of-fashion? What values do you associate with the people based on their clothing?
Is the person wholly or partially undressed? If so, where are they situated and, by extension, where are you, the viewer, supposed to be? Is the person looking at you or away from you? Are you supposed to look at and admire him/her, pity him/her, or envy him/her, feel desire for him/her? Do you?

E.   _Objects_
What kind of object is shown in the image? What is its function – illustration, advertisement, diagram? Can you see all of it or just part? Are you looking from above, below or head-on?
Are you supposed to want it, understand it, make your own, etc? Does the image enable you to do this? What kind of person would need to be able to understand, own or explain such an object? In other words, what kind of viewer are you expected to be?

Does the object have a set of associations? What kind of people would own such an object, or wish to own it? Is it considered to be cheap or expensive, tacky or sophisticated? Why does it have these associations in your culture? Does it have the same associations elsewhere?

Does the object have symbolic value? Does it symbolise values like beauty, youth, passion, temptation, knowledge, power? How did it come to have these values? Does the object have this value in your culture now, or in the past? What about in other cultures?

F. Settings

Is there no apparent setting (i.e. is the object or person shown against a dark or indistinct background)? If not, why do you think you are being invited to focus only on the object or person in the image?

Is the setting identifiable? Is it an urban or a rural setting, a desert or the ocean, public or domestic, etc? Does it look like the kind of place you would wish to be?

Does the setting have any kind of associations – *romantic* mountains, urban *squalor*, garden *paradise* etc.? What kind of people might live, work or visit there?

Is the setting used to illustrate a country or the home of a particular group of people? Do you think it is an accurate representation of the homeland, or is it partial? If it is partial, why has this particular image been selected?

G. Composition

Look at Figure 7.4 earlier in this chapter. It summarises some of the possible meanings which can be given by *placing* one part of the image in relation to the others. The main divisions are:

Centre/Margins: Is there a strong presence in the centre of the picture? If so, what is its significance and how does it relate to the elements (if any) at the margins?

Top/Bottom: The upper part of an image is often used to represent something that is ideal, heavenly, a state to which we aspire. The lower part shows something that is real, practical, 'scientific'. Is your image divided like this?

Left/Right: The left part of an image often gives a context in which the information on the right should be understood (e.g. an 'expert' on the left introduces a product shown on the right). Does your image have a left-right structure? If so, does the left-hand-side information give a context?

H. Framing

Are the elements in the picture shown as a whole, or are they separated in some way by 'frames' (i.e. lines formed by part of the setting, or by tools people are holding, or by shadows, etc.)?

If the elements are shown as a whole, what kind of category do they belong to? Can you give the category a short title?

If the elements are separated by frames, why has this been done? Do they simply belong to separate categories? Are they antagonistic to each other, or is there a problem of communication between them?

I.   Important information

What do you see in the *foreground* and *background* of your image? The important information is usually in the foreground, closer to the viewer. Is this so for you?

Is some element in the picture *foregrounded* in another way – i.e. does some aspect of the lighting, focus or colour bring it to your attention? Why has it been singled out so?

J.   Images of action

In your image, is someone or something acting upon one of the other elements in the image? If so, is this a physical action (e.g. kissing, shooting, following) or a mental action (e.g. watching, desiring, disliking)?

How is the action portrayed – by gesture, gaze, expression on face, or by means of a *vector*, that is, a line tracing a path from one element or character to another, drawn for example by a tool, or a ray of light, or a pattern on the image?

What kind of people/things are the actors or viewers in your images? What kind of actions do they perform? What kind of people/things are acted upon or looked at by others in the frame? Across a variety of images, do *patterns* emerge about the kinds of thing certain cultural groups do (e.g. housework, driving certain cars, particular types of play)?

Are you, the viewer, ever acted upon or observed by an element in the picture? Do fingers, guns, gestures indicate to you? How are you expected to respond to these forms of address, threat and invitation?

K.   Descriptive images

If no vectors or actions are taking place in the image, then you are probably only expected to observe it. Consider the *purpose* of your observation. How are you expected to respond to what is described by the image:

desire it?	be revolted by it?
admire it?	despise it?
use it as a role model?	avoid it?

be amused by it?   ridicule it?
imitate it?   be shocked by it?
understand it?   condemn it?

What does your expected response reveal about the cultural norms assumed by the producers of the image? What kind of images describe admirable qualities, and what kind of images describe qualities to avoid and condemn? Do you always agree with the norms which are assumed? Are they constant over time? Do certain groups in society challenge those norms visually – by exaggerating them or subverting them? If so, how?

L. From reality to abstraction
Does the content of the image seem 'realistic' or 'unrealistic'? How is the degree of 'reality/unreality' achieved?

- use of colour/monochrome film
- sharpness of focus (soft focus to very sharp focus)
- saturation of colour (from very pale, to very rich)
- degree of detail given
- (im)possible perspectives

Does the title help you interpret the image, or is the interpretation deliberately left open? How much does the viewer have to work with the image to create meaning? Do you enjoy working this hard, or do you feel cheated and frustrated by the lack of guidance?

M. Image and text
Look again at the diagram of the composition of an image (Figure 7.4). How is the text positioned with respect to the image? Is it:

- to the left, providing a context?
- to the right, providing an explanation?
- at the top, expressing an ideal state?
- at the bottom, grounding the image in reality?
- at the centre, demanding our attention?
- at the margins, providing a gloss, or extra information?
- superimposed, and at one with the image?
- framed separately, providing complementary info?
- parallel to the image, suggesting similarity?
- at an angle to the image, suggesting otherness?
- supplied by speech or thought bubbles from a character?

Of course, not every image will interact with the text according to the general 'rules' suggested above. However, the suggestions will provide a starting point for considering *how* text and image interact.

Finally, words from another language can be imported, almost as visual images into the texts of another culture. If you can, investigate how French, German, Italian and Spanish words are used in advertising in anglophone countries. Or consider how English is used in advertising in non-anglophone countries. What do your findings suggest about the relative influence of one culture on another, and how one culture perceives the other?

Conclusion

An intercultural approach to ELT demands the fostering of skills of observation, interpretation and critical cultural awareness. Teachers can therefore usefully exploit the potential of visual images to construct messages, often in association with verbal text. The exploitation of visual aids to foster critical cultural awareness is particularly attractive because it extends practices familiar to teachers who currently use images to promote comprehension and to generate spoken and written English. By moving from understanding to more explicit modes of interpretation, however, we move our students into the area of intercultural learning.

The potential of developing visual literacy to raise intercultural awareness is particularly great in an ELT context. If ethnographic visits are too expensive or difficult to arrange, then visual materials can at least be brought into the classroom and compared with visuals from the home culture. This procedure cannot of course replicate or satisfactorily substitute for a visit overseas, but it can nevertheless provide a rich source of intercultural comparison. Visual materials can be supplemented by other cultural phenomena from the target culture – media texts, literature and certain 'ways of behaving'. These phenomena are the focus of the next chapter.

Chapter 8

Using Literary, Media and Cultural Studies

In Chapter 7 we considered the use of visual images as a rich resource for developing the intercultural skills of interpretation and critical awareness. This chapter continues the theme of developing interpretation and critical awareness by exploring insights from a broad subject, namely the application in the intercultural classroom of strategies from the disciplines of literary, media and cultural studies. Topics addressed include:

- *Interpretation in English Language Teaching.*
- *A model of discourse production and processing.*
- *Using 'cultural texts' in the intercultural classroom (i.e. texts from literary, media and cultural studies).*
- *Contrasting 'mediated' and 'unmediated' discourse, with particular reference to television interviews and 'conversational' dialogue in sitcoms.*

Texts, Interpretation and English Language Teaching

Although they are well-established academic fields in their own right, literary, media and cultural studies are historically linked and share, to differing extents, methodologies, practices and controversies. Moreover, notwithstanding their academic origins, many of these practices and methodologies have spilled over into related areas of education, including English language teaching.

English literature now commands such a central position in the study of arts and humanities that it is salutary to remind ourselves of how recent a curriculum innovation it in fact is. Crawford (1998) traces the subject's origins to the founding of professorial chairs in eloquence, rhetoric and *belles lettres* in the 18th-century Scottish universities, and it is not until the late 19th century that English literature became widely taught in English and American higher education. Media studies is even more recent, rising in the wake of broadcast technologies, and achieving wide institutional acceptance only in the final 30 years of the 20th century. Cultural studies is newer still, emerging in Britain, at least, from a cross-fertilisation of sociology and literary studies in the 1950s and1960s and even now not represented independently in many universities at undergraduate or postgraduate level. When cultural studies is taught, it is usually within literature, media or sociology courses, or at postgraduate level in interdisciplinary 'centres' or 'schools'. The developing discipline in the UK is sometimes labelled 'British cultural studies' to distinguish its methodological strategies and disciplinary concerns from its North American counterpart. 'British' cultural studies has nevertheless been effectively exported elsewhere, for example to Australia (Turner, 1990) and Brazil. Despite the 'British' label, the concerns of British cultural studies are as much with American as British popular culture, and it is influenced by European intellectuals, such as Marx and Foucault.

As literary, media and cultural studies have developed in Britain the disciplines have undergone various crises of identity and substantial refashioning of their core beliefs. English literature evolved from a subject concerned with rhetoric into a discipline whose teachers promoted themselves as no less than the guardians of civilised values, values which were themselves stored in the 'great tradition' of writing in English. The energies of the profession were – and in some places still are – directed towards discriminating between those works that enshrine eternal values that deserve to be celebrated and preserved (i.e. 'canonical' texts), and those works that do not. Literary critics from F.R. Leavis to Harold Bloom have taken on the mantle of guardian of the English literary heritage, and, by extension, of Western culture (e.g. Leavis, 1948; Bloom, 1995). As the 20th century progressed, the criteria for canonisation and exclusion were increasingly contested – the celebration and exclusion of texts was seen as motivated more by factors such as class and gender than 'timeless value'. 'English literature' itself became politicised, and was seen as a way in which middle-class white males withheld power from groups such as the working classes, women, and other races. The discipline itself became engaged in examining these processes of inclusion and exclusion, and the way literary texts interact with wider social processes and power relations between different social groups.

The development of media studies can be seen partly as a reaction against the 'high culture' of English literature. The popular media are undoubtedly important and deserving of academic study. However, given their relative novelty and popularity, it was initially difficult to make the case that television programmes or cinema films enshrined the eternal values of a great tradition. One central concern of media studies was (and still to some extent is) the 'effects' of media products. From an initial assumption that media products were dangerous propaganda that corrupted the minds of their consumers, researchers have progressed to a more sophisticated model of how individuals and groups actually process and position themselves in relation to the programmes and films they watch and listen to. In comparison with English literature (which still largely focuses on the reader's personal encounter with the work of art), media studies locates the text in a social situation: the researcher is as likely to consider other people's responses to the programme or film in question, and relate those responses to the perceived ideological content of the text. For example, it is assumed that the middle classes and working classes will 'consume' current affairs programmes in different ways, or that men and women will 'consume' soap operas differently. The student of media therefore explores the way different groups make sense of texts that themselves are the result of complex technological processes of production.

Cultural studies embraces both literary and media studies and further expands the notion of the 'text'. In literary studies, the 'text' is the novel, story, play or poem under investigation; in media studies it is the radio or television programme, the cinema film or pop song, the newspaper report or editorial. In cultural studies, any social practice can be read as a 'text'. 'Texts' in cultural studies can be sports, dances, fashions or even practices like cooking or shopping. As one of the founders of British cultural studies, Raymond Williams, has said, 'culture is ordinary' (Williams, 1958, reprinted in Gray & McGuigan, 1997: 5–6), and it follows that the ordinary practices of people in society can be 'read' in order to show how a culture's values, beliefs, and attitudes systematically pervade and organise everyday life.

These academic disciplines are relevant to intercultural English language teaching in several ways. First, there is a common concern with *texts*. The goal of the language teacher is to help students understand and produce spoken and written texts (in the traditional sense of language products) and to cope with, mediate between or even enter into 'cultural texts' (if seen as social practices). The text, in both its broad and narrow sense, is central to ELT and all the above disciplines. Another directly relevant factor is the *interpretation* of texts. ELT has focused in recent decades on skills-based methodologies, and, in particular, on strategies for developing reading, writing, speaking and listening. Literary, media and cultural studies have together refined a sophisticated set of strategies that are crucial to reading and listening, and also impact upon speaking and writing, namely, strategies of interpretation. Interpretation involves using our cultural knowledge to 'go beyond' the words contained in the text in order to reach a richer understanding of them. The intercultural classroom, then, can use what literary, media and cultural studies have said about the nature of the text in order to foster the crucial skill of interpreting the language and wider social behaviour of the target culture. To do this, we must first look at models of text and discourse processing.

'Encoding and Decoding': A Model of Discourse Production and Processing

One question that has loomed large over literary, media and cultural studies, is the question of who has authority over the meaning of a text. In the early days of academic literary studies, academics assumed that canonical literature emanated from the sensibility of the artistic genius, and that students had to be schooled to understand how the text conveyed this sensibility, and to develop the good taste required to discriminate between proper and second-rate works of art. This view put the author 'in charge' and the role of students was to learn to appreciate the 'right' authors (e.g. Richards, 1929). However, as literary studies evolved, scepticism grew about whether a text could give information directly about the intentions of the author. Therefore the text itself became the authoritative object of study, and a set of strategies called 'close reading' developed. Close reading paid particular attention to the possibility of multiple meanings in literary texts, and to formal features (e.g. rhyme, rhythm, alliteration, and metaphor) which might contribute to this multiplicity of meaning. Meaning was still considered to be inherent in the text, and the job of the critic was to use highly trained reading skills to tease it out (e.g. Brooks & Penn Warren, 1938, 1943). More recently, there has been a shift towards giving the reader authority over the meaning of the text (e.g. Fish, 1980). Nowadays, we privilege the way that the reader actively constructs meaning – or 'deconstructs' meaning, if he or she offers a reading which goes against established tradition but can be shown to have some plausible basis.

More so even than in literary studies, the viewer or text-processor has been the object of detailed scrutiny in media and cultural studies: as we saw in Chapter 5, ethnographic studies have been carried out to observe how people 'consume' media and cultural products. Ethnographers sit, tape-recorders and notebooks at the ready, while their subjects watch television programmes or participate in cultural activities such as dancing or sports. The question motivating the ethnographers is 'how are the subjects making meaning out of the "texts" (i.e. the soap operas, dances or football games) with which they are interacting?'

Clearly, all three parts of the discourse equation (author, text and reader) are important to the communicative event. The author has some control over the meaning to be conveyed, although the direct transmission of his or her meaning is impossible to achieve, and therefore some 'fuzziness' is likely. The text itself is a meaningful construct and it will be open to interpretation, probably in the way that the producer intended (sometimes known as the 'dominant' reading). The reader or viewer, however, brings to the 'blue-print' of the text a set of expectations and conventions which might differ from those of the producer, and so the construction of meaning will always be an individual matter. A sophisticated reader might challenge the ideolog-ical assumptions – the implicit value-system – of the producer and come up with a 'resistant reading', that is, a reading that subverts the attitudes and beliefs which the producer probably intended to convey.

The media commentator Stuart Hall devised a diagram of 'encoding and decoding' which attempted to capture the tripartite structure of the communicative event (Hall, 1980). In a subsequent interview (Hall, 1994), he complained that his diagram only showed half of the process, so Figure 8.1 is an adaptation of his earlier diagram in accordance with his later wishes. It shows that texts are produced by 'encoders' who construct texts using certain cultural assumptions (or 'frameworks of knowledge') and within the constraints of technological possibility. Thus some encoders speak and write, while others take photographs, film or produce record-ings in collaboration with others. The result is an organised text – words, or images, or combinations of the two. This text is then processed by the 'decoders' according to their cultural assumptions and technologies – thus a film produced in the 1930s for cinema distribution might now be processed on a television screen via videotape or DVD, and the changes in cultural context and technology may well alter the way it is viewed and understood. The complete cycle shows that decoders are also encoders, that texts are created, processed, and either adapted or responded to. Someone who views a film might talk to someone about it, or write a review of it, or (given the resources) make a tribute to it, a parody of it, or even a remake. In other words, the texts that we create are conditioned partly by the texts we have already been exposed to. The revised model is thus directly relevant to genre analysis (see Chapter 4), which assumes that people encode texts according to generic conventions formed in part by exposure to other texts.

In Figure 8.1 participants x and y can be seen as variables: the same two people need not always be involved in the chain of discourse. The 'mean-ingful text' is here not only restricted to speech and writing, but can be any media text or even any form of social behaviour, such as dance or fashion. The main point of the diagram is that the production and reception of discourse are always done in a social and cultural context, and are dependent on what we have already heard and said, seen and written. What we can say in different contexts is also dependent on what we know and believe (frameworks of knowledge), the expectations we have about what our audience wants to see and hear (relations of production), and the

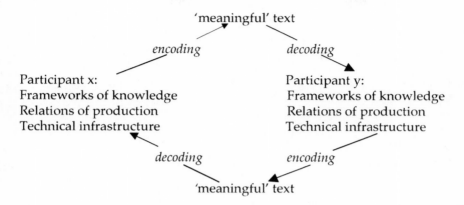

Figure 8.1 Model of discourse production and processing (adapted from Hall, 1980)

technical means of communication at our disposal, from paper and pen to a film or television studio (technical infrastructure).

As cultural critics, we can bring different sets of skills to the analysis of each part of the communication process: we can use our intuition and research skills to seek to understand the motivations of and constraints upon the encoders ('auteur theory'), we can use our semiotic skills to unpack the implications of the text itself ('semiotic analysis' or 'close reading'), and we observe the impact of the text on the audience, the decoders ('ethnography').

Of course every model of text should carry a warning. A model can only ever be a simplification and organisation of a complex reality. However, because it is a simplification and organisation of complex issues, a model such as that in Figure 8.1 can help us to clarify our thoughts and inform the design of classroom activities.

'Cultural' Texts and English Language Teaching

The history of using cultural texts in ELT parallels the history of using such texts in native-speaker education. Earlier last century, the 'canon' of great texts was presented to students in order to transmit the values of 'civilised' anglophone culture. In the context of the anglophone countries, this process can now be seen as the imposition of white, middle-class male values via a literary canon; in an overseas (and especially a post-colonial) context, the process can further be viewed as an imperialistic project, however well-intentioned its proponents might be (cf. Phillipson, 1992). As the tide of empire ebbed, different approaches to the teaching of literature followed. For example, Widdowson (1975) promotes stylistics, effectively a linguistically informed 'close reading' of texts, partly to improve learners' understanding and appreciation of the creative potential of the target language system. Later, articles in Brumfit and Carter (1986) challenge the ethnocentric bias of 'the great tradition' and argue for the recognition in ELT of literatures in World Englishes. More recently, literature books such as Lazar (1993) and McRae (1991) stress 'literature with a small l'. In these books, non-canonical literature is seen as a means of understanding the mind-set of a range of English speakers, as a way of accessing their frames of knowledge, values and presuppositions.

Media and cultural studies have a comparatively shorter history in ELT. Language activities have been designed to take advantage of the widespread use of video in ELT (e.g. Cooper *et al.*, 1991), but comparatively little has been published for teachers on the application of media studies as such. Some impact, however is being made by coursebooks such as Edginton and Montgomery's advanced-level *The Media* (1996), a systematic approach to the study of advertising and news reports in the press and television. At a lower level, the *True to Life* series of textbooks (Gairns *et al.*, 1996) includes activities that suggest the influence of media studies – the Intermediate coursebook, for example, has activities based on the cross-cultural comparison of game shows (units 3 and 4)

As we have seen above, literary and media studies are closely linked to cultural studies, and the few teachers' guides and student coursebooks specifically to focus on cultural studies tend to include literary and media topics too. Bassnett (1997) has a high literary content, although one of the articles included, Durant (1997), is particularly concerned with the process of selection of a broader range of texts for cultural exploration. *Crossing Cultures*, (Chichirdan *et al.*, 1998), a coursebook produced for 12th grade Romanian school pupils, ranges widely across general cultural topics (e.g. Welsh national icons and images of the British monarchy) as well as literary topics ('gendering the canon') and media themes ('the rhetoric of ads', and the role of soaps).

To summarise, then, mediated texts, that is, those texts communicated by some form of mass media, have long been used successfully in ELT, and recent years have seen an upsurge in their use as a cultural resource. What useful generalisations can be made about their use in the 'intercultural' ELT classroom? First, we should not confuse the world-view represented in a book, television programme or spectator event with an 'unmediated' communicative event. The presence of an audience (usually a paying audience, directly or indirectly) changes the nature of the discourse. Given that fact, we can then focus on different aspects of the 'discourse cycle' adapted from Hall (Figure 8.1), remembering as we do so that too narrow a focus on one part of the total discourse process can distort our view of the whole. The model of discourse offers a set of ways of approaching texts; however, it gives no guidance in the selection of appropriate materials. The sections which follow consider in turn literary, media and cultural texts, and suggest ways of exploiting them which are related to their disciplinary traditions, and which also focus on different stages of the 'encoding-decoding' cycle shown in Figure 8.1.

Literature in the intercultural classroom

As noted above, literature has enjoyed mixed fortunes in ELT, owing to different developments within the discipline of literary studies, and also developments within the ELT profession. Just as literary studies was passing through a crisis to do with the justification of the 'great tradition', ELT was moving towards syllabuses determined by the needs of learners – and given the nature of literature, it is difficult to prioritise it as a pragmatic requirement for language study. Since then, however, ELT has moved towards a more eclectic approach to syllabus design, and literature has been rehabilitated, even refreshed, by the disciplinary reinvention of literary studies.

ELT, of course, exploits literature and the insights of literary studies for its own ends. From the perspective of the intercultural classroom, literary texts are selected because they illustrate aspects of the target culture. Pulverness (1996: 11) argues that text selection should focus on the kinds of cultural information literary texts can dramatise:

> period culture – 'the whole way of life'
> social attitudes – *le vice anglais* [i.e. the class system]
> political values – the state of the nation
> language and manners – soundbites

In other words, the practical educational utility of literary texts – Pulverness discusses mainly novels and plays – is that they can vividly illustrate aspects of an entire society, from the rich to the poor, and show, for example, the lived relationships between the classes. Moreover, contemporary plays in particular often contribute to or stimulate topical political debates, and dramatise current issues. At the very least, literature can be trawled for 'soundbites', quotations that vividly sum up the spirit of an epoch, or profound social changes. For example, the 19th century politician Benjamin Disraeli was also a novelist, and in one of his novels, *Sybil*, he sums up the divided condition of England in the mid-1800s in a famous 'soundbite' that is still echoed today in talk of 'one nation' or 'two nation' political policies:

'Two nations; between whom there is no intercourse and no sympathy; who are as ignorant of each other's habits, thoughts and feelings, as if they were dwellers in different zones, or inhabitants of different planets; who are formed by a different breeding, are fed by a different food, are ordered by different manners, and are not governed by the same laws.'
'You speak of – ' said Egremont, hesitatingly.
'THE RICH AND THE POOR.'

The vividness of literature lies in the construction of dramatic voices which, though they are fictional, nevertheless represent the people who inhabit a given culture at a particular time. Pulverness cites, as contrasting examples, the restrained English voice of Stevens, the butler in Kazuo Ishiguro's *The Remains of the Day*, and the defiant English voice of the protagonist Karim Amir, in Hanif Kureishi's *The Buddha of Suburbia*.

There are various published reports into the use of literature in intercultural language education at different levels (e.g. Burwitz-Melzer, 2001; Byram & Fleming, 1998: 143–221; Kramsch, 1993: 130–76). One example will suffice to demonstrate the possibilities and challenges involved in using literature in the intercultural classroom. In a small-scale research project into the use of literature to introduce cultural topics to a group of advanced ELT learners at the University of Stirling, the learners were given a new short story to read every two weeks, supported by worksheets and class discussion (MacDonald, 2000). MacDonald (2000: 150) speculates about the value of this literary experience, based on his students' positive ratings of two of the stories they had read, one by Bernard MacLaverty and the other by Pauline Melville:

> It is possible that stories in which learners can identify quite strongly with a central character who is an outsider working through a sense of disengagement and alienation with the target culture might reflect their own state of suspension between native and target value systems. In positioning themselves in relation to the stance of the characters in such a story, the learners might become engaged in the process of exploring and questioning their own worldviews in relation to those presented in the story.

It is a fundamental goal of an intercultural approach to language teaching that learning about a culture is learning about its values and beliefs, and how these are expressed. Certainly an advantage of 'cultural texts' (whether literature, film or other social practice) is that they dramatise the target value system by showing its tensions and conflicts, and this fact may indeed motivate learners who are negotiating their own tensions and conflicts as they encounter the new culture.

MacDonald and his colleagues adopted a four-phase learning cycle adapted from Gajdusek (1988). Each story was covered in four hours, the first being devoted to pre-reading activities designed to activate relevant schemata by relating the theme and subject matter of the story to the students' own experience and / or knowledge of similar stories. At the end of the first class, the story was given out. The second phase consisted of students filling in a worksheet of questions checking on the 'basic facts' of the story – point of view, character, setting, time, place, and so on. This phase included discussion of these aspects of the story. The third phase in the cycle involved small-group discussion of key issues in the story – plot climaxes, themes and style. Each group would focus on specific issues and feed back to the class. The students then choose from a menu of follow-up activities, designed to extend and enrich their personal involvement with the text. They might retell part of the story from a different point of view, or write a dialogue between characters, or relate the story to their own experiences. Finally the students returned to a discussion which related the themes of the story to problematical issues in British culture – for example, class conflict (Pulverness's *vice anglais*), racial, ethnic or sectarian tensions, colonisation, or general alienation.

The four-phase cycle described above and the action research which accompanied it give a valuable model for using literary texts of some length to explore culture in an ELT setting and monitor the effect of the exploration. The goals of the course were varied: to extend the students' linguistic skills, develop their cultural awareness, learn a little about literary theory, and contribute to personal enrichment. Student feedback suggests that the learners felt that all four goals were being achieved.

The four-phase model proposed by the University of Stirling team focuses mainly on the latter part of the 'encoding-decoding' cycle. The first phase – 'activating the learners' schemata' – paves the way for the individuals' discourse-decoding strategies by activating and moulding their frames of knowledge. The second part of the cycle, checking facts, is again concerned with monitoring the decoding process, to the extent that the content of the stories is understood. Phase three is an opportunity to begin to compare the individual's reading of the story with that of his or her peers – the different interpretations are discussed in small groups. The follow-up activities allow learners to refashion and extend their interpretations, with reference to further changes in their frameworks of knowledge, and further understanding of the language system that underlies the text. In the final phase these revised interpretations are again tested against a discussion of the story's relationship to wider British issues. The process described accords with the current tendency in literary studies to focus on the 'text decoding' part of the discourse cycle. There is little discussion of what the author *really* meant, or the author's belief system – which would probably have been the focus of literary studies classes, earlier last century. The focus instead is on understanding the creative potential of the linguistic system, and on constructing continually revised (and richer) meanings from the texts in a series of structured discussions.

Media studies in the intercultural classroom

In media studies, like literary studies, different interpretative traditions focus on different aspects of the 'encoding-decoding' cycle. 'Auteur' theory privileges the role of the film or television director in guaranteeing a coherent text by communicating a personal vision in the way he or she organises the enormous technical and human resources involved in making a feature film. Auteur theory has been challenged by those who argue that no one person can be held responsible for the 'personal vision' of such a complex product. Other theorists argue that a particular studio or even a particular actor is largely responsible for the style of a film and therefore is better placed than the director to be considered the 'auteur', that is, the originator of the discourse. Auteur theory attempts to account for the thematic or stylistic elements of a film by relating them to the concerns, usually of the director, but occasionally of other key participants in the film-making process. Strangely, the screenwriter is seldom considered to be an 'auteur', a fact which underlines the non-literary aspects of the medium.

Other traditions in media studies run parallel to 'close reading' and 'stylistics' in literary studies by focusing on the text itself. However, a text which involves a rich array of visual and aural signs needs a set of interpretative strategies different from those used to interpret words on a page. Television and film critics draw upon the discipline of 'semiotics', the science of signs, to support their interpretations, particularly of the visual elements of a text (cf. Bignell, 1997; van Leeuwen, 1996). They pay attention to factors such as whether the actor is shown in close, medium or long-shot; the quality of the lighting in a scene; how music and sound-effects are used; the fluidity of the camera movement; and how scenes are edited. Each of these factors is assumed to have an effect on audience reaction. For example, in still images, an intimacy is achieved when actors are shown in close-up, and we are less likely to identify with characters shown only in medium or long-shot. If an actor's face is lit from below, he or she appears distorted and therefore sinister. Rapid cutting is characteristic of action movies, while long, leisurely takes slow the pace of a film down. As in still images, our perspective of characters is important: characters shot from

below are invested with authority, while those shot from above seem relatively weaker. Kramsch (1993: 189–96, 211–23) reports on the exploration of
the deep-rooted ideological messages conveyed by film conventions. This
exploration was stimulated by cross-cultural comparisons of a short
French documentary on truffle-hunting and an American commercial for
Coca-Cola.

As noted in Chapter 5, a further strand of media studies draws upon ethnography to focus not on the discourse producers, or the text itself, but on the
discourse processors, or the audience. Ethnographic media researchers are
interested in how audiences position themselves in relation to the texts: do
they accept or resist the 'dominant' interpretations? Do men and women
read certain types of text differently? Ethnographic evidence of how viewers
and listeners actually respond to media texts has enriched our understanding of media effects, although there is continuing debate on exactly what to
make of this evidence. Rose (2001: 198–9) reports on the controversy that
arose from Walkerdine's (1990) observations of a working-class family's
viewing of the film, *Rocky II* –her initial revulsion at the celebration of male
violence, and her later, more considered reflection upon her earlier
emotional response. Lull (1990) recommends that the ethnographer adopts
a less engaged, less judgemental approach to ethnographic observation;
however, as Walkerdine notes, a detached, neutral stance is in fact impossible to achieve. The learner who attempts an ethnographic project needs to
bear in mind that the report will be coloured by his or her own attitudes,
and try to mediate between the 'frames of knowledge' that inform the
viewers' responses, and those 'frames of knowledge' that inform his or her
own response.

The research methods adopted by the media researcher again depend on
the stage in the discourse cycle they focus on: text-encoder (the territory of
the auteur theorist), text itself (semiotician) or or text-decoder (ethnographer). We must recall, too, that the cycle is an idealisation: anyone wishing
to discuss mainstream Hollywood films today must realise that the final
shape of the movie must partly be determined by the studio's own
'ethnographic' research. Small-group audience testing might help decide
whether certain scenes should be added or edited, and even whether
scenes should be reshot and the ending changed. In Brazil, the evolving
plotlines of soap operas, the famous 'telenovelas', are also determined
partly by ongoing research into audience reaction. If certain characters are
popular, their roles will be developed in the story; unpopular characters
might well be dropped. There is in fact a more intimate relationship
between producer and consumer in the shaping of the text than an
idealised model can capture.

Until relatively recently, media research techniques have understandably had less influence than techniques of literary studies on ELT. However, the English language teacher and student can learn and adapt some of the strategies of media research for their own uses, and to serve their own interests. Like researchers in media studies, they can decide what their focus will be: those interested in auteur theory will search out interviews with directors in film magazines, or on film-related websites. Those interested in the semiotics of film will have to begin to learn the 'discourse' of visual signs (for an introduction, see Bignell, 1997). Those interested in audience responses can use ethnographic techniques; for example, they can sit with an audience watching a British or American situation comedy and note the comments they make and where and for how long they laugh. If the class is in email contact with other classes elsewhere, they can compare responses across cultures: the availability of cable and satellite television means English-language programmes are available in many countries on a daily basis. An interesting question for small-scale 'action research' might be whether audiences in different countries laughed in the same place while watching, say, globally distributed situation comedies like *Friends* or *Absolutely Fabulous*, and how they understood and responded to different characters. Within a single country, an ethnographic project might observe the responses of different age-groups or genders to the same programme.

The 'encoding-decoding' discourse cycle can therefore be used to structure the way that ELT courses organise materials and activities related to media texts. Attention to discourse obviously does not exhaust the possibilities for exploring media texts. For example, the fact that they *are* media texts – i.e. that they 'mediate' a world-view for the benefit of an audience – radically differentiates them from 'unmediated' texts, which function in the private sphere. This aspect of media texts is discussed further below.

Cultural studies in the intercultural classroom

'Cultural' texts obviously include literary and media texts; however, this section focuses specifically on those forms of social behaviour which fall outside the definition of literature or media, but which nevertheless can be read as 'texts'; for example, dance, fashion and sport. Cultural studies, as an academic discipline, has grown up as a self-consciously rebellious field of study, taking as its subjects subcultural groups such as hooligans, punks, and rastafarians, partly in order to elevate the status of hitherto marginalised groups (Murdock, 1997: 180).

The selection process of researchers into cultural studies has favoured as subjects the relatively powerless in society: the working-classes, women, blacks and youth (often in combination). There is no reason why subcultures involving, say, older privileged white males could not be subjected to similar inquiry; however, the political interests of researchers into cultural studies have led to a proliferation of studies into relatively disadvantaged subcultures. Much of the research in cultural studies follows a similar pattern to that in literary and media studies: the social practices of a subcultural grouping are considered as a 'text' to be analysed and explained. Such research can again be related to different stages of the encoding-decoding discourse cycle. There is, however, more of a problem in cultural studies of determining the 'auteur' and the 'audience' of the text. In *Subculture: The Meaning of Style*, Hebdige (1979: 122–3) distinguishes between the 'self-conscious innovators', the 'originals' who develop a sub-culture, and the 'hangers-on' who later appropriate the symbols of the subculture, without consciously or deliberately adopting its ideology. This distinction is echoed in the complaints of Widdiecombe and Wooffitt's subcultural informants about 'plastic goths', 'pseudo goths' and other 'shallow' or 'inauthentic' subcultural members. In both cases, it seems, there is a small group of 'auteurs' whose behaviour and style are taken up by a larger group, or audience, but in the process the core beliefs of the orig-inators are diluted or lost. However, McRobbie (1993) has questioned such distinctions, by arguing for a fusion in the categories of consumption and production. For example, when cultural practices such as fashion are concerned, the consumer can combine and adapt ready-made garments in order to produce something 'original'. The cyclical version of the encoding-decoding discourse model is adaptable enough to account for this *bricolage* (i.e. the improvisatory use of given materials to make new meanings): the decoder feeds new encodings back into the discourse system and contrib-utes actively to the dialogic evolution of texts.

Methods of analysis in cultural studies therefore downplay the roles of auteur and audience as distinctive categories, and focus instead on the semiotic analysis of the texts, and the ethnographic analysis of members of the subculture as *both* consumers and producers of meaning. As an illustra-tion of how researchers in cultural studies have approached social practice as semiotic text and as ethnographic data, I shall look at two approaches to dance. First, McRobbie (1993) considers the social practices of young female dancers at the mass raves which flourished in Britain in the early 1990s. These took place in large, disused warehouses and hangars, to the sound of hypnotic 'techno' music, and were associated with the use of the drug Ecstasy. Girls danced in hot pants and bra tops, and some wore babies' dummies or whistles, in their mouth or around their neck. The dances lasted for long periods – some for several days – and tired dancers were provided with 'chill-out' rooms where ice-lollies were sold. McRobbie's description of the girls' dress and behaviour utilises the vocabulary of text analysis: for example, the dances and fashions 'articulate' social tensions (McRobbie 1993: 25–6):

The tension in rave for girls comes, it seems, from remaining in control, and at the same time losing themselves in dance and music. Abandon in dance must now, post-AIDS, be balanced by caution and the exercise of control in sex. One solution might lie in cultivating a hyper-sexual appearance, which is, however, symbolically sealed off through the dummy, the whistle or the ice lolly. This idea of insulating the body from 'invasion' is even more apparent in the heavy duty industrial protective clothing worn by both male and female fans of German techno music, a European variant of rave.

McRobbie argues that the overt 'childlike' connotations of the dummy and the ice-lolly serve to construct a message: namely, that rave subculture explicitly rejected the world of adult concerns, thereby simultaneously expressing its anxiety about them.

The techniques used to 'read' the social practices (the enthusiastic dancing, the fashion, the preferred foodstuff) consist of a sophisticated set of strategies for decoding signs – again they are related to the techniques used to interpret literary, visual and media texts. In isolation from ethnographic practices, such interpretations of subcultures (especially relatively powerless subcultures) have been criticised as further impositions, this time of academics who force their own meanings onto the ambiguous signs of the subcultural members themselves. Widdiecombe and Wooffitt's (1995) interviews with subculture members contain examples of those members' irritation with outsiders' interpretations of their activities (see Chapter 6). However, as Murdock notes above, taken as sophisticated discussions of the meaning potential of the social practices, such semiotic interpretations have the merit of defending subcultural behaviour from the charge that it is shallow and random. The clothing and behaviour of the young girls is dignified by McRobbie's analysis of it as part of a larger system of meanings that respond to current social pressures.

Cultural studies today tends to combine semiotic analysis with ethnographic surveys. McRobbie (1993) makes a strong plea for a 'thick' description of girls' involvement in subcultural activity that portrays in depth how they are actively contributing to the economic and social system in which they are situated (e.g. subcultural activity offers some girls opportunities to adapt and sell on second-hand clothing designed for use in raves). In another study of dancers, Thomas (1993, 1997) used ethnographic techniques to explore how a young multicultural, mixed-sex dance group explored issues of race and gender through their membership of a London jazz-dance performance group. Although some semiotic skills are in evidence in her analysis of three dances (Thomas, 1997), the burden of the research lies in her observation of the dancers and her interviews with them on how *they* interpret the dancing. Her general findings are that British culture 'feminises' dancing, so that the males in the group, while fiercely proud of their performance, were more anxious than the females about the extent to which they had to exhibit emotion on stage. She also found that the black women felt more constrained than the black men by a white-dominated society whose expectations tend to stereotype them as sexual caricatures. Thomas' research, like most ethnography, privileges not her own interpretation of the dances, but how the dancers themselves make meaning from their practices.

Again, there are challenges and possibilities in such research for ELT teachers, particularly teachers of older teenagers and young adults. The attraction of cultural studies for many of its researchers is that it takes youth seriously. There are problems – as McRobbie and others note – for adults in 'invading' the arena of youth subcultures (anxieties which can be extended to any outsiders imposing themselves on a subcultural community), and indeed members may resist categorisation and interpretation by outsiders. However, sensitively handled, social practices can become 'textual resources' for use in the ELT classroom. The stylistic analyses used in literary, visual and media texts can be adapted to the analysis of social practice, and ethnographic techniques can be employed to explore subcultures. Obviously, an intercultural ELT curriculum can usually only provide for small-scale projects; nevertheless, there is scope for intercultural exploration even within the constraints of an ELT course. The encoding-decoding model of discourse can once more help organise investigations of the subculture in question and guide relevant questions: Who are the originators? How did their styles and behaviours originate? What are the economic and technological constraints upon the production of styles and behaviours? What might the styles and behaviours mean? What are the communication patterns between originators and consumers? How do the originators and consumers make sense of their behaviours?

'Mediated' and 'Unmediated' Discourse

It is important not to confuse 'spontaneous' discourse of the kind discussed in Chapters 3 and 4 with conversations and interviews as represented in literature and the media. Literary and media texts, and many of the 'texts' considered in cultural studies, can be said to be *mediated*, that is, they are constructed with an audience in mind. This simple fact is important to remember, because it fundamentally affects the nature of the discourse found in these types of text. In 'unmediated' discourse, a number of friends might gossip to affirm their social and group identities. In a play, novel, film or television programme, a group of characters might be presented as gossiping – but for reasons that go beyond the negotiation of group values. The author might be satirising the characters, holding them up to ridicule, or alternatively, he or she might be demonstrating their high moral fibre. The gossip itself might simply be a strategy for revealing hitherto undivulged information, and therefore heightening suspense or explaining some plot development. The purpose of gossip in mediated texts is therefore not what it would be in unmediated texts.

The nature of mediated texts means that we cannot simply apply the discourse rules of unmediated texts to them. The 'conversation' between the guest and host in a televised chat show may seem in some respects to be like a conversation between old friends, but the presence of a studio audience and a wider unseen audience means that it has different goals, and so different rules and linguistic choices will be adopted. Even the presence of television cameras at a political conference will alter the nature of the communicative event: as well as being a rallying cry to the party faithful, the conference will also become a television advertisement for the unity and coherence of the party. Internal debate may therefore be suppressed and restricted to off-camera events.

The analysis of mediated texts has to take into consideration their function as entertainment or propaganda. However, mediated texts also enter into the ongoing social negotiation of what it is to be a member of a given culture at a particular time. For example, characters in television soap operas can confirm or even overstep the bounds of social propriety, and therefore become objects of unmediated 'gossip' among viewers, an activity often fuelled also by tabloid press coverage (Blum-Kulka, 2000: 219–20). A gay relationship, a betrayal, physical violence under duress – all these mediated events can prompt informal re-negotiation among groups of viewers about what is acceptable or unacceptable behaviour in society. In a way, the character in popular fiction, film or television, 'stands in for' the absent friend who might also be the subject of gossip. By a process of transference, the life-style of the actor who plays the character might also become the subject of gossip. There is therefore an interaction between some mediated texts and unmediated discourse – the former prompts cultural debate and perhaps shifts in a society's attitude to represented individuals or groups.

I have chosen to look in slightly greater detail below at some mediated texts from situation comedies and talk shows, partly because these two media genres are typically played in front of a live audience, which parallels (and is sometimes used to prompt) the home audience, and partly because the staples of these media genres (conversations and interviews) parallel the speech genres discussed elsewhere in this book (Chapters 3 and 6).

Mediated interviews

Media texts containing interviews are themselves varied in generic purpose: they range from current affairs interviews with politicians and personalities in the news, to talk shows with personalities from the world of entertainment. The generic purpose of the first type of programme would (ideally) be to elicit information which would enlighten the viewing public, while the purpose of the second is increasingly, in the view of Tolson (1991), to engage in 'banter' for the amusement of the studio and home audience. As Tolson points out, hybrid forms exist, and a serious interview might at certain points switch into banter, and vice versa.

The viewing audience is crucial to the form of the mediated interview. Whereas in an interview conducted for research purposes, the interviewer seeks to elicit information or confirm hypotheses, the media interviewer often seeks to elicit known information for the purposes of display. This is evident in, for example, a programme from the series *Inside the Actor's Studio*, in which the host, James Lipton, interrogates Robert de Niro, in front of a live audience of trainee actors, directors and writers. In some ways, the interview format in this programme is related to current-affairs interviewing: the focus of the talk is not banter but information. However, a recurring feature of the interview is that Lipton seems to know much more about the information he is eliciting than de Niro does. At one point they are discussing de Niro's Oscar-winning performance as the boxer Jake La Motta in the film *Raging Bull*:

JL: You were there to accept that award, were you not?
RdN: Yes.
JL: Whom did you thank? You thanked some – it was very interesting.
RdN: Oh I think my my mother and my f- my father, and who else?
JL: I think you also thanked La Motta and all his –
RdN: Of course, I –
JL: Everybody.
RdN: I thanked his brother even though he was suing us.
          [Audience laughter]

Here it is evident that Lipton knows the story which de Niro seems temporarily to have forgotten. At one point de Niro actually questions the interviewer, who in turn prompts him by recalling the relevant details, and on cue, de Niro produces the punchline, to which the studio audience responds with laughter. The interaction between the pair – the exchange of information and chat – is therefore directed primarily towards the audience. It is for display. The live audience in a typical talk show thus becomes an active participant in the interaction – not only by laughing, but by indirectly shaping the form of the questions and answers directed towards them. In the de Niro interview, they also applaud every time de Niro first mentions a significant film he has starred in, and they back-channel in other ways too. One of the familar legends about de Niro is the story of how he gained weight in order to play the older La Motta:

JL	[Referring to script]: I know you've told this story many many many times but it is it is as you've said fundamental. You actually broke off in the middle of the film so that you would gain the weight. How did you gain it? You had –
RdN:	I just ate – [Some audience laughter] big breakfast, big lunch, big dinner. It it was fun, you know, the first fifteen pounds are okay and it's… but after that it's [low voice] drudge drudgery –
JL:	How much did you gain because at the end you were immense.
RdN:	I gained I gained sixty pounds.
Audience:	Oooooh! [Laughter and then applause]
JL	(to Audience): Remember what he looked like at the beginning of the movie? You can see every muscle in his body.

The audience here becomes even more of an active participant in the interaction, to the extent that Lipton concludes the exchange by addressing them directly. An interesting contrast can be made between this interview and a Brazilian chat show filmed in front of a Portuguese-speaking audience, in which the host, Jo Soares, interviewed the American actor Patrick Swayze, in English. When shown on television the interview had subtitles, but, clearly, few in the live audience understood English sufficiently to follow the exchanges. In this situation, where the studio audience could participate less directly, the interviewer had to provide much more of the immediate back-channelling for his guest. There were further differences in the programme. In the de Niro interview, James Lipton sat to the left of the screen (a position of authority, in which news interviewers, for example, are usually situated), in front of a large table, about ten feet away from de Niro, who had his own small table with a glass upon it. Lipton had a script on his table, from which he occasionally read. Since the participants were so distant from each other, they could only be shown together in long shot: medium shots and close-ups showed the interviewer and interviewee alone. The overall set-up gave a sense of formality to the interview – this was more than just 'chat' – a tone heightened by Lipton's rather formal grammar (e.g. the full tag sentence, 'were you not' and use of 'whom'). By contrast, Soares sat to the left of Swayze, easily close enough to touch him (which he occasionally did). Both interviewer and interviewee remained together in shot, except when the camera cut to show members of the audience. To the far right of the screen was a desk on which a mug was placed. Soares did not read from his script so obviously, and from all these elements, the typical informality of the 'chat show' as opposed to the 'formal interview' was largely maintained. Tolson (1991; reprinted in Marris & Thornham, 1996: 190) characterises 'chat' in chat shows as follows:

> First there is an often topical shift towards the 'personal' (as opposed to the institutional), or towards the 'private' (as opposed to the public). Secondly, this shift may be accompanied by displays of wit (e.g. foregrounded lexical ambiguities) or humour (double entendres, etc,). But thirdly, and this is the vital point, in any context, 'chat' always works by opening up the possibility of transgression. Chat does not simply reproduce norms and conventions, rather it flirts with them, for instance it opens up the possibility of the interviewee putting questions to the interviewer.

According to this classification, the 'formal' de Niro interview approaches 'chat' when de Niro starts good-humouredly quizzing Lipton about facts in his life he himself has forgotten. The Soares interview with Swayze is less serious from the start, and focuses more on the revelation of the personal, or 'psuedo personal'. For instance, Swayze explicitly makes the point that his career is governed by personal rather than institutional factors:

JS: You've you've played ah very different roles . . . and ah you've played a bouncer, surfer, doctor, a dancer ah what makes you choose a role from a script?

PS: For me, my heart.

JS: Yeah.

PS: Em I I choose roles by instinct. Em I feel very lucky that I lived through the Hollywood hit machine mentality you know –

JS: Mmhmm

PS: – where you make decisions only according to how much money something's going to make at the box office.

JS: Mmhmm

PS: You know, I need to do roles and characters that are going to further me as an actor and are going to open my heart up in some way . . . you know like that's the reason I did a film like *Dirty Dancing*, like *Ghost*, like eh, like eh eh like *To Wong Foo*, you know because it's not a movie about drag queens, it's a movie about human beings and people and the dignity we we all all possess and everyone deserves a chance at happiness no matter who we are.

The studio audience is silent throughout Swayze's response (whereas an

American or even a British audience would probably have at least one or two members whooping at the names of favourite films), leaving Swayze to receive his encouragement only from Soares. The silent audience is even more apparent when Swayze attempts humour:

JS: [touching PS's arm briefly]: When when you started as an actor, because of being a dancer, did people think that you were gay, because of all the enormous prejudice that –

PS: Well . . . my point of view is [deep voice] let 'em call me gay [JS laughs broadly; Audience murmurs] and see what happens.

JS: [still laughing] No pro – and see what happens! And you you study martial arts too.

PS: All my life.

JS: Well, let's see, let's see, let's see eh first let's talk about eh *City of Joy*. It's a complete different kind of movie, right? [PS nods] And I have –

PS: I I'm very proud of it.

JS: I have here, I have here some scenes also.
            [A clip is shown from *City of Joy* featuring Swayze's character assisting with a difficult birth. Audience applauds]

JS: Beautiful.

There are a number of points in this exchange which deserve comment. First, in passing, we see another example of the 'feminisation' of dance, referred to by Thomas above, which, perhaps in conjunction with Swayze's reference to drag queens earlier, prompts Soares' question about Swayze's sexuality. This subject clearly broaches the chat show convention about revealing 'synthetic' personality rather than 'real' personality (and so is in danger of transgressing the norms of the genre). Soares therefore couches the question between two justifying subordinate clauses ('Because . . . because . . . '). Swayze chooses to respond humorously, adopting a macho voice to articulate a challenge to the question. The uncomprehending studio audience understandably fails to respond to the humour. The audience silence leaves Soares to support Swayze with his own loud laughter, which might prompt the studio audience's murmur. His follow-up question is irrelevant, except in so far as it acknowledges that the question about Swayze's sexuality has challenged the chat show conventions too strongly, and so is an obvious attempt to re-establish his guest's macho masculinity. The interviewer then introduces a clip of Swayze's latest film, after which the audience, on cue, applauds.

Mediated interviews, then, like unmediated interviews, are clearly about much more than the simple exchange of information and ideas. First of all, the interviewer often knows in advance the answers he or she desires from the guest, and the questions are simply prompts to elicit the desired response for the audience in the studio and at home. Secondly, when the interviewee discloses information, it is not necessarily 'sincere' but must be interpreted within a set of conventions whereby the guest seems to be revealing aspects of his or her 'essential' personality. However, he or she is actually constructing what Tolson (1991) calls a 'synthetic' personality, that is, a personality for public consumption. That said, there are variations within the talk show genre: the formality of the Lipton interview and the informality of the Soares interview are partial indicators of the degree of 'sincerity' we can expect of the interaction. For example, when Lipton prompts de Niro to recall, later in the interview, that his father died a few months before the completion of de Niro's first film as director (de Niro plays a father in the movie, and the film is dedicated to his own father) de Niro is moved almost to tears. This exhibition of sincere emotion, while touching, would be transgressive in the 'chat show' format, where revelation of personality is typically controlled and, indeed, expected to be largely fictional – thus the banter between Soares and Swayze.

Mediated dialogue in sitcoms

As is the case in interviews, the discourse of televised drama or comedy is radically altered by the presence of an audience. Most sitcoms, like most interviews, have a studio audience present, representing the home audience, and its responses in some instances prompt that of the home audience. 'Canned laughter' after all, refers to the artificial heightening of the live studio response in a bid (sometimes counter-productive) to shape the response of the home audience. Unlike interviews, however, which are still spontaneous interactions (no matter how polished the guest's anecdotes might be), comedies are scripted. In some ways, the dialogues presented in drama and comedy simulate everyday conversations, but the presence of a studio audience and an audience at home changes the nature of the exchanges. Comedy, in particular, can arise from (among other things) the subversion and parody of the discourse structures of everyday conversation. Dialogue at cross-purposes is largely a complication of basic information exchange. In the discussion of 'second-storying' (Chapter 3), a *Monty Python* comedy sketch was mentioned, which featured four Yorkshiremen competing to tell the most absurd story about their childhood poverty. A similar parody is used in the first episode of the US sitcom *Friends*. This comedy, about a group of six twenty-somethings, sharing adjacent apartments in New York, revolves, as the title suggests, around their friendships and relationships. We would therefore expect much of the language to have a bonding function. It is not surprising, then, that poor-girl Pheobe supports the rich newcomer, Rachel, by telling a story of shared experience. The comedy here lies in the audience's recognition of the inappropriateness of the story (a fact acknowledged by the character, Ross). Rachel's flatmates are urging her to cut up the credit cards which tie her to her family (a symbolic act which will put her on a par with her new-found, hard-working 'friends'):

Monica: Come on, you can't live off your parents your whole life.
Rachel: I know that. That's why I was getting married!
[Audience laughter]
Phoebe: Give her a break. It's hard being on your own for the first time.
Rachel: [surprised] Thank you.
Phoebe: You're welcome. I remember when I first came to this city. I was fourteen. My mom had just killed herself and my stepdad was back in prison. [Audience laughter] And I got here and I didn't know anybody. And I ended up living with this albino guy who was like cleaning windshields outside Port Authority, and then he killed himself. [Audience laughter] And then I found aromatherapy, so believe me, I know exactly how you feel. [Audience laughter; Rachel looks confused.]
Ross: The word you're looking for is 'Anyway . . . ' [Loud audience laughter]

The audience's loudest laughter here is reserved for Ross's punchline, which, by overtly changing the topic, acknowledges that Pheobe's story (which initially promised to offer sympathy by sharing an experience) transgresses the cultural function of such stories by quickly moving far beyond the shared experiences of most middle-class Americans. The comedy, as in the *Monty Python* sketch, lies mainly in the exaggerated transgression of an everyday conversational genre.

The question that mediated discourse such as this raises about 'real' discourse, as presented in the family mealtime discussion in Chapter 3, is that the taped conversation there, too, was in a sense 'mediated'. At least one of the participants in all the conversations reported in Eggins and Slade (1997) must have known that the interaction would go beyond the immediate participants, at least insofar as it would be scrutinised by discourse analysts, and possibly eventually published for a wider audience. In the collection of 'everyday' conversational data, mediation is sometimes explicitly acknowledged by the participants, for example, in the following exchange between a child, Shlomit, and an adult male friend of her family, Yoash, recorded and translated from Hebrew by Blum-Kulka (2000: 232). Shlomit and Yoash are discussing the child's history teacher, whose husband is an acquaintance of Yoash.

Shlomit: Does he talk a lot? She is a terrible talker.
Yoash: He is a very educated man.
Shlomit: She is completely dumb.
Yoash: She is dumb?
Shlomit: Excuse me, it's being recorded.

Shlomit's comment acknowledges that she is aware that this conversation is also being directed at an outside 'audience', and her awareness of this audience influences what can be said. The question of whether recordings are made with or without the knowledge of participants is therefore crucial. Eggins and Slade do not give many details about the means of data collection, particularly the degree to which it was 'covert'. In some of their data direct mention is made of the recording apparatus, but it is unclear under what conditions each recording was made. Certainly, over time, in domestic situations, people may lose an awareness of being recorded; however, with all recorded data there may be a sense in which one or more participants is playing to the unseen audience. This changes the nature of the interaction, as we have seen; however, it need not automatically disqualify it as 'artificial'. After all, some everyday conversations may be partly conducted in the consciousness that other people are eavesdropping. Mediated and unmediated discourses are perhaps best seen as being on a continuum, where awareness of a wider audience is high or low, and the exchanges are more or less directed towards an immediate or remote 'public'. Purely unmediated interactions are perhaps impossible to record, at least ethically. However, it is important to remember that the nature of the interaction changes depending on whether the interaction is directed towards an immediate audience or a broader, 'eavesdropping' public.

Mediated discourse in the intercultural classroom

The above discussion demonstrates that the English language teacher and student should always remember that mediated discourse is different from unmediated conversation, and does not offer an ideal model for, say, everyday conversation or ethnographic interviewing strategies. Tolson (1991), for example, observes that in one analysed section from a popular British chat show, the guest asked more questions than the nominal interviewer. However, their distance from unmediated discourse clearly does not disqualify mediated exchanges from use in the intercultural language classroom, especially if the goal is to explore cultural attitudes and beliefs. For example, the interviews and sitcoms discussed above can be considered from several viewpoints. First of all, the laughter of the audience can be analysed. An unannotated script of an exchange can be given to the students, and they can be asked to predict where laughter will occur and suggest why.

Their predictions can then be matched with a video presentation, and discussion can ensue as to the cross-cultural differences in the comedy.

Mediated dialogues which parody conversational genres can also be used to teach those genres – not least because parodies clearly expose, and even criticise common generic structures. The structures of information exchange, second-storying and gossip can be found in sitcoms and dramas, although here the point will not be primarily to negotiate values but to drive a plot, contribute to characterisation, or raise a laugh. The complex mixture of witty banter and pseudo-revelation which characterises chat shows can also be exploited (indeed parodied) in the ELT classroom. Jo Soares' interview with Patrick Swayze gives examples of both the construction of a 'synthetic' self-revelation ('For me, it's my heart') and the witty avoidance of 'real' self-revelation ('Let them try'). An understanding of the cultural conventions of talk-show discourse can help target the likely language to be used (value-laden, personal, ambiguous, frequently sexual) and the discourse conventions (the probing for revelation on the part of the interviewer; the strategies used to counter this on the part of the interviewee). In the end, mediated texts also play a prominent role in the real world of discourse, and, for many learners, they are the most readily available examples of the target language to be found outside the classroom, in films and on cable television or satellite channels.

Conclusion

It would clearly take many volumes to do justice to a discussion of literary, media and cultural texts and the variety of ways in which the 'cultural texts' of literature, film, television, and social practice can be used to explore the target language and culture. This chapter has narrowed the discussion to two main points, both to do with the discourse conventions of various 'cultural' texts. First, an adaptation of Stuart Hall's 'encoding-decoding' model of discourse production and reception, though idealised, can help clarify the aims and outcomes of intercultural activities. Projects – and small-scale classroom activities (such as reading and listening comprehensions, and class surveys) – can either focus on encoders ('auteurs'), the texts themselves (through 'close reading' or 'semiotics'), or the receivers ('audiences'), using appropriate research methodologies (e.g. biographical research, stylistic or semiotic analysis, or ethnography). Secondly, a recognition of the mediated nature of literary and media texts, in particular, can lead to an understanding of the special conventions of such discourses, and prompt further enquiry into how different audiences from different cultures make sense of them.

Chapter 9

Assessing Intercultural Communication

> The question 'what is a good test?' is a question of ideology – because a 'good test' depends on clear identification of target competence, and target competence is a composite of goals and ideals. (Spiro, 1991: 16)

The penultimate chapter in the book turns to the issue of assessing intercultural communicative competence. Topics addressed include:

- *The role of assessment in intercultural learning and ELT.*
- *Test formats (objective and subjective tests, with examples).*
- *Formative and summative assessment.*
- *How to determine learners' progress.*

The Role of Assessment

So far this book has been largely concerned with understanding the ways in which language constructs, maintains and represents social identities and group relationships, and how an understanding of these processes can inform intercultural English language education. This chapter considers assessment issues raised by an intercultural approach to English language teaching and learning. Much has been published to guide teachers in how to understand and construct language tests (e.g. Alderson & North, 1991; Hughes, 1989). In the literature on assessment and testing, a test is considered *valid* if it assesses what it is meant to test, and not something else (for further details, see Hughes, 1989: 22–8). The explicit incorporation of a cultural element into a language course raises obvious questions about the means of assessment used in the course: for instance, should they test language or culture, simultaneously or separately? A test that focuses on language alone might have the undesirable effect of downgrading the status of the cultural component of a course – why should teachers and students spend valuable curricular space on something for which the students will not receive tangible credit? On the other hand, why should a topic like culture (which might be seen as akin to history, geography or literary studies) be tested through a second language at all?

Indeed, some writers raise the question of whether culture can be tested explicitly. Kramsch (1993: 257) makes the point that the real value of reaching an intercultural perspective (which she describes as a 'third place', transcending both home and target culture) is an intensely individual quest, whose value might not be realised until long after a course of study has ended:

> Nobody, least of all the teacher, can tell [students] where that very personal place is; for each learner it will be differently located, and will make different sense at different times. For some, it will be the irrevocable memory of the ambiguities of the word 'challenge'. For others, it will be a small poem by Pushkin that will, twenty years later, help them make sense out of a senseless personal situation. For others still, it will be a small untranslatable Japanese proverb that they will all of a sudden remember, thus enabling them for a moment to see the world from the point of view of their Japanese business partner and save a floundering business transaction.

Kramsch is, of course, right to avoid reducing the value of intercultural exploration to those elements that can be codified and tested before, during and after the course. Nevertheless, assessment does have an institutional and individual use: state educational systems demand assessment to measure the performance of schools and the individuals who attend them. Teachers and learners also demand assessment as a means of measuring their progress, charting future needs, and diagnosing problems. In addition, recognition by an institution that a subject like culture is worth assessing can act as a stimulus for teachers and students to take it seriously.

If we accept that a language course should at least contain an intercultural component, and that the intercultural component should therefore be routinely assessed as an integral part of the course, then, to ensure test validity, it is necessary to specify the kinds of knowledge and skills that we are judging. Spiro (1991) gives a useful account of the kinds of knowledge and skills required to measure a potentially nebulous concept: 'literary competence'. She shows that literature tests demand a high degree of cultural knowledge (usually about canonical writers, literary history and literary theory), as well as the skills required to produce acceptable responses including the articulation of an aesthetic response that involves the appropriate use of quotation, paraphrase and summary. Or, to take a more general instance, communicative language teaching has generally focused on the 'four skills' of speaking, listening, reading and writing, and communicative test design has therefore concentrated on the construction of reliable tasks that measure students' performance in such a way as to make inferences about the state of their communicative competence. The various position papers in Alderson and North, (1991) show, however, that although communicative language teaching has been broadly accepted within ELT, communicative language testing is still a site of considerable unresolved controversy. The testing of culture can only add to the ongoing professional debate.

Byram (1997b: 87–111) looks in detail at the types of evidence and test formats that can be drawn upon to assess the various intercultural *savoirs* he identifies (see Chapter 2 for details). It is evident that an intercultural approach to language teaching and learning, as proposed here, extends and reshapes many of the goals of a communicative language course. Communicative language tests tend to break the global skill of language behaviour into four (still quite general) subskills: speaking, listening, reading and writing. The activities suggested in this book also promote these 'general' language skills in a number of ways. For example, the chapters on everyday conversation and interviewing further the acquisition of speaking and listening skills; and the chapter on written genres targets the acquisition of writing and reading skills. These three chapters together also provide information and practice in how members of the target culture interact in different contexts (*savoir 1*); that is, they focus on interactions between gossiping friends, and between specialists and their peer group or popular readerships. The chapter on ethnography focuses on ways of using observation and interview to discover cultural information (*savoir 4*), and the chapters on images and on literary, media and cultural studies illustrate ways of interpreting and relating different types of information (*savoir 2*). Throughout the book, critical reflection has been promoted, rather than unthinking adoption of, say, the interaction patterns of the target culture (*savoir 3*). Moreover, the ethos of open-minded inquiry is meant to promote understanding and tolerance of linguistic and cultural difference (*savoir 5*). Intercultural education is, of course, overtly designed to result in attitudinal and behavioural changes on the part of learners; however, although language courses should make explicit the values of the target culture, and do so in a sympathetic light, they should not impose those values upon unwilling students. As Byram recommends, understanding, critical reflection and mediation should be the watchwords.

Intercultural communication should be a clearly defined option in language education. The goals of any course should specify whether learners, teachers and institutions are concerned with (1) increasing language proficiency, (2) gaining factual knowledge about the target culture, (3) acculturating, and / or (4) mediating between cultures. This book has consistently argued that teaching and testing from an intercultural perspective can enrich a language course. If tests are then matched to curricular goals, then the tests should be valid. The following section will suggest ways in which a cultural perspective can be assessed.

Test Formats

Formal assessment can come in different parts of a course: a pre-test can find out the level of the students' knowledge and ability before the course starts, and so perform a useful diagnostic function; tests during a course can gauge progress and increase motivation, and act as a further diagnostic; while post-tests can both measure individual students' skills and knowledge when a course has ended, and give some indication of the effectiveness of the course. (See further, the section on 'Formative and Summative Assessment', below.) Different types of test format might be chosen at different stages, depending upon the purpose of the teacher.

The test formats discussed in this section do not depart greatly from those with which most language teachers will be familiar. Language tests fall into two general types: objective and subjective tests. The former type (which includes multiple-choice, true–false, and short question–answer tests) can be marked easily and often automatically. They do not require the marker to make a personal evaluative judgement. Subjective tests, however, do involve some kind of personal evaluation of the candidate's performance. Objective tests are good at testing knowledge but not necessarily skills; for a deeper and more global test of students' abilities, subjective tests are often preferable.

Objective tests

In the United States, objective tests of culture were used in New York State education tests of a foreign language up until June 1976, when they were discontinued (Valette, 1986: 180–1). Candidates for the Regents examinations were asked to answer 10 of 15 multiple-choice questions on points of cultural knowledge or etiquette; for example, about the population of France or the significance of a theatre audience whistling. The administrators of these tests dropped the culture section after expressing misgivings about its effects on candidates' learning – it was felt that students were simply memorising facts, rather than organising their cultural knowledge and relating it to their second-language behaviour (Dammer, 1975; cited in Valette, 1986: 181). Valette's examples of objective test items suggest why they fell from institutional favour in New York State. She gives the following example of a matching test item (1986: 184):

FAMOUS PEOPLE

Match the following persons with their contributions:

(1) Rochambeau	(a) poet and president of Senegal
(2) Senghor	(b) feminist writer
(3) De Beauvoir	(c) pioneer aviator and novelist
(4) Curie	(d) discoverer of radium
	(e) commander of French troops during the American revolution

Correct responses: 1e, 2a, 3b, 4d

This kind of test item, and the kind of knowledge it represents, is easy prey to the criticism that it tests a motley assembly of facts, here connected only in so far as the celebrities involved were French speakers. More focused questions of this type can, however, test relevant cultural knowledge, given that the knowledge concerned has been (or will be) taught as an integral part of the course. For example, the following matching test could be given to students before, during or after a course that included anglophone youth culture as a main theme:

POPULAR MUSIC TRENDS

Match the name of the following groups/singers with (a) the type of music they play, (b) the city with which they are associated, and (c) the decade they rose to fame:

The Supremes	Mersey Beat	London	1960s
Bob Marley	Brit Pop	Detroit	1970s
The Beatles	Reggae	Seattle	1980s
Oasis	Motown	Liverpool	1990s
The Sex Pistols	Grunge	Kingston	
Nirvana	Punk	Manchester	

The difference between this test item and the previous one is that it is focused on a topic: namely, popular music trends. Texts about popular music trends, and about youth cultures, will normally presuppose a level of background knowledge of music styles, key representatives, and associated locations and periods. It is therefore easier to demonstrate the usefulness of such a test item in terms of its relation to a course component on popular music. One advantage of a topic-focused test item like this is that it can function as a pre-test, eliciting the level of background knowledge learners have before a course component begins. The completion of such a test would also have the pedagogical purpose of orienting the students towards texts on the subject.

Even so, there are obvious dangers of too heavy a reliance on objective test items such as those above. First of all, they can only test 'shallow learning', such as the memorisation of facts, and not 'deep learning', which would involve the ability to organise, synthesise and relate information (cf. Entwhistle *et al.*, 1992: 4–9). Sometimes, shallow learning needs to be tested, but it should not be the final goal of a course on culture. Secondly, because they stress facts and generalisations, objective test items can too easily encourage stereotyping, as a further example from Valette demonstrates (1986: 185):

DESCRIBING ETIQUETTE

What is the traditional American pattern when a man and a woman are walking down a city street?
Correct response: The man always walks on the *curb* side.

This test item may be true, in so far as it describes traditional, and even desirable, views of some Americans' etiquette; however, presented out of context as a 'fact', it encourages the false inference that all 'traditional' Americans behave in this way. Clearly this is too simplistic a view, even of this aspect of gender relations. Deeper learning would contextualise this nugget of etiquette socially and historically, and use observation and interview to find out how widely it is actually observed in contemporary society. Is there, for example, a generation divide in American views of this aspect of etiquette? Has feminism impacted upon chivalric behaviour such as men keeping to the kerb, offering women seats on buses, and holding doors open for them to pass through? Objective test items cannot test deeper learning of this type.

Subjective tests

Subjective tests demand that the marker evaluates a more complex response by the candidate. They are subjective in so far as they call upon the judgement of the marker: differences of opinion are therefore possible, although the test specification should give markers clear guidance about the criteria used in grading. There is in fact no absolute distinction between objective and subjective tests – some elicitation techniques have characteristics of both types. As Spiro (1991: 65–6) demonstrates, even matching tests can be devised that can elicit evidence of deeper learning: the candidate can be asked to match the beginnings of a selection of stories with their endings, and to justify the matches made. Such a test is partly objective in that the matches would be right or wrong, but the justification element would involve recognition of cultural markers and consistency of style. The marker might even give some credit to a wrong match if the justification for it were plausible.

The following test types (which draw on Byram, 1997b; Spiro, 1991; and Ur, 1996) give suggestions for ways of testing candidates subjectively on the topics that have formed the substance of this book.

(a) Identifying genres

The candidate is given a selection of excerpts from, say, popular and learned scientific texts, or personal and business letters, and has to group them according to genre. If the candidate is also required to justify his or her choice, the test becomes more subjective, since the judgement of the candidate (rather than simply the product of that judgement) is taken into consideration. This test would mainly involve reading, and possibly oral or written production (in either the first or second language), if justification of the identification is required.

(b) Selecting appropriate language

A familiar question type in language examinations is the gap-filling, or cloze, test. An adaptation of this test type requires students to select appropriate language (possibly from a range of given options) to fill a gap in a generic text. As in (a), this test becomes subjective if the candidate has to write rather than choose the gap-fillers, and also if he or she has to justify the response. The skills of reading, and optionally writing, would be involved here, and again sensitivity to generic conventions would be the point at issue.

(c) Transformation and rewriting tasks

Transformation and rewriting tasks again test the candidate's ability to recognise and produce genre-specific texts. Here, the student can be given a text which is stylistically inconsistent – e.g. a letter which is a mixture of personal and business styles – and he or she might be required to edit it according to given instructions (i.e. to make it more like a business or personal letter). A more complex task would involve rewriting an entire text so that it shifts genres: e.g. an extract from a research-oriented article might be popularised, or vice versa. Again, oral or written justification for the changes can also be demanded. The justification should indicate the candidate's awareness of the conventions of the target discourse community (see Chapter 4).

(d) Reflective essay tasks

The reflective essay is itself a genre and can be taught as such. However, it may also be a vehicle for reflection upon the state of the candidate's intercultural awareness, and so constitute valuable evidence of the learning process thus far. Topics for reflective essays might include (Byram, 1997b: 95–103):

- analysing one's personal experience of the target culture;
- describing 'key characteristics' of the target culture;
- seeing a familiar situation from another's point of view;
- evaluating the value systems of different cultures / texts;
- identifying and explaining cultural misunderstandings in a given text / situation;
- identifying and accounting for ethnocentric perspectives in a given text / situation;
- mediating between conflicting interpretations of a text or situation;
- analysing data elicited in small-scale ethnographic research.

It will be evident from these topics that the reflective essay is a complex task type, demanding considerable control of the target language. The demands of the genre include the ability to organise elements of description, narration, explanation and evaluation into a coherent and plausible whole. In more 'academic' contexts, quotation and paraphrase might also be demanded (with sources properly referenced). The testing of reflective essays should be integrated into a course in which the skills of essay-writing are being explicitly taught: the purpose of the genre (as an index of the state of the student's learning process) should be made clear to all the candidates.

If the process of redrafting is a prominent aspect of the course, this can also be reflected in the testing. The first draft of a reflective essay can be awarded a grade, and comments made by the marker which would lead to an improved grade. The redraft is then evaluated in accordance with the degree to which the candidate has responded to the constructive advice of the marker.

(e) Role-plays/Simulations

Most of the above test formats involve the use of writing, which is the most common mode of testing in anglophone culture. However, some of the skills and techniques discussed in this book can only be properly tested orally, most probably by role-play or simulation. These skills include:

- using everyday conversation to construct and maintain individual identity within a group;
- using formal and informal interviews to elicit cultural knowledge.

The type of conversational role-plays described in Chapter 3 can be adapted for assessment purposes. The evaluation of the candidates' participation would not rest solely on whether information has been transferred using accurate and fluent language. The evaluation would also take into consideration the candidate's ability to, say, pick up on a topic from a participant's narration, and tell an appropriate 'second story'.

Interviewing techniques are useful in pragmatic ethnography and therefore also testable. Standard ELT oral testing procedures can also be modified to assess interviewing skills, particularly since this skill does involve the transfer of information. In some ELT oral examinations, candidates work in pairs to prepare and rehearse an information-gap activity, which is then acted out before an assessor with the additional participation of a staff interlocutor. Typical tasks include choosing a holiday from a given range, under the constraint of a given budget. An intercultural interviewing task would specify the kind of informant, and the nature of the 'ethnographic' information sought; for example, a supermarket manager or a shopper might be quizzed with a view to finding out cultural information about patterns of consumption in a certain area. Working individually or in pairs, the candidates would have to brainstorm the kind of questions to be asked of the informant, and then interview the teacher or other interlocutor, who would play the part of the manager or shopper. The candidates could be assessed on the appropriateness and delivery of their questions, and, optionally, on the accuracy of their notes and recall. The scope of this test does not allow for time for a more considered analysis of the informant's responses.

In addition to conversational interaction and interviewing techniques, interpretative skills can be displayed by adapting other well-established oral testing techniques. For example, a long-standing feature of general ELT examinations is to require candidates to talk about a given picture or photograph. The visual literacy skills discussed in Chapter 7 can be tested by selecting pictures or photographs that convey the kind of cultural information that candidates have been exploring (e.g. newspaper photographs, or advertisements) and eliciting the kind of formal analysis that has been taught on the course (i.e. the 'vocabulary' and 'grammar' of the images). The test obviously presupposes that this kind of activity has been practised during the course itself.

(f) Projects and portfolios

The tests described above are constrained by limited time-frames. A reflective essay, or an oral test of interviewing techniques, for example, cannot probe the full extent of a candidate's ability to organise a project, implement data gathering, analyse the data, and report back in speech and/or writing. Group or individual projects can therefore be staged and continually assessed over longer periods of time. Projects and portfolios are useful in assessing a number of types of skills and knowledge more expansively and thoroughly than a reflective essay can. For example, they can demonstrate the following skills:

- planning a small-scale research project;
- allocation of tasks (teamwork);
- implementation of research (data gathering);
- analysis of data;
- writing up and/or oral presentation of data.

Each stage of the research process can be separately evaluated and graded by the marker. The content of the research can also be graded for those aspects of intercultural competence identified by Byram (1997b); for example, affective responses to 'culture shock', ability to 'decentre' one's cultural assumptions, and to evaluate critically behaviour in both the home and the target culture. Once again, the marker should make it explicit to the candidate that these aspects of the project will be assessed.

Portfolios need not be structured as ethnographic projects. The aims of different kinds of courses will favour different kinds of testable products. A short course in English for Specific Purposes might be more concerned with students' abilities to write genre-specific texts – a portfolio of coursework, then, might provide samples of drafts and redrafts across favoured genres (e.g. business letters, business reports, notes towards oral presentations, tapes of oral presentations, handouts and visuals used, etc.). Such a portfolio would not be an investigation of some aspect of a target culture; rather it would demonstrate the candidate's ability to conform to the expectations of the target culture. However, it is strongly recommended that such portfolios should contain an element of critical reflection (perhaps in the familiar form of a learner journal) – learners may deliberately opt not to conform to the expected norms of the target culture, and they should have that freedom. However, it is sometimes difficult for a marker to infer whether a deviation from expected norms is a deliberate choice or not, and some self-analysis (or discussion of the portfolio, if time permits) can clarify whether the student is or is not aware of the cultural norms which are being subverted.

Finally, projects and portfolios have the advantage of drawing upon useful 'transferable' skills other than linguistic control and intercultural awareness. In educational environments that provide adequate technological support, data-gathering and project presentation can increasingly draw on electronic resources. Students seeking information on a discourse community can gather data from websites, internet discussion groups, and email contacts, and projects can be presented in disk form with textual information and analysis supported by sound and image files. Even the structure of projects can vary: for example, hypertext assignments might be preferred to more traditional, linear reports and essays. Clearly, the extent to which technological skills are tested depends upon the resources available to the teacher, learners and institutions; however, they can be directly relevant to cultural learning. Finding a useful email discussion group and gathering data about, say, fans of a soap opera from that discussion group, is as relevant an ethnographic research technique as, say, interviewing a native speaker. Where such resources are available, they can be exploited, and the efficiency of their exploitation can clearly become part of the overall course assessment.

Formative and Summative Assessment

There is a danger in over-assessing students during a course, and in this context a useful distinction can be made between formative and summative assessment. The former gives students guidance on their performance during a course, while the latter evaluates their skills and knowledge by the end of the course. Students' linguistic and intercultural competence changes at different rates over the course of time, and continuous assessment in particular does not always adequately reflect these differential variations. Furthermore, if a student knows that his or her work at the beginning of a course is to count towards the final assessment, they may take the work more seriously, but there is also less freedom to experiment and take risks than there would otherwise be, and consequently the educational process can actually be hindered rather than supported. There is therefore a balance to be struck in how much continuous assessment to demand, and how much of that should be counted towards a final course grade.

The choice and implementation of test formats depends on many factors, such as the length of the course, its aims, the number and language level of the students, and (not least) the time that the teacher is willing and able to devote to assessing students' work. In the general organisation of assessment, however, it might be useful again to consider the culturally contextualised, encoding/decoding model of discourse suggested in this book. The exploration of culture by language learners can proceed on two general fronts: exploration of the possible meanings of texts (semiotics), and/or exploration of the discourse communities that produce and consume the texts (ethnography). This book suggests that an intercultural ELT curriculum should incorporate a mixture of interpretative and ethnographic skills if it aims to equip learners to discover and understand the target culture. 'Good language tests', then, should initially support learners in their acquisition of interpretative and ethnographic skills (formative assessment), and then evaluate the degree to which they have acquired them (summative assessment). The choice of test formats at any stage in this process should be based on the type of skills and knowledge being formed, or summatively evaluated. For instance, genre identification is best suited to an early stage in formative assessment, when teachers are supporting students' growing awareness of how the linguistic form of texts is shaped by the requirements of different discourse communities. Transforming texts from one genre to another might be more suited to summative assessment, once the student has greater familiarity with and control over the linguistic forms expected by different discourse communities. As noted above, a portfolio can incorporate samples of student writing across different genres (ideally including reflections upon the writing process itself), and give a more extensive profile still of the candidate's control of a range of culturally shaped texts. With the reservations expressed earlier, such a portfolio can be used either in formative or summative assessment.

Determining Progress

As noted at the beginning of this chapter, Kramsch (1993) cautions against too narrow an assessment of the cultural element of a language course, arguing that its benefit might not be realised (in both senses of the word) until long after the course has ended. Byram (1997b: 75) also warns against viewing cultural education as a step-by-step progression up a metaphorical ladder – he argues that a jigsaw puzzle is a better metaphor for the process of learning, whereby the earlier stages of learning provide points of reference ('the edges and the corners'), and a richer, more detailed picture emerges at later stages of learning. Byram (1997b: 75–6) observes that:

> Learners often need to revisit issues and encounter them in different contexts and perspectives. Furthermore, their needs may suggest a different order from that usually taken, and their needs may change and require different priorities at different points in their learning process, particularly when that process is life-long.

Byram also notes, for example, that younger learners may not benefit as much as older ones from cultural content in their lessons. The ability to abstract content from experience, and even to perceive difference, is partly dependent on maturity. As a case in point, various research projects suggest that dialect-speaking children under the age of 10 have not acquired a full awareness of the differences between their own speech variety and the standard language (see the articles collected in Cheshire *et al.*, 1989). Evidently, the kinds of cultural exploration which depend upon a comparison between language varieties and their relation to their speech community would need either to be radically modified for younger children, or postponed until they are in their early teens.

Although he grants that all aspects of the *savoirs* that he defines as elements of intercultural competence are related, Byram is currently working with colleagues across Europe to specify a 'threshold' of intercultural competence, that is, a point at which it might be argued that learners have achieved an institutionally sanctioned blend of cultural knowledge and skills. The desire to specify a threshold level of intercultural competence itself reflects Byram's background in the state education sector, and his involvement in the Council of Europe's ongoing project to harmonise language learning goals across the European Community (cf. Byram & Zarate, 1997; van Ek, 1975). Even so, Byram acknowledges that such a threshold would vary from context to context, depending in part upon (1) the social demands upon learners to acquire language for purposes such as commerce and diplomacy, as well as for personal recreation; (2) the orientations of the home country towards those cultures (national and professional) where the second language is used either as a mother tongue or as an auxiliary means of communication; (3) the resources available in the educational institution where the language is taught (materials, methods, trained teachers, technology, etc.); (4) a specification of the situations in which the learners are likely to use their communicative and intercultural skills (e.g. on study trips, in personal contacts, or in secondary exposure through the media or internet contacts).

At present, the specification of readily available curriculum objectives, and work towards a consensus about a threshold for intercultural competence, are in their infancy. No widely used ELT examination, such as the UCLES or Oxford examinations, currently specifies or tests intercultural competence as here defined, and so it is up to the individual teacher and institution to decide if or how a cultural component in their teaching should be tested. This chapter has been able only to offer general guidance to the issues surrounding assessment in the cultural classroom. However brief the discussion must be here, the topic remains of fundamental importance to the concept of language teaching more widely. In a lively critique of language assessment up to the 1990s, Harrison (1991: 97) comments:

> One of the first consequences of looking at a language from a communicative point of view is the realisation that the context of an utterance

has a vital importance in establishing its meaning. A question for testing is whether this context is necessary for the assessment of communicative skills.

It is a point which, unfortunately, Harrison does not pursue in detail: he proceeds, instead, to remind his readers that test-taking, like theatre, is about performance and display, as much as it is about the performance of 'real-life' tasks, and that good tests should engage the candidates' creativity and allow them to be 'spontaneously appropriate' (1991: 104). Tests of intercultural competence face many of the same questions as communicative language tests: how best to specify context, and how best to construct test formats in which knowledge of the cultural functions of language inform but do not straitjacket students' creativity. Implicit in Harrison's observations is a reminder that testing, too, is a cultural variant: it takes time for the culture of testing to bend itself to the prevailing winds of teaching and learning. The test formats suggested in this chapter do not stray far beyond those well-established already in the language testing literature, and so teachers and students should not balk at their unfamiliarity. However, the tasks have been modified to probe more specifically the cultural aspects of language knowledge and use, and the candidates who undertake such culturally oriented assessments should be clearly briefed about what is required of them, and the criteria to be used in grading their performance. Until general examinations in intercultural proficiency become widely available, it must be the responsibility of local curriculum planners and teachers to flesh out the details of the most appropriate goals, formats and grading criteria for the assessment of the intercultural content of their language courses.

Chapter 10

Prospects for Teaching and Learning Language and Culture

This book has attempted to describe the intellectual contexts and practical means of implementing an intercultural approach to English-language teaching, much of it associated with Michael Byram and his colleagues. The literature on intercultural language learning now encompasses detailed descriptions of intercultural skills and how to assess them (Byram, 1997b), explorations of learning as ethnography (Roberts *et al.*, 2001), and practical examples of classroom practice from around the world (Alred, Byram & Fleming, 2003; Byram & Fleming, 1998; Byram *et al.* 2001). The International Association for Languages and Intercultural Communication (IALIC), has been formed to further research and practice in intercultural education, and it has launched the *Journal for Language and Intercultural Communication*. A review of the expanding literature on intercultural approaches to language education shows that, with notable exceptions (e.g. Kramsch, 1993), much of it has been concerned with teaching and learning languages and cultures other than English. Where English *is* the target language, teaching has been based mainly in state institutions – the state primary, secondary, further and higher education systems rather than commercial language schools. For example, Byram's work has centred on modern languages teaching in the European Community, and some of his work on defining the goals of the intercultural curriculum has been connected with the Council of Europe's ongoing harmonisation of the objectives of language and culture teaching throughout the Community (e.g. Byram & Zarate, 1991). The contributors to Byram *et al.*'s (2001) anthology of case studies of intercultural approaches teach in schools or colleges, in Britain, Denmark and Bulgaria, where an intercultural curriculum has been developed by a teachers' network over the years, with support from the British Council (Davcheva & Docheva, 1998). It is not surprising that, as discussed in Chapter 1, intercultural language education has been developing apace in the public sector, while its impact so far has been less evident in commercial language schools. The curricular goals of intercultural education embed language teaching and learning in a wider educational project that has explicit ethical implications. Byram (1997b: 50) sets out the 'attitudes' that intercultural education seeks actively to promote – and assess:

- willingness to seek out or take up opportunities to engage with otherness in a relationship of equality; this should be distinguished from attitudes of seeking out the exotic or of seeking to profit from others;
- interest in discovering other perspectives on interpretation of familiar and unfamiliar phenomena both in one's own and in other cultures and cultural practices;
- willingness to question the values and presuppositions in cultural practices and products in one's own environment;
- readiness to experience the different stages of adaptation to and interaction with another culture during a period of residence;
- readiness to engage with the conventions and rites of verbal and nonverbal communication and interaction

Behind these attitudes is the assumption that learners and teachers are working in a liberal democracy that upholds values like equality, and the tolerance of difference, and that it is the teacher's job to foster these values overtly in the language classroom, and assess them alongside the 'four language skills'. The teacher, then, becomes a moral guide, a role that more traditionally suits the state school teacher (who represents institutional authority) than the commercial school teacher (who is ultimately an employee of the learner). Intercultural approaches to language education are perhaps less likely to be implemented in totalitarian regimes where the self-reflective and self-critical components of the curriculum might well be discouraged or indeed repressed.

Even so, intercultural approaches have caught on in countries with no long history of liberal democratic government. Intercultural language education has become popular in parts of eastern Europe, such as Bulgaria, which, since 1989, have undergone a major social and cultural upheaval: the language classroom became a place in which new ways of constructing one's own and other cultures could be explored. The issues at stake have never been more topical or urgent. Intercultural language education has also become established, usually at university level, in some countries whose regimes have traditionally been less open to criticism. The intercultural comparison of the role of women in British and American culture, as reflected in, say, popular women's magazines, can lead to indirect criticism of the treatment of women in one's own country.

Intercultural language education in such circumstances can become a relatively safe way of indirectly talking critically about one's own society.

There is an understandable anxiety about the moral role taken by
English-language educators in a world where English has become the
global lingua franca. Pennycook (1998, 2001) and Phillipson (1992) are
powerful critiques of ELT in state educational contexts where the imposition of English-medium education effectively creates obstacles for learners'
further education, while simultaneously alienating them from their home
culture. The contexts in question are not societies where the home language
is well established and relatively unthreatened by the advance of global
English. Rather, the brunt of Phillipson's wrath is reserved for certain post-
colonial countries in Africa where a range of tribal languages is spoken, and
where, he argues, English-medium education has become imperialism by
another name. First of all, it creates a disadvantaged majority, and a
minority elite that has been socialised to be sympathetic to Western values.
Secondly, English-medium education provides a continuing source of
employment for British-educated teachers, and a ready market for Anglo-
American publishers. Finally, the disadvantaged majority whose mastery
of English is not sufficient to bring them the rewards of educational and
social advancement are nevertheless dislocated from their tribal backgrounds, since their link with tribal language and culture has been severed.
They become rootless, and consequently might drift into menial jobs in the
cities or into petty crime (cf. Graddol & Goodman, 1996, on the threat of
English-medium education on traditional culture in Papua New Guinea).
Recent perspectives on linguistic imperialism, including a critique of
Phillipson's position, can be found in Canagarajah (1999).

It would of course be facile to suggest that intercultural language
education can solve the problems of global inequality. However, it is
possible that an intercultural approach can help solve the dilemma facing
English-language teachers in educational contexts such as those described
by Phillipson, Graddol and others. The dilemma is that in the modern
world, teaching English has the potential to empower learners by giving
them access to broader education. However, by imposing proficiency in
English as a prerequisite for such access, many learners are denied further
education and their sense of pride both in themselves and in their home
culture may be diminished. An intercultural approach to English education
in such contexts would acknowledge that knowledge of English is a useful
qualification in contemporary society. However, it would revise the goal of
'mastery' of English as a curricular aim. The strict imposition of 'English-
medium' education would be reviewed in contexts where home languages
are under threat, and space would be found to foster English language
skills alongside mother tongue skills. This could be done, for example, by

exploring story-telling or conversational strategies in both cultures. The reflective component of the intercultural curriculum requires specialist knowledge of the home culture – with the learner and non-native teacher as specialist. The key curriculum goal becomes a process of mediation, whereby the home culture is explored and explained to members of anglophone culture, and anglophone culture is also investigated critically. Instead of becoming 'minority elites' who have absorbed enough of the target culture to replicate its beliefs, social structures, and inequalities, successful learners become 'intercultural diplomats', negotiating between the contrasting world-views of home and target culture. Less successful learners should not be alienated from the home culture – though their linguistic and cultural expertise might not be so advanced, they should still have had the opportunity to explore aspects of both home and target culture with sensitivity and respect. Learners' attitudes and beliefs will necessarily change as they come into contact with a new culture, especially one as potentially dominating and destructive as anglophone culture – but that is an inescapable fact of contemporary life. The challenge is to manage that change of belief and attitude so that – inevitably to different degrees – it empowers rather than subjugates the learner and the society to which he or she belongs. This principle holds for all contexts in which English is learnt world-wide, even those in which the home language and culture are less under threat (cf. Pennycook, 1994). In comparison with the state sector, the commercial sector has traditionally had less of a stake in the moral education of its learners. This is not to say that commercial ELT is value free. White (1988: 24) acknowledges that ELT curricula reflect different general systems of value:

> Views on the nature and purpose of education include those which emphasize the transmission of an esteemed cultural heritage; which stress the growth and self-realization of the individual; and those which regard education as an instrument of social change. Respectively, these three orientations or ideologies have been termed classical humanism, progressivism and reconstructionism.

White goes on to associate the main ELT methodologies with these orientations (cf. Clarke, 1981). Grammar-translation aimed to transmit an esteemed cultural heritage (classical humanism); audiolingualism and notional-functionalism both aimed to effect social change by producing individuals with a mastery of the target language system (reconstructionism); and task-based or 'process-based' approaches to language teaching aimed to foster individual growth by challenging the learner with problems they must solve by developing their linguistic competence (progressivism). For the commercial sector, the progressive curriculum provides a suitable 'fit' for the contractual relationship the institution has with its clients: the unspoken agreement is that the learner (or the learner's sponsors) will pay for a form of teaching that will facilitate his or her linguistic development. To caricature the relationship broadly, commercial schools provide a service; they do not aim to 'brainwash' clients into liberal thinking or to challenge the ideological basis of their existence.

There may, therefore, be understandable suspicion of intercultural approaches particularly among some educators in the commercial sector. This suspicion may result from some of the following reasonable anxieties:

- it is not the job of the commercial English language school to inculcate moral values;
- intercultural education might have unsavoury associations with a crude classical humanist model that esteemed western cultural values at the expense of non-western values (cf. Phillipson, 1992);
- intercultural education might also have associations with 'enculturation' or the desire to impose a possibly unwanted cultural identity on the learner;
- 'culture' is a notoriously vague concept at the best of times;
- ways of approaching culture academically – through ethnography and cultural studies – are unnecessarily bewildering and they seem to have little practical application;
- if intercultural language education does have a place, it is in the state sector, which has the time to explore moral issues and, in some cases, the resources to allow educational visits to the target culture, where learners can engage in 'face to face' ethnography if they so desire.

Intercultural language education is a curriculum option, competing with other types of curriculum; however, most of the anxieties raised above can be allayed. While it is the goal of the intercultural curriculum to foster certain values, those values are expressly designed to respect rather than threaten learners' own systems of belief. The key values promoted by the intercultural curriculum are open-mindedness, curiosity, tolerance of difference, and respect – for self and others. As noted above, properly implemented, the intercultural curriculum should empower learners, and promote their self-confidence. The intercultural curriculum should be distinguished from other curricula that in the past have promoted 'culture' – for example, the classical humanist curriculum that presented 'great works' of the English literary canon for translation and appreciation. As Chapter 8 showed, literary, media and cultural texts form an integral part of the intercultural curriculum (as they do with many 'communicative' approaches to ELT), but they serve as occasions for cultural exploration and intercultural comparison, not as reservoirs of eternal 'civilised values'. Nor does the intercultural curriculum aim to construct 'model Americans' or 'model Europeans', although, as noted, some of Byram's work has been conducted within the umbrella of the Council of Europe, which links language education with an evolving notion of 'European citizenship' encompassing both eastern and western Europe (Byram, 1997b: 25–6). 'Model citizens' in an intercultural curriculum would not be individuals with specific beliefs on particular topics, but rather individuals who could reflect upon the attitudes and behaviour of self and others, and engage in an ongoing negotiation between them. Not all intercultural negotiations will be susceptible to resolution: after all, different groups in a single society hold strongly divergent views on topics such as capital punishment, the right to life, the traditional roles of men and women in society, and how children should be educated. The intercultural learner learns how to explore the beliefs of others without recourse to crass stereotyping, to respect these beliefs in their context (without necessarily subscribing to them), and to respond to them in such a way that the others will be inclined to understand and respect the learner's own position.

Few language teachers will argue with an approach to teaching and learning that promotes mutual respect. However, the remaining anxieties are significant ones: that culture is a vague concept and that ethnography and cultural studies are complex disciplines that add unnecessary burdens to the teacher's already considerable workload. For some teachers, of course, the vagueness of the concept of culture is liberating. The variety of classroom practices developed in the name of 'cultural learning' bears witness to the fact that many teachers and learners find intercultural exploration stimulating and creative precisely because it *is* broadly conceived. For those teachers who demand a more focused curriculum, Byram's *savoirs* offer a careful, consistent and, above all, practical guide to the construction of an intercultural curriculum. It is nevertheless true that some of the academic disciplines that contribute to intercultural exploration – for example, ethnography, visual literacy and cultural studies – are often dauntingly theoretical and abstract. However, as I hope I have shown in Chapters 5–8 in this book, once you have a grasp of their basic principles and the history of their development, they become much more accessible, and their application to teaching and learning becomes clearer. Moreover, the classroom activities adopted in an intercultural approach do not very often stray from those activities familiar from much 'communicative' teaching and learning: role-plays, simulations, project work, debates and questionnaires, with attendant reading, listening and viewing tasks. Chapters 3 and 4 show that a 'cultural turn' has already influenced much that has been happening in the development of written and spoken skills in the mainstream ELT classroom. An intercultural approach does not demand a wholesale revolution in teaching practices – it requires a redirection towards a significantly altered set of goals, goals that, for the majority of learners, are more readily realised than slow progress towards a vaguely conceived 'native speaker proficiency'.

It is true that few commercial language schools can arrange for learners to visit the target culture and engage in the direct forms of ethnography discussed in Chapters 5 and 6. However, this does not invalidate an intercultural approach. As demonstrated in Chapter 5, 'home ethnography' is equally viable, and 'distance' or 'virtual ethnography' is sometimes possible through 'tandem' projects involving email or 'snailmail' correspondence (Dodd, 2001). These can be combined with an analysis of the products of English speaking culture as available in the media, advertising, literature and other cultural phenomena such as art, dance, fashion and music (Chapters 7 and 8). At the heart of the intercultural curriculum are practices of observation, analysis and explanation – and both the home and anglophone culture provide manifest opportunities for the development of these practices. For better or worse, wherever you are in the world, the opportunities are usually there for observation and analysis of anglophone cultures through television, film, video, radio, and the World Wide Web. Viewers with access to cable television in Latin America, for example, have ample opportunity to compare the conventions of home-grown 'telenovelas' with American (and occasionally British) soap operas. Websites devoted to the programmes also allow a certain amount of 'virtual ethnography' through audience research.

English-language teachers who might be anxious about the intercultural curriculum, then, can in principle be reassured about the motivations underlying it and the consequences of introducing it. On a more positive note, an intercultural approach can validate current classroom practices that otherwise might seem removed from the communicative goal of native-speaker proficiency – e.g. exploration of the home culture, or analysis of the conventions of advertising or television programmes. The motivation of teachers and learners can be enhanced by the realisation that the language class is part of a larger exploration of everyday cultural practices, at home and abroad.

An intercultural approach embraces and transforms all three types of educational curriculum that White (1988: 24) identifies. It might best be described as 'neo-humanist', since it places respect for individuals and their many cultures at the heart of its enterprise. The intercultural learner moves among cultures, in a process of continual negotiation, learning to cope with the inevitable changes, in a manner that is ultimately empowering and enriching. The home culture is never denied nor demeaned, yet the intercultural learner will find his or her attitudes and beliefs challenged by contact with others, and the process of interaction will lead to the kind of personal growth characterised by 'progressive' curricula. The social (or 'reconstructionist') outcome will be a generation of learners who are trained (to different degrees) in 'intercultural diplomacy' – who will consequently have learnt to cope with the stresses of living in the multicultural global village that the world has become.

Taken to extremes, the vision may well seem utopian, and, as noted earlier, it would be facile to suggest that intercultural language education alone can make people kinder, more tolerant and open. However, if adopted more widely, it may offer a modest contribution to that process. Much has still to be done, for example to incorporate intercultural strategies into the kinds of textbooks used commonly in commercial language schools. Ideally, 'intercultural' textbooks would be targeted more specifically at particular communities, and result from partnerships between native-speaker and non-native speaker contributors. They would offer support for project work and ethnography as well as specific lessons giving language support. Commercial language examinations (such as those run by UCLES, Oxford and others) also need to take account of advances in the assessment of intercultural skills reviewed briefly in Chapter 9, and offer appropriate tests, if intercultural education is to advance in the commercial sector in the next few decades.

However, as I hope this book has shown, much has also been achieved in the past few decades. At the very least, intercultural language education has reached a level of maturity sufficient to inform a coherent set of classroom practices whereby language improvement is allied to more general ways of understanding our world.

Bibliography

Alderson, C. and North, B. (eds) (1991) *Language Testing in the 1990s: The Communicative Legacy*. London: Macmillan, Modern English Publications and the British Council.

Alptekin, C. and Alptekin, M. (1990) The question of culture: EFL teaching in non-English-speaking countries. In R. Rossner and R. Bolitho (eds) *Currents of Change in English Language Teaching* (pp. 21–6). Oxford: Oxford University Press.

Alred, G., Byram, M. and Fleming, M. (eds) (2003) *Intercultural Experience and Education*. Clevedon: Multilingual Matters.

Anderson, B. (1991) *Imagined Communities: Reflections on the Origin and Spread of Nationalism*. London: Verso.

Anderson, M., Jerald, M. and Turpin, L., (1997) Ethnographic study: Dynamic seeing for culture learning. In A.C. Fantini (ed.) *New Ways in Teaching Culture* (pp. 119–21). Alexandria, VA: TESOL.

Arnold, M. (1960) *Culture and Anarchy*. J. Dover Smith (ed.). Cambridge: Cambridge University Press.

Aronson, R. (1987) A murder mystery from the Mesozoic. *New Scientist* 8 October, 56–9.

Aronson, R. and Harms, H.D. (1987) The palaeoecological significance of an anachronistic ophiuroid community. In W.C. Kerfoot and A. Sih (eds) *Predation: Direct and Indirect Impacts on Aquatic Communities* (pp. 355–66). Hanover, NH: University Press of New England.

Austin, J.L. (1962) *How to Do Things with Words*. Cambridge, MA: Harvard University Press.

Ballard, B. and Clanchy, J. (1991) Assessment by misconception: Cultural influences and intellectual traditions. In L. Hamp-Lyons (ed.) *Assessing Second Language Writing in Academic Contexts* (pp. 19–36). Norwood, NJ: Ablex.

Bakhtin, M. See Volosinov, V.N.

Barnak, P. (1979) Critical incidents exercise. In D. Hoopes and P. Ventura (eds) *Intercultural Sourcebook: Cross-cultural Training Methodologies*. Chicago: Intercultural Press.

Barnard, R. and Cady, J. (1992) *Business Venture 1*. Oxford: Oxford University Press.

Barrat, D. (1986) *Media Sociology*. London: Tavistock.

Barro, A., Jordan, S. and Roberts, C. (1998) Cultural practice in everyday life: the language learner as ethnographer. In M. Byram and M. Fleming (eds) *Language Learning in Intercultural Perspective: Approaches Through Drama and Ethnography* (pp. 76–93). Cambridge: Cambridge University Press.

Barrow, R. (1990) Culture, values and the language classroom. In B. Harrison (ed.) *Culture and the Language Classroom* (pp. 3–10). London. Macmillan and Modern English Publications/British Council.

Barthes, R. (1977) *Image/Music/Text*. Edited and translated by S. Heath. London: Fontana.

Barton, D. (1994) *Literacy: An Introduction to the Ecology of Written Language*. Oxford: Blackwell.

Bassnett, S. (ed.) (1997) *Studying British Cultures*. London: Routledge.

Bazerman, C. (1988) *Shaping Written Knowledge: The Genre and the Activity of the Experimental Article in Science*. Madison: University of Wisconsin Press.

Becher, T. (1989) *Academic Tribes and Territories*. Milton Keynes: Open University Press.

Bell, A. (1996) Text, time and technology in news English. In D. Graddol and S. Goodman (eds) *Redesigning English: New Texts, New Identities* (pp. 3–26). London: Routledge.

Bernstein, B. (1971) *Class, Codes and Control* (vol. 1). London: Routledge and Kegan Paul.

Bex, T. (1996) *Variety in Written English: Texts in Society: Society in Texts*. London: Routledge.

Bhatia, V.K. (1993) *Analysing Genre*. Harlow: Longman.

Bickner, R. and Peyasantiwong, P. (1988) Cultural variation in reflective writing. In A.C. Purves (ed.) *Writing Across Languages and Cultures: Issues in Contrastive Rhetoric* (pp. 160–76). Newbury Park: Sage.

Bignell, J. (1997) *Media Semiotics: An Introduction*. Manchester: Manchester University Press.

Bloom, H. (1995) *The Western Canon: The Books and the School of the Ages*. London: Papermac.

Bloomfield, L. (1933) *Language*. New York: Holt, Rinehart & Winston.

Blum-Kulka, S. (2000) Gossipy events at family dinners: Negotiating sociability, presence and the moral order. In J. Coupland (ed.) *Small Talk* (pp. 213–40). London: Longman.

Boas, F. (1911) Linguistics and ethnology. In F. Boas (ed.) *Handbook of American Indian Languages*. Washington DC: Smithsonian Institute.

Bosher, S. (1997) Exploring cross-cultural miscommunication. In A.E. Fantini (ed.) *New Ways in Teaching Culture* (pp. 169–73). Alexandria, VA: TESOL.

Bouton, L. (1999) Developing nonnative speaker skills in interpreting conversational implicatures in English: explicit teaching can ease the process. In E. Hinkel (ed.) *Culture in Second Language Teaching and Learning* (pp. 47–70). Cambridge: Cambridge University Press.

Breen, M. and Littlejohn, A. (eds) (2000) *Classroom Decision-Making: Negotiation and Process Syllabuses in Practice*. Cambridge: Cambridge University Press.

Brooks, C. and Warren, R. Penn (1938) *Understanding Poetry*. New York: Holt, Rinehart & Winston.

Brooks, C. and Warren, R. Penn (1943) *Understanding Fiction*. New York: Appleton-Century-Crofts.

Brouwer, D., Gerritsen, M. and Dettan, D. (1979) Speech differences between women and men: on the wrong track? *Language and Society* 8, 33–50.

Brumfit, C. (ed.) (1991) *Assessment in Literature Teaching*. London: Macmillan, Modern English Publications and the British Council.

Brumfit, C.J. and Carter, R.A. (1986) *Literature and Language Teaching*. Oxford: Oxford University Press.

Burwitz-Melzer, E. (2001) Teaching intercultural communicative competence through literature. In M. Byram, A. Nichols and D. Steven (eds) *Developing Intercultural Competence in Practice* (pp. 29–43). Clevedon: Multilingual Matters.

Butler, C. (1985) *Systemic Linguistics: Theory and Applications*. London: Batsford.

Byram, M. (ed.) (1993) *Germany: Its Representation in Textbooks for Teaching German in Great Britain*. Frankfurt / Main: Diesterweg.

Byram, M. (1997a) Cultural studies and foreign language teaching. In Bassnett (ed.) *Studying British Cultures* (pp. 53–64). London: Routledge.

Byram, M. (1997b) *Teaching and Assessing Intercultural Communicative Competence*. Clevedon: Multilingual Matters.

Byram, M. and Fleming, M. (eds) (1998) *Language Learning in Intercultural Perspective: Approaches Through Drama and Ethnography*. Cambridge: Cambridge University Press.

Byram, M., Morgan, C. *et al.* (1994) *Teaching-and-Learning Language-and-Culture*. Clevedon: Multilingual Matters.

Byram, M., Nichols, A. and Stevens, D. (eds) (2001) *Developing Intercultural Competence in Practice*. Clevedon: Multilingual Matters.

Byram, M. and Zarate, G. (1997) Defining and assessing intercultural competence: Some principles and proposals for the European context. *Language Teaching* 29, 14–18.

Canagarajah, A.S. (1999) *Resisting Linguistic Imperialism in English Teaching*. Oxford: Oxford University Press.

Candlin, C. and Hyland, K. (eds) (1999) *Writing: Texts, Processes and Practices*. London: Longman.

Cann, R.L., Stoneking, M. and Wilson, A.C. (1987) Mitochondrial DNA and human evolution. *Nature* 325, 31–6.

Carel, S. (2001) Students as virtual ethnographers: Exploring the language-culture connection. In M. Byram, A. Nichols and D. Stevens (eds) *Developing Intercultural Competence in Practice* (pp. 146–61). Clevedon: Multilingual Matters.

Carter, R. and Nunan, D. (eds) (2001) *The Cambridge Guide to Teaching English to Speakers of Other Languages*. Cambridge: Cambridge University Press.

Casanave, C.P. (1992) Cultural diversity and socialization: A case study of a hispanic woman in a doctoral program in sociology. In D.E. Murray (ed.) *Diversity as Resource: Defining Cultural Literacy* (pp. 148–182). Alexandria, VA: TESOL.

Chalmers, A.F. (1982) *What is This Thing called Science?* Milton Keynes: Open University Press.

Cheshire, J. *et al.* (eds) (1989) *Dialect and Education*. Clevedon: Multilingual Matters.

Chichirdan, A. *et al.* (1998) *Crossing Cultures: British Cultural Studies for Romanian 12th Grade Students*. Bucharest: The British Council.

Chomsky, N. (1957) *Syntactic Structures*. The Hague: Mouton.

Clarke, J.L. (ed.) (1981) *Educational Development: A Select Bibliography*. London: Kogan Page.

Cohen, P. (1980) Subcultural conflict and working class community. In S. Hall, D. Hobson, A. Lowe and P. Willis (eds) *Culture, Media, Language* (pp. 78–87). London: Hutchinson.

Collie, J. and Slater, S. (1987) *Literature in the Language Classroom*. Cambridge: Cambridge University Press.

Connor, U. (1988) A contrastive study of persuasive business correspondence: American and Japanese. In S.J. Bruno (ed.) *Global Implications for Business Communications: Theory, Technology and Practice* (pp. 57–72). Houston: School of Business and Public Administration, University of Houston.

Connor, U. (1996) *Contrastive Rhetoric: Cross-cultural Aspects of Second-language writing.* Cambridge: Cambridge University Press.

Cooper, R., Lavery, M. and Rinvolucri, M. (1991) *Video.* Oxford: Oxford University Press.

Corbett, J. (1997) Language, genre and culture. In *LABSA Journal* 1 (2), 21–8.

Corbett, J. (1999) *Written in the Language of the Scottish Nation.* Clevedon: Multilingual Matters.

Corbett, J. (2000) Culture, variety and ELT. In K. Seago and N. McBride (eds) *Target Language – Target Culture?* (pp. 156–76). London: AFLS/CILT.

Council of Europe (1989) *Language Learning in Europe: The Challenge of Diversity.* Strasbourg: Council of Europe Press.

Coupland, J. (ed.) (2000) *Small Talk.* London: Longman.

Crawford, R. (1997) Redefining Scotland. In S. Bassnett (ed.) *Studying British Cultures* (pp. 83–96). London: Routledge.

Crawford, R. (1998) *The Scottish Invention of English Literature.* Cambridge: Cambridge University Press.

Culler, J. (1997) *Literary Theory: A Very Short Introduction.* Oxford: Oxford University Press.

Damen, L. (1987) *Culture Learning: The Fifth Dimension in the Language Classroom.* Reading, MA: Addison Wesley.

Dammer, P. (1975) A rationale for the elimination of the culture section from the Regents examination in modern foreign languages. In *Language Association Bulletin* 27, 2.

Davcheva, L. and Docheva, Y. (eds) (1998) *Branching Out: A Cultural Studies Syllabus.* Sofia: British Council and Tilia.

Davies, A. (1991) *The Native Speaker in Applied Linguistics.* Edinburgh: Edinburgh University Press.

Dawkins, R. (1986) *The Blind Watchmaker.* Harlow: Longman.

De Jong, W. (1996) *Open Frontiers: Teaching English in an Intercultural Context.* Oxford: Heinemann.

Dodd, C. (2001) Working in tandem: An Anglo-French project. In M. Byram, A. Nichols and D. Stevens (eds) *Developing Intercultural Competence in Practice* (pp. 162–75). Clevedon: Multilingual Matters.

Drakakis, J. (1997) Shakespeare in quotations. In S. Bassnett (ed.) *Studying British Cultures* (pp. 152–72). London: Routledge.

Dudley-Evans, T. (ed.) (1987) *Genre Analysis and ESP.* Birmingham: University of Birmingham Dept of English.

Duff, A. and Maley, A. (1990) *Literature.* Oxford: Oxford University Press.

Durant, A. (1997) Facts and meanings in British Cultural Studies. In S. Bassnett (ed.) *Studying British Cultures* (pp. 19–38). London: Routledge.

Eco, U. (1976) *A Theory of Semiotics.* Bloomington, IN: Indiana University Press.

Edginton, B. and Montgomery, M. (1996) *The Media.* Manchester: The British Council.

Eggins, S. and Slade, D. (1997) *Analysing Casual Conversation.* London: Cassell.

Entwhistle, N., Thompson, S. and Tait, H. (1992) *Guidelines for Promoting Effective Learning in Higher Education.* Edinburgh: University of Edinburgh Centre for Research on Learning and Instruction.

Erickson, F. (1996) Ethnographic microanalysis. In S.L. McKay and N.H. Hornberger (eds) *Sociolinguistics and Language Teaching* (pp 283–306). Cambridge: Cambridge University Press.

Fairclough, N. (1989) *Language and Power.* London: Longman.

Fairclough, N. (ed.) (1992) *Critical Language Awareness.* London: Longman.

Fairclough, N. (1995) *Critical Discourse Analysis.* London: Longman.

Fantini, A.E. (ed.) (1997) *New Ways in Teaching Culture.* Alexandria, VA: TESOL.

Fish, S. (1980) *Is there a Text in this Class?* Cambridge, MA: Harvard University Press.

Fiske, J. and Hartley, J. (1978) *Reading Television.* London: Methuen.

FitzGerald, H. (2003) *How Different Are We? Spoken Discourse in Intercultural Communication.* Clevedon: Multilingual Matters.

Fogarty, D. (1959) *Roots for a New Rhetoric.* New York: Russell & Russell.

Forceville, C. (1999) Educating the eye? Kress and Van Leeuwen's *Reading Images: The Grammar of Visual Design* (1996). In *Language and Literature* 8 (2), 163–78.

Foucault, M. (1981) The order of discourse. In R. Young (ed.) *Untying the Text: A Post-Structuralist Reader* (pp. 48–78). Boston: Routledge & Kegan Paul.

Gajdusek, L. (1988) Towards a wider use of literature in ESL. *TESOL Quarterly* 22, 227–57.

Gairns, R. and Redman, S. with Collie, J. (1996) *True to Life: Intermediate Class Book.* Cambridge: Cambridge University Press.

Garfinkel, H. (1967) *Studies in Ethnomethodology.* Englewood Cliffs, NJ: Prentice Hall.

Genova, M.M. (2001) Visual codes and modes of presentation of television news broadcasts. In M. Byram, A. Nichols and D. Stevens (eds) *Developing Intercultural Competence* (pp. 60–76). Clevedon: Multilingual Matters.

Ghadessy, M. (ed.) (1988) *Register Analysis: Theory and Practice.* London: Pinter.

Ghadessy, M. (ed.) (1993) *Registers of Written English.* London: Pinter.

Goodman, S. (1996) Visual English. In D. Graddol and S. Goodman (eds) *Redesigning English: New Texts, New Identities* (pp. 38–72). London: Routledge.

Graddol, D. and Goodman, S. (eds) (1996) *Redesigning English: New Texts, New Identities.* London: Routledge.

Gramsci, A. (1971) *Selections from the Prison Notebooks of Antonio Gramsci* (ed. and trans by Q. Hoare and G. Nowell Smith). London: Lawrence and Wishart.

Gray, A. and McGuigan, J. (eds) (1993) *Studying Culture: An Introductory Reader* (2nd edn). London: Edward Arnold.

Guilherme, M. (2002) *Critical Citizens for an Intercultural World: Foreign Language Education as Cultural Politics.* Clevedon: Multilingual Matters.

Gumperz, J.J. (1977) Sociocultural knowledge in conversational inference. In M Saville-Troike (ed.) *28th Annual Round Table Monograph Series on Languages and Linguistics.* Washington, DC: Georgetown University Press.

Gumperz, J.J. (1984) The politics of conversation: Conversational inference in discussion, with Jenny Cook Gumperz. *Berkeley Cognitive Science Report* No. 23.

Hall, J.K. (1993) Oye, oye lo que ustedes no saben: Creativity, social power and politics in the oral practice of chismeando. *Journal of Linguistic Anthropology* 3 (1), 75–98.

Hall, J.K. (1999) The prosaics of interaction: The development of interactional competence in another language. In E. Hinkel (ed.) *Culture in Second Language Teaching and Learning* (pp. 137–51). Cambridge: Cambridge University Press.

Hall, S. (1980) Encoding/Decoding. In S. Hall, D. Hobson, A. Lowe and P. Willis (eds) *Culture, Media, Language* (pp. 128–38). London: Hutchison. Reprinted in part in P. Marris and S. Thornham (eds) *Media Studies* (pp. 41–50). Edinburgh: Edinburgh University Press.

Hall, S. (1994) Reflections upon the encoding/decoding model: An interview with Stuart Hall. In J. Cruz and J. Lewis (eds) *Viewing, Reading, Listening: Audiences and Cultural Reception.* Boulder, CO: Westview Press.

Hall, S. and Whannel, P. (1964) *The Popular Arts.* London: Hutchinson Educational.

Hall, S., Hobson, D., Lowe, A. and Willis, P. (eds) (1980) *Culture, Media, Language.* London: Hutchinson.

Halliday, M.A.K. and Hasan, R. (1989) *Language, Context and Text* (2nd edn). Oxford: Oxford University Press.

Halliday, M.A.K., McIntosh, A. and Strevens, P. (1964) *The Linguistic Sciences and Language Teaching.* London: Longman.

Halliday, M.A.K. and Martin, J.R. (1993) *Writing Science: Literacy and Discursive Power.* London: The Falmer Press.

Harrison, A. (1991) Language assessment as theatre: Ten years of communicative testing. In C. Alderson and B. North (eds) *Language Testing in the 1990s* (pp. 95–105). London: Macmillan.

Harrison, B. (ed.) (1990) *Culture and the Language Classroom.* London: Macmillan and Modern English Publications/British Council.

Hasan, R. (1984) *The Nursery Tale as Genre.* Nottingham Linguistics Circular No. 13.

Heath, S.B. (1983) *Ways with Words.* Cambridge: Cambridge University Press.

Hebdige, D. (1979) *Subculture: The Meaning of Style.* London: Methuen.

Hinkel, E. (ed.) (1999) *Culture in Second Language Teaching and Learning.* Cambridge: Cambridge University Press.

Hirsch, E.D. Jr (1987) *Cultural Literacy: What Every American Needs to Know.* Boston: Houghton Mifflin.

Hirsch, E.D. Jr, Kett, J.F. and Trefil, J. (1988) *The Dictionary of Cultural Literacy.* Boston: Houghton Mifflin.

Hobson, D. (1980) Housewives and the mass media. In S. Hall, D. Hobson, A. Lowe and P. Willis (eds) *Culture, Media, Language* (pp. 105-14). London: Hutchinson. Partially reprinted in Marris and Thornham (eds) (1997) *Media Studies* (pp. 307–12). Edinburgh: Edinburgh University Press.

Hoggart, R. (1957) *The Uses of Literacy.* Harmondsworth: Penguin.

Holliday, A. (1994) *Appropriate Methodology and Social Context.* Cambridge: Cambridge University Press.

Howard, M.C. (1989) *Contemporary Cultural Anthropology* (3rd edn). London: HarperCollins.

Hughes, A. (1989) *Testing for Language Teachers.* Cambridge: Cambridge University Press.

Hyland, K. (2000) *Disciplinary Discourses: Social Interactions in Academic Writing.* London: Longman.

Hymes, D. (1972) On communicative competence. In J.B. Pride and J. Holmes (eds) *Sociolinguistics* (pp. 269–93). Harmondsworth: Penguin.

Hyon, S. (1996) Genre in three traditions: Implications for ESL. *TESOL Quarterly* 30 (4), 693–722.

Johns, A.M. (1992) Towards developing a cultural repertoire: A case study of a Lao college freshman. In D.E. Murray (ed.) *Diversity as Resource* (pp. 183–201). Alexandria, VA: TESOL.

Jones, L. (1977) *Functions of English*. Cambridge: Cambridge University Press.

Jong, W. de (1996) *Open Frontiers: Teaching English in an Intercultural Context*. Oxford: Heinemann.

Judd, E.L. (1999) Some issues in the teaching of pragmatic competence. In E. Hinkel (ed.) *Culture in Second Language Teaching and Learning* (pp. 152–66). Cambridge: Cambridge University Press.

Kachru, B. (1986) *The Alchemy of English: The Spread, Functions and Models of Non-Native Englishes*. Oxford: Pergamon Press.

Kachru, Y. (1999) Culture, context and writing. In E. Hinkel (ed.) *Culture in Second Language Teaching and Learning* (pp. 75–89). Cambridge: Cambridge University Press.

Kay, H. and Dudley-Evans, T. (1998) Genre: What teachers think. *ELT Journal* 52 (4), 308–13.

Klippel, F. (1984) *Keep Talking*. Cambridge: Cambridge University Press.

Kramsch, C. (1993) *Context and Culture in Language Teaching*. Oxford: Oxford University Press.

Kramsch, C. (1998) *Language and Culture*. Oxford: Oxford University Press.

Kramsch, C. (2001) Intercultural communication. In R. Carter and D. Nunan (eds) *The Cambridge Guide to Teaching English to Speakers of Other Languages* (pp. 201–6). Cambridge: Cambridge University Press.

Kress, G. and van Leeuwen, T. (1996) *Reading Images: The Grammar of Visual Design*. London: Routledge.

Lakoff, G. and Johnson, R. (1980) *Metaphors We Live By*. Chicago: University of Chicago Press.

Lavery, C. (1993) *Focus on Britain Today: Teachers Book*. London: Macmillan.

Lazar, G. (1993) *Literature and Language Teaching*. Cambridge: Cambridge University Press.

Leavis, F.R. (1930) *Mass Civilization and Minority Culture*. Cambridge: Gordon Fraser.

Leavis, F.R. (1948) *The Great Tradition*. London: Chatto & Windus.

Lecompte, M. and Goetz, J. (1982) Problems of reliability and validity in ethnographic research. *Review of Educational Research* 52(1), 31–60.

Loveday, L. (1981) *The Sociolinguistics of Learning and Using a Non-Native Language*. Oxford: Pergamon.

Lucas, T. (1992) Diversity among individuals: Eight students making sense of classroom journal writing. In D.E. Murray (ed.) *Diversity as Resource* (pp. 202–32). Alexandria, VA: TESOL.

Lull, J. (1990) *Inside Family Viewing: Ethnographic Research on Television's Audiences*. London: Routledge.

Macaulay, R.K.S. (1991) *Locating Dialect in Discourse*. Oxford: Oxford University Press.

Macaulay, R.K.S. (1995/6) Remarkably common eloquence: The aesthetics of an urban dialect. *Scottish Language* 14/15, 66–80; reprinted in R.K.S. Macaulay (1997) *Standards and Variation in Urban Speech* (pp. 139–62). Amsterdam: John Benjamins.

MacDonald, M. (2000) Strangers in a strange land: Fiction, culture, language. In K. Seago and N. McBride (eds) *Target Language – Target Culture?* (pp. 137–155). London: AFLS/CILT.

Maley, A. and Moulding, S. (1981) *Learning to Listen*. Cambridge: Cambridge University Press.

Marris, P. and Thornham, S. (eds) (1996) *Media Studies: A Reader*. Edinburgh: Edinburgh University Press.

Martin, J.R. (1985) *Factual Writing: Exploring and Challenging Social Reality*. Victoria: Deakin University Press.

Maule, D. (1989) *Focus on Scotland*. London: Macmillan.

McCrone, D *et al.* (1995) *Scotland – The Brand: The Making of Scottish Heritage*. Edinburgh: Edinburgh University Press.

McGuigan, J. (ed.) (1997) *Cultural Methodologies*. London: Sage.

McKay, S.L. and Hornberger, N.H. (eds) (1996) *Sociolinguistics and Language Teaching*. Cambridge: Cambridge University Press.

McRae, J. (1991) *Literature With a Small 'l'*. London: Macmillan.

McRobbie, A. (1981) Settling accounts with subcultures: A feminist critique. In T. Bennett, G. Martin, C. Mercer and J. Woollacott (eds) *Culture, Ideology and Social Process: A Reader* (pp. 112–24). London: Open University Press.

McRobbie, A. (1993) Shut up and dance: Youth culture and changing modes of femininity. *Youth* 1 (2), 13–31.

Melde, W. (1987) *Zur Integration von Landeskunde und Kommunikation in Fremdsprachenunterricht*. Tubingen: Gunter Narr Verlag.

Milroy, J. and Milroy, L. (1991) *Authority in Language* (2nd edn). London: Routledge.

Milroy, L. (1987) *Language and Social Networks* (2nd edn). Oxford: Blackwell.

Mitchell, C. (1984) Case studies. In R. Ellen (ed.) *Ethnographic Research: A Guide to General Conduct* (pp. 237–9). London: Academic Press.

Monaco, J. (1981) *How to Read a Film*. New York and Oxford: Oxford University Press.

Montgomery, M. (1986) *An Introduction to Language and Society*. London: Routledge.

Montgomery, M. (1995) Institutions and discourse. In *British Studies Now, Anthology 1–5* (pp. 25–8). Manchester: British Council.

Montgomery, M. (1998) What is British cultural studies anyway and why are people saying such terrible things about it? *British Studies Now* 10, 3–6.

Montgomery, M. and Reid-Thomas, H. (1994) *Language and Social Life*. Manchester: British Council.

Morgan, C. (2001) The international partnership project. In M. Byram, A. Nichols and D. Stevens (eds) *Developing Intercultural Competence in Practice* (pp. 11–28). Clevedon: Multilingual Matters.

Morgan, J. and Rinvolucri, M. (1986) *Vocabulary*. Oxford: Oxford University Press.

Morley, D. (1980) *The Nationwide Audience: Structure and Decoding*. London: British Film Institute.

Morley, D. (1986) *Family Television*. London: Routledge.

Murdock, G. (1997) Thin descriptions: Questions of method in cultural analysis. In J. McGuigan (ed.) *Cultural Methodologies* (pp. 178–92). London: Sage.

Morrow, K. and Johnson, K. (1981) *Communication in the Classroom*. London: Longman.

Murray, D.E. (ed.) (1992) *Diversity as Resource: Redefining Cultural Literacy*. Alexandria, VA: TESOL.

Murray, D.E., Nichols, P.C. and Heisch, A. (1992) Identifying the languages and cultures of our students. In D.E. Murray (ed) *Diversity as Resource* (pp. 63–84). Alexandria, VA: TESOL.

Myers, G. (1989) The pragmatics of politeness in scientific articles. In *Applied Linguistics* 10, 1–35.

Myers, G. (1990) *Writing Biology.* Madison: University of Wisconsin Press.

Neelankavil, J.P., Mummaleni, V. and Sessions, D. (1996) Use of foreign language and models in print advertisements in East Asian countries: A logic modelling approach. *European Journal of Management* 29 (4), 24–38.

Nightingale, V. (1989) What's ethnographic about ethnographic audience research? *Australian Journal of Communication* 16, 50–63.

Nunan, D. (1988) *The Learner Centred Curriculum.* Cambridge: Cambridge University Press.

Nunan, D. (1989) *Designing Tasks for the Communicative Classroom.* Cambridge: Cambridge University Press.

Nunan, D. (1992) *Research Methods in Language Learning.* Cambridge: Cambridge University Press.

Pennycook, A. (1994) *The Cultural Politics of English as an International Language.* London: Longman.

Pennycook, A. (1998) *English and the Discourses of Colonialism.* London: Routledge.

Pennycook, A. (2001) *Critical Applied Linguistics.* London: Erlbaum.

Perelman, C.H. (1982) *The Realm of Rhetoric* (translated by W. Kluback). Notre Dame: University of Notre Dame Press.

Phillipson, R. (1992) *Linguistic Imperialism.* Oxford: Oxford University Press.

Phipps, A. (2000) Reading theory, reading praxis: Critical understanding through complex texts. In K. Seago and N. McBride (eds) *Target Language – Target Culture?* (pp. 119–36). London: AFLS/CILT.

Pinker, S. (1994) *The Language Instinct.* Harmondsworth: Penguin.

Platt, J., Weber, H. and Lian, H.M. (1984) *The New Englishes.* London: Routledge & Kegan Paul.

Poulton, J. (1987) All about Eve. *New Scientist* 14 May, 51–3.

Pride, J. (1982) *New Englishes.* New York: Newbury House.

Prodromou, L. (1990) English as cultural action. In T.R. Rossner and R. Bolitho (eds) *Currents of Change in English Language Teaching* (pp. 27–39). Oxford: Oxford University Press.

Pulverness, A. (1996) Worlds within words: Literature and British Cultural Studies. In David A. Hill (ed.) *Papers on Teaching Literature from The British Council's Conferences in Bologna 1994 and Milan 1995.* The British Council, Italy.

Radway, J. (1988) Reception study: Ethnography and the problems of dispersed audiences and nomadic subjects. *Cultural Studies* 2 (3), 359–76.

Raw, L. (1994) *Changing Class Attitudes.* Manchester: British Council.

Reynolds, M. (1998) Genre analysis: What is it and what can it do? *LABSA Journal* 2 (1) 72–7.

Richards, J.C. and Nunan, D. (eds) (1990) *Second Language Teacher Education.* Cambridge: Cambridge University Press.

Richards, I.A. (1929) *Practical Criticism.* London: Routledge & Kegan Paul.

Rickford, J.R. (1987) The haves and have-nots: Sociolinguistic surveys and the assessment of speaker competence. *Language in Society* 16 (2). 149–77.

Risager, K. (1998) Language teaching and the process of European integration. In M. Byram and M. Fleming (eds) _Language Learning in Intercultural Perspective_ (pp. 242–54). Cambridge: Cambridge University Press.

Roberts, C., Davies, E. and Jupp, T. (1992) _Language and Discrimination: A Study of Communication in Multi-Ethnic Workplaces_. Harlow: Longman.

Roberts, C., Byram, M., Barro, A., Jordan, S. and Street, B. (2001) _Language Learners as Ethnographers_. Clevedon: Multilingual Matters.

Rose, G. (2001) _Visual Methodologies_. London: Sage.

Rossner, R. and Bolitho, R. (eds) (1990) _Currents of Change in English Language Teaching_. Oxford: Oxford University Press.

Sapir, E. (1958) _Culture, Language and Personality_. Berkeley: University of California Press.

Saville-Troike, M. (1989) _The Ethnography of Communication_ (2nd edn). Oxford: Basil Blackwell.

Scollon, R. (1999) Cultural codes for calls: The use of commercial television in teaching culture in the classroom. In E. Hinkel (ed.) _Culture in Second Language and Learning_ (pp. 181–95). Cambridge: Cambridge University Press,

Scollon, R. and Scollon, S.W. (2001) _Intercultural Communication_ (2nd edn). Oxford: Blackwell.

Scrivener, J. (1994) _Learning Teaching_. Oxford: Heinemann.

Seago, K. and McBride, N. (eds) (2000) _Target Language – Target Culture?_ London: AFLS/CILT.

Searle, J.R. (1969) _Speech Acts: An Essay in the Philosophy of Language_. Cambridge: Cambridge University Press.

Sercu, L. (1998) In-service teacher training and the acquisition of intercultural competence. In M. Byram and M. Fleming (eds) _Language Learning in Intercultural Perspective_ (pp. 255–89). Cambridge: Cambridge University Press.

Skuttnab-Kangas, T. (2000) _Linguistic Genocide in Education_. London: Erlbaum.

Spiro, J. (1991) Assessing literature: Four papers. In C. Brumfit (ed.) _Assessment in Literature Teaching_ (pp. 16–83). London: Macmillan.

Spradley, J. (1979) _The Ethnographic Interview_. New York: Holt, Rinehart & Winston.

Stern, H.H. (1992) _Issues and Options in Language Teaching_, edited by P. Allen and B. Harley. Oxford: Oxford University Press.

Storey, J. (1993) _An Introductory Guide to Cultural Theory and Popular Culture_. London: Harvester Wheatsheaf.

Swales, J. (1981) _Aspects of Article Introductions_. Aston ESP Research Reports No 1, The Language Studies Unit, University of Aston in Birmingham.

Swales, J. (ed.) (1985) _Episodes in ESP_. Oxford: Pergamon.

Swales, J. (1990) _Genre Analysis_. Cambridge: Cambridge University Press.

Swales, J. (1998) Discourse communities, genres and English as an international language. _World Englishes_ 7, 211–20.

Tannen, D. (1984) _Conversational Style: Analyzing Talk Among Friends_. Norwood, NJ: Ablex.

Tannen, D. (1986) _That's Not What I Meant! How Conversational Style Makes or Breaks Your Relations with Others_. New York: Morrow.

Taylor, D. (1992) _Global Software: Developing Applications for the International Market_. Heidelberg: Springer Verlag.

Thomas, H. (1993) An-other voice: Young women dancing and talking. In H. Thomas (ed.) _Dance, Gender and Culture_. Basingstoke: Macmillan.

Thomas, H. (1997) Dancing. In J. McGuigan (ed.) *Cultural Methodologies* (pp. 142–54). London: Sage.

Thompson, E.V. (1963) *The Making of the English Working Class*. London: Gollancz.

Tolson, A. (1991) Televised chat and the synthetic personality. In P. Scannell (ed.) *Broadcast Talk* (pp. 179–87). London: Sage. Partially reprinted in Marris and Thornham (eds) *Media Studies* (pp. 189–197). Edinburgh: Edinburgh University Press.

Tomalin, B. and Stempleski, S. (1993) *Cultural Awareness*. Oxford: Oxford University Press.

Toulmin, S. (1958) *The Uses of Argument*. Cambridge: Cambridge University Press.

Toulmin, S., Rieke, R. and Janik, A. (1979) *An Introduction to Reasoning*. New York: Macmillan.

Trudgill, P. (1994) *Dialects*. London: Routledge.

Trudgill, P. and Hughes, A. (1979) *English Accents and Dialects*. London: Edward Arnold.

Turner, G. (1990) *British Cultural Studies: An Introduction*. London: Routledge.

Ur, P. (1996) *A Course in Language Teaching: Practice and Theory*. Cambridge: Cambridge University Press.

Valdes, J.M. (ed.) (1986) *Culture Bound: Bridging the Cultural Gap in Language Teaching*. Cambridge: Cambridge University Press.

Valdes, J.M. (1990) The inevitability of teaching and learning culture in a foreign language course. In B. Harrison (ed.) *Culture and the Language Classroom* (pp. 20–30). London: Macmillan.

Valette, R.M. (1986) The culture test. In J.M. Valdes (ed.) *Culture Board* (pp. 179–97). Cambridge: Cambridge University Press.

van Ek, J.A. (1975) *The Threshold Level*. Oxford: Pergamon.

van Leeuwen, T. (1996) Moving English: The visual language of film. In D. Graddol and S. Goodman (eds) *Redesigning English* (pp. 81–105). London: Routledge.

Vasquez, O.A. (1992) A Mexicano perspective: Reading the world in a multicultural perspective. In E.D. Murray (ed.) *Diversity as Resource* (pp. 113–34). Alexandria, VA: TESOL.

Ventola, E. (1983) Contrasting schematic structures in service encounters. *Applied Linguistics* 4 (3), 242–58.

Volosinov, V.N. [M. Bakhtin] (1973) *Marxism and the Philosophy of Language* (trans. L. Matejka and I.R. Titunik). New York: Seminar Press.

Wadham-Smith, N. (1992) Editorial. *British Studies Now* 1. On WWW at http://www.britcoun.org/studies/bsn_pdfs/bsn01.pdf.

Walkerdine, V. (1990) *Schoolgirl Fictions*. London: Verso.

Walters, K. (1992) Whose culture? Whose literacy? In D.E. Murray (ed) *Diversity as Resource* (pp. 3–29). Alexandria, VA: TESOL.

White, R.V. (1988) Introduction. In R.V. White (ed.) *Academic Writing: Process and Product* (pp. 4–16). London: British Council.

Whorf, B.L. (1956) *Language, Thought and Reality*. Cambridge, Mass: MIT Press.

Wiegand, P. (1992) *Places in the Primary School*. London: Falmer Press.

Widdiecombe, S. and Wooffitt, R. (1995) *The Language of Youth Subcultures*. Hemel Hempstead: Harvester Wheatsheaf.

Widdowson, H.G. (1975) *Stylistics and the Teaching of Literature*. London: Edward Arnold.

Widdowson, H.G. (1994) The ownership of English. *TESOL Quarterly* 28 (2), 377–89.

Wilkins, D.A. (1972) *The Linguistic and Situational Content of the Common Core in a Unit/Credit System*. Strasbourg: Council of Europe.

Wilkins, D.A. (1976) *Notional Syllabuses*. Oxford: Oxford University Press.

Williams, R. (1958) Culture is ordinary. Reprinted in A. Gray and J. McGuigan (eds) *Studying Culture* (pp. 5–14). London: Edward Arnold.

Williams, R. (1961) *The Long Revolution*. Harmondsworth: Penguin.

Williams, R. (1962) *Communications*. Harmondsworth: Penguin.

Williams, R. (1974) *Television: Technology and Cultural Form*. London: Fontana.

Williams, R. (1976) *Keywords: A Vocabulary of Culture and Society*. London: Fontana.

Willis, D. and Willis, J. (2001) Task-based language learning. In A. Carter and D. Nunan (eds) *The Cambridge Guide to Teaching English to Speakers of Other Languages*. Cambridge: Cambridge University Press.

Willis, J. (1996) *A Framework for Task-Based Learning*. Harlow: Longman.

Willis, P.E. (1977) *Learning to Labour: How Working Class Kids Get Working Class Jobs*. Farnsborough: Saxon House.

Woollacott, J. (1986) Fictions and ideologies: The case of situation comedy. In T. Bennett, C. Mercer and J. Woollacott (eds) *Popular Culture and Social Relations* (pp. 196–218). Milton Keynes: Open University Press. Partially reprinted in Marris and Thornham (eds) *Media Studies* (pp. 169–79). Edinburgh: Edinburgh University Press.

Index

225

CPSIA information can be obtained at www.ICGtesting.com
Printed in the USA
BVOW07s1953090114

341260BV00001B/2/A